W9-ADP-783

BARRIO-LOGOS

HISTORY, CULTURE, AND SOCIETY SERIES
CENTER FOR MEXICAN AMERICAN STUDIES
UNIVERSITY OF TEXAS AT AUSTIN

BARRIO-LOGOS

Space and Place in Urban
Chicano Literature and Culture

RAÚL HOMERO VILLA

 UNIVERSITY OF TEXAS PRESS, AUSTIN

Second paperback printing, 2001

Requests for permission to reproduce material from this work should be sent to Permissions, University of Texas Press, Box 7819, Austin, TX 78713-7819.

∞ The paper used in this book meets the minimum requirements of ANSI/NISO Z39.48-1992 (R1997) (Permanence of Paper).

LIBRARY OF CONGRESS CATALOGING-IN-PUBLICATION DATA

Villa, Raúl.
    Barrio-logos : space and place in urban Chicano literature and culture / Raúl Homero Villa. — 1st ed.
       p.   cm. — (History, culture, and society series)
    Includes bibliographical references (p.   ) and index.
     ISBN 0-292-78741-3 (cloth : alk. paper) — ISBN 0-292-78742-1 (pbk. : alk. paper)
     1. American literature—Mexican American authors—History and criticism.
2. Hispanic American neighborhoods in literature.   3. Mexican Americans—Intellectual life.   4. City and town life in literature.   5. Mexican Americans in literature.   6. Space and time in literature.   7. Local color in literature.
8. Setting (Literature) I. Title. II. Series.
PS153.M4V55   2000
810.9'86872—dc21   99-30871

DEDICATORIO

Como dice el dicho, "cada loco con su tema."
Este producto del mío lo dedico a mi familia,
con afecto especial para mis padres,
Raúl Aníbal Villa y Yolanda Rivera Villa;
y a todos los barrios, presentes y ausentes.

BARRIO VIEJO

Viejo barrio, barrio viejo, sólo hay lugares parejos,
Donde un día hubo casas, donde vivió nuestra raza.
Sólo quedan los escombros de los hogares felices,
de las alegres familias de esa gente que yo quise.

Por las tardes se sentaban, afuera a tomar el fresco,
yo pasaba y saludaba, ya parece que oigo el eco.
"¿Cómo está, doña Juanita? Buenas tardes, Isabel.
¡Hola! ¿Qué dices, Chalita? ¿Cómo están Arturo y Manuel?"

Viejo barrio, barrio viejo, que en mi infancia te gocé,
y con todos mis amigos iba descalzo y a pie.
De la Meyer hasta el Hoyo, desde el Hoyo hasta la acequia,
de la acequia hasta el río, ése era el mundo mío.

Dicen que éramos pobres, pues yo nunca lo noté,
yo era feliz en mi mundo, de aquel barrio que adoré.
Bonitas las serenatas a las tres de la mañana,
que le cantaba a mi chata, pegadito a su ventana.

Por la calle del convento, una casa destruida
quedó como monumento al gran amor de mi vida.
Pobrecito viejo barrio, cómo te debe doler,
cuando en nombre del progreso, derrumban otra pared.

Viejo barrio, barrio viejo, yo también ya envejecí,
y cuando se hace viejo, nadie se acuerda de ti.
Vámonos muriendo juntos, que me entierren en tu suelo.
Y seremos dos difuntos, rodeados de mil recuerdos.

EDWARD "LALO" GUERRERO

CONTENTS

ACKNOWLEDGMENTS

I can only begin to suggest the range of people, places, and institutions that knowingly and unknowingly helped me to realize this project. With apologies to the majority who go unnamed, I wish to thank the following.

For institutional support: the Office of the Dean of Faculty and the Louis and Hermione Brown Humanities Support Fund at Occidental College; the President's Postdoctoral Fellowship Program of the University of California; the Literature Board of the University of California at San Diego; the Scholars Program of the Getty Research Institute for the Study of Art and the Humanities; and the John Randolph Haynes and Dora Haynes Foundation.

For intellectual energy and professional guidance: Jorge Mariscal, Yvonne Yarbro-Bejarano, María Herrera-Sobek, George Lipsitz, Helena María Viramontes, ADOBE L.A., Lawrence Herzog, José E. Limón, José Saldívar, James Clifford, and my colleagues in English and Comparative Literary Studies at Occidental College.

For enriching my spirit: *los artistas de Aztlán, mis amigos,* L.A., the Arizona-Sonora Desert, Fausto and Pepita.

For wisdom, patience, love, and sweat: Rita Cano Alcalá.

We must be insistently aware of how space can be made to hide consequences from us, how relations of power and discipline are inscribed in the apparently innocent spatiality of social life, how human geographies become filled with politics and ideology.

— EDWARD SOJA, *Postmodern Geographies*

. . . place expresses how a spatially connected group of people mediate the demands of cultural identity, state power and capital accumulation.

— SHARON ZUKIN, *Landscapes of Power*

. . . the barrios of our cities are truly the contemporary sites of our complex identities. Here between freeways and industrial warehouses, displaced by urban renewal and exiled by economics, large Mexican communities continue their day to day lives. Barrios filled with Spanish speaking businesses and . . . vibrant cultural activities are also touched by the alienation and poverty of city life. Many of these historic barrios are the earliest landmarks of Mexican culture in the United States, predating the annexation.

—AMALIA MESA-BAINS, "LAND AND SPIRITUALITY IN THE DESCANSOS"

From the analytical standpoint, the spatial practice of a society is revealed through the deciphering of its space.

—HENRI LEFEBVRE, *The Production of Space*

BARRIO-LOGOS

Introduction

*Spatial Practice and Place-Consciousness
in Chicano Urban Culture*

GEOGRAPHY MADE DESTINY:
THE STRUGGLE OVER SOCIAL SPACE

The consequences of geographic displacement loom large in Chicano historical memory, characterized, among other things, by the determining effects of
land loss, shifting and porous national borders, coerced and voluntary migra-
tions, and disparate impacts of urban development. The 1848 annexation of
former Mexican territory—as a result of the Mexican-American War—into
what is now the United States Southwest is the originary moment in the
general subordination of *mexicanos*-cum–Mexican Americans. Their resulting
second-order citizenship was compelled by a variety of legal and extralegal
social processes that contributed to the "racial formation" (Omi and Winant
1986) of American society in which they were situated. As one example, Carl
Gutiérrez-Jones (1995:1) has critically evaluated the foundational Chicano
experience of being interpellated as a criminal population by the institutional
and ideological apparatuses of Anglo-American culture, noting that it has "a
long and complex history that is intimately related to their [Chicanos] very
construction as a social group in the United States." In like fashion, the experience of being displaced in multiple ways from a perceived homeland has
been an essential element of Chicanos' social identity in this country. By extension, the centrality of such deterritorialization to Chicanos has guaranteed
its importance as a theme in their expressive practice—in both "high" and
"low" cultural forms—most commonly figured through imagery and rhetoric of "the lost land" (Chávez 1984).

While geography has indeed proven to be destiny for many Chicanos, its consequences have not been arbitrary caprices of fate. Rather, they have been purposefully effective as manifestations of the "spatial practice" of the new American rulers of the land. Since, as Henri Lefebvre explains, "in *spatial practice*, the reproduction of social relations is predominant," the consequences of deterritorialization for *mexicanos* in the newly annexed territories literally put them in their designated place within the emergent social space of Anglo-American capitalism (1991:50; original emphasis). In California, which is the geographic field of my study, the United States' victory in the Mexican-American War of 1846–1848 brought in its wake manifold mechanisms to dispossess the native Californio elites of their economic land base and political authority while simultaneously divesting the majority laboring class of their cultural lifeways and legacy. Throughout the late 1800s, local, state, and federal legislation; judicial duplicity; overt racist violence; and more surreptitious intercultural conflict combined to prepare the way for, and quell any resistance to, the new order of things. The conjunction of dominating social processes—public and private land loss, racial conflict, cultural denigration, legal and extralegal social control, economic disenfranchisement, and political disempowerment—structured the increasing subordination of both the elite Californios and the laboring *pobladores* (settlers), though not immediately at the same rate or in equal measure.

Historians of Chicano culture, as well as of California and the western United States more broadly, have noted the persistence into the present of the dominant social patterns produced in this moment of epochal transition from northern Mexico to American Southwest.[1] While this legacy is broadly evident throughout the region, this study focuses on the urban manifestation of these social patterns in California. Major attention is given to their enactment in Los Angeles, as it experienced continuous social-spatial transformations from El Pueblo de Nuestra Señora la Reina de Los Angeles de Porciúncula through its various "American" metamorphoses—from an early Anglo township to the world city of today. A detailed discussion of the city's historical morphology constitutes the first section of this study in Chapters 1 and 2. This singular attention to Los Angeles is called for, as the city is a paradigmatic site of urban Chicano social history (Camarillo 1979:199; Acuña 1984). Since the early twentieth century, the original barrio neighborhoods of downtown and later East Los Angeles have been the most populous and, in many respects, exemplary spaces of urban Chicano settlement. As a result, they have also been the most studied of the many significant barrio communities in the United States.

was not imposed without significant response by the *mexicanos* living within, and acting on behalf of, their developing residential milieus. The situating powers of the landscape, law, and media effects have been regularly, if not uniformly, contested or circumvented by Chicanos. Barrio residents have consciously and unconsciously enacted resistive tactics or defensive mechanisms to secure and preserve the integrity of their cultural place-identity within and against the often hostile space regulation of dominant urbanism. These related and antagonistic forces *together* define the dialectical production of barrio social space, which from the beginning was "shaped not only by external factors associated with the rapid pace of urbanization in southern California, but also by internal changes within the barrio population. The process was an ongoing dynamic one, especially in cities where the Mexican population was increasing rapidly" (Camarillo 1979:198).

Social commentators have long noted the importance of the barrio's internal "geographical identity." This identity, manifest in the unique conjunctural forms of its residents' cultural practices and consciousness, has been a vital mode of urban Chicano community survival against the pressures of a dominant social formation. Richard Griswold del Castillo has characterized this well-developed place-consciousness, present from the earliest period of the Los Angeles barrio, as follows: "whatever its implications for the socioeconomic fortunes of Mexican-Americans, the creation of the barrio was a positive accomplishment. The barrio gave a geographical identity, a feeling of being at home, to the dispossessed and poor. It was a place, a traditional place, that offered some security in the midst of the city's social and economic turmoil" (1979:150). And yet, the barrio was not then, nor is it now, a space of pure security and wholly positive cultural practices. Griswold del Castillo reminds us of this when he notes that even as the barrio represented "a place of familial warmth and brotherhood, it was also a place of poverty, crime, illness and despair. To this day, many Chicanos continue to feel ambivalent about the barrio. The *comunidad* is the basis of a dynamic cultural upwelling, but it also continues to be a place of exploitation and poverty" (ibid.:140). This qualification avoids shining a singularly idealizing light upon barrio culture that would render its expressive manifestations as always necessarily positive or politically contestative. Nevertheless, many of the cultural practices produced and exercised in the barrios have tended toward positive articulations of community consciousness, which contribute to a psychologically and materially sustaining sense of "home" location.

In the same manner and toward the same collective end as the users of those resistive spatial "operations" and "tactics" that Michel de Certeau speaks of in

FIGURE 1.   "El Barrio, Love It or Leave It." Drawing by Sergio Hernández. Courtesy of the artist.

The Practice of Everyday Life, barrio residents have always practiced numerous ways of "establishing a kind of reliability within the situations imposed on . . . [them], of making it possible to live in them by reintroducing into them the plural mobility of goals and desires" (1984:xxii). Manifesting alternative needs and interests from those of the dominant public sphere, the expressive practices of barrio social and cultural reproduction—from the mundane exercises of daily-round and leisure activities to the formal articulation of community defensive goals in organizational forums and discursive media—reveal multiple possibilities for re-creating and re-imagining dominant urban *space* as community-enabling *place.* Thus, they contribute to a cumulative "antidiscipline" that subverts the totalizing impulse of the dominant social space containing the barrios. Collectively, these community-sustaining practices constitute a tactical ethos (and aesthetic) of *barriology* ever engaged in counterpoint to external barrioization.

First coined in the late 1960s by the associated members of the *Con Safos* magazine and artist collective in East Los Angeles, *barriology* was a playful but serious promotion of the cultural knowledge and practices particular to the barrio (Ybarra-Frausto 1978:98–100). The linguistic hybridization of the Spanish root term *barrio* with the Latin suffix *logos*, combining and juxtaposing Chicano popular associations of social space with elite connotations of academic disciplines, was itself a representative barriological practice.

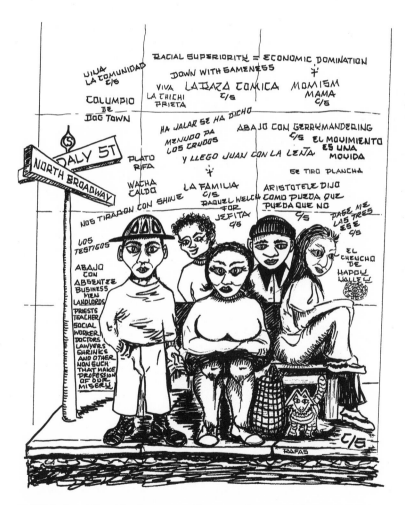

FIGURE 2. The wall as barrio text. Illustration from *Con Safos* magazine by Ralph López-Urbina, a.k.a. Rafas. Courtesy of the artist.

In light of the institutional denigration of Chicano experience in education and the media, *Con Safos* was directly contesting the marginalization of barrio culture, as its editors made clear:

> The *Con Safos* title of the magazine is a symbol adopted from the *Con Safos* of "Caló." Chicano walls in every barrio of the great Southwest, with their graffiti dress of Cholo print, are protected by this symbol of *Con Safos* (C/S) [see Fig. 2]. . . .
>
> Thus, *Con Safos* symbolizes for the magazine the rejection of the "American identity," and the beginning of a Chicano literary genre, a definition of Chicano identity, and an assertion of the moral and aesthetic values of the barrio experience. (Quoted in Ybarra-Frausto 1978:99)

A recurring feature of their published magazine was the "barriology exam" (see Fig. 3), which tested readers' knowledge of barrio traditions and culture, with the highest scores earning a "Ph.D. in Barriology."

As I reassert it here, barriology evokes a whole range of knowledge and practices that form the historical, geographical, and social being-in-consciousness of urban Chicano experience. By retroactively applying a concept and term from the 1960s to practices first manifest in the 1860s, I wish to reiterate my main proposition, albeit in reverse: to broadly identify a historical continuity between past and present circumstances influencing the production of barrio social space and its representations. Only in identifying the tense relationship between socially deforming (barrioizing) and culturally affirming (barriological) spatial practices—which together produce the form and meaning of the barrio—will we come to understand the nuances of this recurring dialectic.

THE MATERIALITY OF PLACE-ATTACHMENT: SENTIMENT, EXCHANGE, AND REPRESENTATION IN THE BARRIO

If the barrio is a complex and contradictory social space for its residents, the motives for defending its territorial and cultural integrity against external disruption must be similarly variegated. The nature of these complexities begs the question: Why is this vulnerable urban milieu so important to Chicanos? Ernesto Galarza, a pioneer in academic Chicano studies, has addressed this question about the substance and significance of the barrio in various capacities as scholar, writer, political advocate, and community adviser. In an interview on the topic of urban displacement in San Jose, California, he was asked

BARRIOLOGY EXAM

BY ANTONIO GÓMEZ
C/S, PhD, BARRIOLOGIST EMERITUS

1. What does the barrio sidewalk mechanic utilize to support his car above ground? _____

2. What does the barrio mechanic use to remove grease from his hands after completing his task? _____

3. What is the greatest single cause of interruptions in street games? _____

4. If someone is said to be *encanicado*, it means that he is
   A. disguised.
   B. a marble fetishist.
   C. in love.
   D. in jail.

5. If you have a cough, what medicine will your *abuelita* be most likely to prescribe?
   A. limonada con miel.
   B. pulmotol.
   C. gordo lobo.
   D. all of the above.

6. According to your *abuelita*, soon after taking a shower or bath you should not
   A. go to a wake.
   B. get a haircut.
   C. cut your nails.
   D. A & B.

7. *Menudo* is made from tripe, which is
   A. the cow's stomach.
   B. the cow's flank.
   C. horse meat.
   D. mutton.

FIGURE 3. Courtesy of the Con Safos Editorial Collective and Sergio Hernández (illustrator).

whether he saw "the preservation of the barrio . . . as desirable." Galarza's response reveals his materialist orientation toward understanding Chicano urban place politics:

> . . . the preservation of a barrio is not the ultimate answer to anything. It's the same sort of thing you get when people talk about preserving a way of life. It's a pretty meaningless phrase. . . . Now there are always *sentimental reasons* for wanting to help people not lose their homes. These are *powerful feelings* but they don't give you much of an intellectual idea of what's going on. (Quoted in Barrera and Vialpando 1974: 13; emphasis added)

I doubt that his reply was meant to devalue or disempower local mobilizations against the disparate impacts of urban restructuring. Rather, I believe he was stressing that an uncritical sentimentality should not be the limit of consciousness informing or resulting from such defensive struggles. This point is clarified in the interview, as Galarza subsequently interrogates the barrio's sociospatial location in the political and economic order of the San José metropolitan system.

To follow his prescription for materially analyzing the barrio's sociospatial situation does not, however, require dismissing "sentimental reasons" and "powerful feelings" as forms of false consciousness. In fact, affective motivations for preserving the integrity of working-class community places may be richly, if not always consciously, attuned to the political economy of urban growth. This point is argued by John Logan and Harvey Molotch, who note that

> [p]oor people . . . are not in a position to effectively claim that their
> neighborhood, *as used by them,* is either a national resource or useful
> for attracting capital. Instead they must make a more "emotional," a
> less "public-regarding" . . . case for their rights to their homes and
> shops. Their claims can be dismissed as idiosyncratic, even if under-
> standable, efforts to intervene in legitimate market and governmental
> planning processes. (1987:135–136; original emphasis)

This characterization of emotionally driven interventions in urban planning also raises the question of how "public-regarding" claims and interests are defined. In their study *Urban Fortunes: The Political Economy of Place,* Logan and Molotch offer ample evidence that these definitions, couched in the positivist rhetoric of cost-benefit analysis and clinical discourses of blight removal, are socially constructed and almost always in the service of private developers and other "place entrepreneurs" who, with their business, media, and government allies, are principal actors in the metropolitan growth coalitions. The material and discursive power of these coalitions allows them to control urban form and meaning such that whatever is good for business is, *ipso facto,* rendered synonymous with the civic interest. Consequently, the escalation of land values and the deepening of the tax base through increased property tax revenues are seen to be inherently good for the city and its citizens.

It has been abundantly demonstrated, however, that urban-renewal and redevelopment projects are usually quite selective in their distribution of associated costs and benefits, beginning with the fact that federal urban-renewal projects "demolished more homes than they built and displaced more neighborhood residents and activities than they relocated" (Boyer 1983:275). Of the 57,300 acres of central-city land made available through federal subsidies between 1954 and 1969, "60 percent of the disposable land went to nonresidential uses" (Mollenkopf 1983:42). With regard to urban highway construction, numerous studies concur with Mark I. Gefland's summary observation that "[n]o federal venture spent more funds in urban areas and returned fewer dividends to central cities than the national highway program" (1975:222). Further account must be taken of the specific loss of low-income housing through neighborhood gentrification, of the various uncompensated material costs of relocation (Downs 1970), of the disruption of place-bound social and economic networks (Logan and Molotch 1987), and of the psychologically devastating "grief response" (Fried 1963) commonly accompanying the severance of home and neighborhood attachments. All told, it becomes clear that while private developers and contractors profit handsomely from their participation in "public" redevelopment projects, their material and psychological costs are borne most heavily, if not exclusively, by the poor and working-class former residents of the areas in which they are sited.

Under the reigning imperatives of cities as engines of surplus accumulation, the use-value orientations to residential place of the poor and working classes can never hope to be equated with the greater good of the city, since, as Logan and Molotch point out, they are not "useful for attracting capital" (1987:135). Ironically, the very fact that the barrios are so often situated in the destructive path of urban restructuring makes their residents exceptionally well positioned to observe and analyze the machinations of capitalist urbanism. Consequently, the "less public-regarding" arguments made by Chicanos in defense of their home turf can be read as *counter*–public arguments, which critically interrogate exchange-value definitions of metropolitan benefit, thus contesting the powerful collective representations of urban-growth coalitions. Cities are thus characterized by competing needs and interests, with those on the side of surplus accumulation having the predominant capacity to shape public opinion or redevelop the city in spite of it.

While it is clear that economic profit drives the engine of growth interests, it is not as apparent what sort of profit barrio residents derive from their inner-city neighborhoods. In a coauthored study with Herman Gallegos and Julian Samora, Ernesto Galarza has provided an excellent summary of the phenomenological substance that constitutes the barrio's "social and cultural capital" (Fernández-Kelly 1995), bringing to the foreground those "intangible" considerations for preserving place that are offered by barrio and other low-income residents against the plans to make "higher and better use" of the land on which their communities are located.

> The intangibles relate to values or preferences which have little to do with the physical redistribution of assets. There appears to be something eminently proper about urban planning that in one process scatters the blight of the downtown slums and rekindles the sparkle of the central city with high-rising chrome. What makes it germane, nevertheless, to discuss intangibles is that all this is happening in the name of Community; and the successful crash of urban redevelopment through the Mexican-American *barrios* is demolishing such community as the ethnic minority had been able to contrive.
>
> This is a crucial matter. If the city offers anything valuable it is those physical points of intercourse, of exchange, of reciprocity and mutual influence, of services and information, of model and example, of variety in styles. When these points of contact disappear, community has faltered. And that is what has been happening in the Mexican-American low-income *barrios.* These were the taverns, the restaurants, the "joints," the motion picture theaters, the barbershops, the small grocery stores, the dance halls upon which the grapevine of the *colonia* was strung. Usually unprepossessing, often tawdry, never luxurious, they were the best in the way of public life that the neighborhood could afford, and the neighbors were comfortable in them. But their very appearance condemned them to destruction along with the deteriorating housing in which their customers lived. (Galarza, Gallegos, and Samora 1969: 23; original emphasis)

This critical analysis details the place-based interpersonal networks that make barrios such important resources—physically, culturally, and economically—for their residents. As such, it offers us "an intellectual idea of what's going on" in the everyday production of barrio social space, thus respecting Galarza's own advice against adducing purely "sentimental reasons for wanting to help people not lose their homes." Of course, the very practices and places of community building he describes are what generate the deeply affective attachments that so often cast an emotional patina over people's perceptions and recollections of their home environments.

According to Raymond Williams, when such expressed attachments to urban working-class milieus are mediated in literature, they embody a particular "structure of feeling" that derives its urgency and affective force precisely as such places are displaced or threatened with erasure under the pressures of capitalism's ceaseless restructuring of space, or what David Harvey (1993) describes as the recurring "spatial fix" of capital:

> The old urban working-class community; the delights of corner-shops, gas lamps, horsecabs, trams, piestalls: all gone, it seems, in successive generations. These urban ways and objects seem to have, in the literature, the same real emotional substance as the brooks, commons, hedges, cottages, festivals of the rural scene. And the point of saying this is not to disprove or devalue either kind of feeling. It is to see the real change that is being written about, as we discern its common process. (Williams 1973:297)

Here, as throughout his theoretical writings, Williams is calling for a materialist reading practice in which the "operations of criticism themselves become an integral part of 'what the text says'" (Silk 1984:165–166). He is careful not to claim that the critical significance of such feelings is transparently manifest in their narrated text form, but rather, is subject to interpretation from them. Rendered as literature, the "real emotional substance" of working people's attachments to urban place can and must be analytically mined, following Williams—and echoing Galarza's prescription for materially situating the "powerful feelings" of barrio residents—to identify "the real change that is being written about, as we discern its . . . process" (Williams 1973:297).

As it happens, Galarza himself produced a literary account of those "intangible . . . values and preferences" specific to the barrio that help ensure its residents' survival while inspiring their affective place-attachments. In "Life in the Lower Part of Town," a chapter from his memoir of early childhood, *Barrio Boy*, Galarza recalls the practices and ethos of everyday life in his immigrant community in early-twentieth-century Sacramento, California. I will treat some of his text in specific detail in Chapter 1. For now, I wish to broadly note that his narration of youthful occupations and pastimes in the barrio expresses a subdued but present nostalgia, inspired by his recollection of how the nascent barrio provided a nurturing social space within the margins of the city's larger social map. Galarza's recollections of life in downtown Sacramento are thus similar to those narratives of "[t]he old working-class community," with its "urban ways and objects," described by Williams. Both acquire critical social meaning not from the manner in which their respective milieus are figured, but, once more, insofar as their figurations can be read as "response[s] to a specific social deformation":

> It is not so much the old village or the old back-street that is significant. It is the perception and affirmation of a world in which one is not necessarily a stranger and an agent, but can be a member, a discoverer, in a shared source of life. . . . For we have really to look, in country and city alike, at the real social processes of alienation, separation, externality, abstraction. And we have to do this not only critically, in the necessary history of rural and urban capitalism, but substantially, by affirming the experiences which in many millions of lives are discovered and rediscovered, very often under pressure. (1973:298)

In *Barrio Boy*, the intimate and nurturing quality of social relations in the lower part of town mediates substantial "experiences of directness, connection, mutuality, sharing, which alone can define, in the end, what the real deformation may be" (ibid.). Focused on the recollection of Galarza's youthful experiences, *Barrio Boy* offers no perspective of the adult Galarza returning to observe the changes that eventually transpired in his downtown neighborhood. However, in his larger corpus of reflections on the situation of urban barrios, he does "come home," in a manner of speaking, to document the social and spatial deformations that would befall poor and working-class Chicano communities across the Southwest.

Galarza's scholarly analyses of barrio social space consequently derive some of their critical strength from an intimate knowledge of its place-making dynamics. When he observes that "the successful crash of urban redevelopment through the Mexican-American *barrios* is demolishing such community as the ethnic minority had been able to contrive" (Galarza, Gallegos, and Samora 1969:23), there is little doubt that his formative years as a "barrio boy" contributed an experiential element to his critique. Although restrained, an affective tone is manifest in revealing figurative language within his otherwise dispassionate scholarly discourse. Consider as an example the indignation coming through his account of a particular barrio's fate against the urban-growth machinery:

> I see what has been happening in Alviso [in Greater San Jose, California] as part of a very broad trend towards the super-urbanization of America. The *urban giants* being created now are not "communities" in any real sense. The people there feel no sense of community. This

process is in fact *destroying what does remain of human communities.* The Mexican communities are very vulnerable to *this kind of cannibalism.* They've been cut off for many decades from their cultural and institutional roots. What is happening in Alviso has already happened to many barrios in the Southwest. (Quoted in Barrera and Vialpando 1974:14; emphasis added)

Rendered by Galarza as malevolent behemoths, the "Sunbelt" metropolises devour those vulnerable communities in the path of their aggressive expansion. His collective literary and scholarly texts on Chicano social-geographic experience range between such deconstructions of macro-urban systems and narrative reconstructions of micro-urban processes. As such, they exhibit two of the principal rhetorical tendencies—understanding "rhetoric" in the expanded sense that Michel de Certeau suggests—that inform the structure of feeling in much barriological expressive culture: an affirmative orientation toward community place practices and a critical orientation toward dominant spatial practices.

These tendencies will variously appear and reappear in my examination of the everyday cultural production of barrio social space (principally in Chapters 1 and 2) as well as of the textual representations of the barrio's past and present transformations under the pressures of capitalist urban development (principally in Chapters 3 through 5). Specific variations of these affirmative and critical rhetorics will also be addressed, most notably with regard to the barrio's internally generated cultural milieu. As I noted earlier, the social dynamics within barrios produce their own pressures and contradictions. Recognizing this, I will variously discuss textual mediations of intracultural tensions associated with changing patterns of immigration, economic restructuring, internecine gang violence, and the cultural hegemony of patriarchy and normative heterosexuality. With their complicated conjuncture of internal and external forces, the barrios of Los Angeles and other California cities have been real and rhetorical locations from which, and about which, to enact ideologically expressive critiques of domination, whether this comes from within or from outside their social spaces. The collective Chicano communities, past and present, as well as the specific activists, writers, and artists discussed in *Barrio-Logos* are, in varying balance, intervening in this intimate social space while interrogating the larger landscapes of power through the political culture of their expressive works.

If the everyday practices of cultural and social reproduction in the barrios are often unselfconscious responses to the external degradations of Chicano social space, the mediations of space and place by those Chicano artists and writers discussed in the latter half of *Barrio-Logos* reveal a fundamental critical consciousness reminiscent of *fin de siècle* avant-garde artists in Europe. Edward Soja praises the latter for having "perceptively sensed the instrumentality of space and the disciplining effects of the changing geography of capitalism" (1989:34). I argue that much the same perception is at work in the texts of urban Chicano artists. This critical consciousness is akin to the contestative impulse that Ramón Saldívar describes as the "dialectics of difference."

> The language of narrative, especially that of Chicano narrative in its place of difference from and resistance to American cultural norms, can best be grasped as a strategy to enable readers to understand their real conditions of existence in . . . America.
>
> This narrative strategy for demystifying the relations between minority cultures and the dominant culture is the process I term "the dialectics of difference" of Chicano literature. (1990:5)

Substituting *culture*—with its reference to multiple expressive media and practices—for *narrative* in Saldívar's description, my study of everyday practices and textual discourses argues that we must understand the urban barrio as a literal "place of difference" and a complex site of material and symbolic production. A brief summary of the contents of the subsequent chapters should serve as a map for the reader's traversal of *Barrio-Logos.*

The first chapter, "Creative Destruction: Founding Anglo Los Angeles on the Ruins of *El Pueblo*," traces the early period (1860s–1930s) of struggle between barrioization and barriology in Los Angeles, and functions as a pair with Chapter 2, which extends the discussion to the present. I detail how Los Angeles was initially transformed into an Anglo city and illustrate the physical, repressive, and ideological strategies—the landscape, law, and media effects—through which Chicanos were subordinately located in the dominant social space. These strategies principally consisted of urban-planning practices, police vigilance and containment methods, and hegemonic representations of the "Spanish romance" and the "Mexican problem." Alternately, I discuss the tactics of everyday life and self-help institutions with which Chicanos laid claim to cultural and civic space for their needs and interests. Similarly, I analyze the discursive production and defense of barrio social space by Spanish-language journalists.

Chapter 2, "From Military-Industrial Complex to Urban-Industrial Complex: Promoting and Protesting the Supercity," is structured similarly to Chapter 1 in its movement between discussing dominant strategies of sociospatial repression (barrioization) and subaltern tactics of sociospatial resistance (barriology). Presenting World War II as a watershed for both tendencies, I reveal the intensification of their dialectic in this period. At its repressive pole, powerful growth coalitions first imagined then began to reconstruct Los Angeles as the supercity of the future, rallying their attendant ideological and repressive apparatuses to the cause. Once more, Chicanos found themselves squarely in the path of this monumental urban morphology: their residential places were coveted by planners and developers as prime spaces for massive urban-renewal and freeway constructions. But as before—and with many of the same discursive, institutional, and popular cultural tactics—Chicanos in the central-city barrios repeatedly defended their use-value orientations to place against the exchange-driven imperatives of the urban-growth machine. A new addition to the barriological tool kit in the postwar period was the development of specifically *literary* forms of discursive intervention by which Chicanos critiqued, with increasing aesthetic sophistication, the instrumentality of dominant spatial practices in marginalizing their communities.

The third chapter, "'Phantoms in Urban Exile': Critical Soundings from Los Angeles' Expressway Generation," focuses on texts of significant critical geographic consciousness produced by writers and artists who came of age during Los Angeles' supercity growth from the late 1950s on. The narrative imaginations of these artists—who are cognizant of the continuing erasure of Chicano cultural landscapes—are haunted by spectral figures of various sorts, as suggested in the chapter title. The artists treated in this chapter are short-story writer Helena María Viramontes, poet Gloria Alvarez, lyricists Willie Herrón and Jesús Velo of the rock band Los Illegals, performance artist and playwright Luis Alfaro, poet and writer Gil Cuadros, and multimedia conceptual artist and writer Harry Gamboa. While these artists carry on the discursive tradition of critiquing external domination first practiced by their Californio journalistic forebears, they do not hesitate to interrogate the corruption of social space by intracultural conflicts. In light of this, I allude to Chicana literary critiques of patriarchal community space, an issue I take up more fully in Chapter 5. I deal more substantially here with how selected writers respond to the alienation of homosexual difference within the normative heterosexuality of Chicano familial culture. Similarly, I discuss the mediated community-disruptive effects of internecine conflicts and intrabarrio tensions tied to the contemporary exacerbation of Chicano gang subculture.

Chapter 4, "Art against Social Death: Symbolic and Material Spaces of Chicano Cultural Re-creation," looks at significant efforts by Chicanos to defend and enrich their aggrieved community spaces in three different urban areas: Elysian Valley in Los Angeles; the Logan Heights barrio of San Diego; and the downtown barrios of Sacramento. With regard to Los Angeles, I will be looking at the literary representations of space produced by Ron Arias through a fantastic narrative makeover of the barrio in his novel *The Road to Tamazunchale*. For Barrio Logan I will discuss the grassroots construction and aesthetic embellishment of a Chicano "people's park" in the heart of the barrio as a community space of representation, as well as its discursive representations in the documentary film *Chicano Park* and the poetic memoir "Logan Heights and the World" by Juan Felipe Herrera. And, most substantially, with reference to Sacramento, I will consider how the community artist-activists of the Rebel Chicano Art Front meld practical interventions in urban place politics with textual representations of the same into a particularly rich form of barriological praxis. This chapter thus illustrates the multiform re-creative practices by which Chicanos have attempted to materially and symbolically reconstitute places of community well-being in the face of the degradations to which they have been subject.

The final chapter, "Between Nationalism and Women's Standpoint: Lorna Dee Cervantes' Freeway Poems," considers a group of poems from Cervantes' prize-winning 1981 collection, *Emplumada*. These poems—"Poema para los californios muertos," "Freeway 280," and "Beneath the Shadow of the Freeway"—variously figure the destructive impact of the Interstate 280 freeway as it cuts through the Greater Santa Clara Valley region and central San Jose barrio of Cervantes' youth. While she reveals a broad social-geographic consciousness akin to her contemporaries in other cities, Cervantes further specifies the constraints experienced by working-class women within Chicano communities. Her texts, therefore, variously focus on the historical violations (and the violation of history) done to the broad Californio-cum-Chicano population through intercultural conflict, and the violations done specifically to Chicanas through intracultural gender conflict. Cervantes alternately expresses a nationalist critique in defending the present and historical interests of *la raza* ("the race," or Chicano people), then decries the patriarchal oppressions within the same *raza*. This ideological variety is plotted across the poems as they map a tightening circumference of social geographies traversed by the freeway: from the Greater Santa Clara Valley through a San Jose barrio and into a matriarchal home.

Creative Destruction

ONE   *Founding Anglo Los Angeles*
on the Ruins of El Pueblo

> . . . *if in discourse the city serves as a totalizing and*
> *almost mythical landmark for socioeconomic and politi-*
> *cal strategies, urban life increasingly permits the re-*
> *emergence of the element that the urbanistic project*
> *excluded. The language of power is in itself "urbanizing,"*
> *but the city is left prey to contradictory movements that*
> *counterbalance and combine themselves outside the reach*
> *of panoptic power.*
> — MICHEL DE CERTEAU, *The Practice of Everyday Life*

MI CASA YA NO ES MI CASA

Bandido Blues: Terror and the Law Effect in Early Anglo Los Angeles

Although California became a state in the American union (1850) shortly after the end of the Mexican-American War, the full cultural dislocation of the laboring *poblador* class and the displacement from power of the elite, landowning Californios was not immediately effected in Southern California, isolated as it was from the national economic system by the lack of a connection to the growing national railroad network. The demographic and infrastructural machinery for a generalized *mexicano* deterritorialization did not gain steam until the completion of the first transcontinental railroad trunk line from San Francisco in 1876, and the subsequent arrival of direct transcontinental links in

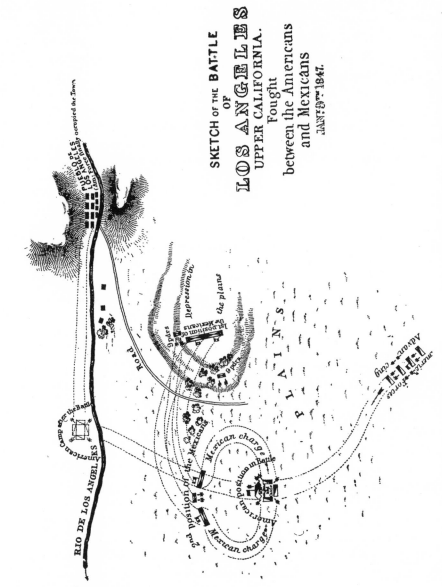

FIGURE 4. "Sketch of the Battle of Los Angeles." Courtesy of the Seaver Center for Western History Research, Los Angeles County Museum of Natural History.

1883 (Southern Pacific line) and 1886 (Sante Fe line). These determining developments compelled a massive in-migration of eastern and midwestern Anglos (whose uninterrupted and voluminous flow would not be checked until the 1930s), the wholesale reorganization of land use by residential subdivision, a radical makeover of the built environment, and the nascent industrialization of the regional economy.

Prior to these dramatic trends, however, the residue of racial animosity from the war produced a protracted intercultural conflict for a quarter century and beyond that sometimes verged on race war. This lingering and violent antagonism served a foundational purpose in consolidating the sociospatial regime of power for the conquering "Americans." Its first major expression, though, took place in northern California. There, the demographic minoritization and general subordination of *mexicanos* (and other non-Anglo "foreigners" such as the Chinese, Basques, and Chileans) began almost immediately, with the massive influx of Anglo-American miners, claim jumpers, and other opportunists drawn to the gold rush in 1849 (Barrera 1979:20). This original restructuring of the ethnic-cultural balance of population was not simply produced by the sheer quantity of the Anglo-American arrivals. Equally compelling were the legal and extralegal strategies for *mexicano* expulsion. For example, the 1850 Foreign Miners Tax was an administrative mechanism employed to pressure "alien" miners out of the region. Carey McWilliams notes that with this "act as the spearhead, a systematic campaign was launched to oust the Mexicans from their claims" (1976:58). Not content with the questionable legality of such ascendant political and juridical apparatuses, many Anglos took independent expropriating initiative to deadly extremes:

> In 1850 a mob of 2,000 American miners descended on the Mexican mining camp of Sonora and, "firing at every Mexican in sight," proceeded to raze the town. The rioting lasted for nearly a week, with scores of murders and lynchings being reported. Following this major assault, individual Mexicans were singled out for attack. Every mysterious offense was promptly blamed on some unhappy Mexican. . . . Juries would convict greasers [sic] on very moderate evidence indeed, and the number of lynchings has never been computed. (McWilliams 1976:58–59)

The consequent effects were felt in Southern California in at least two ways that were significant to the developing *mexicano* spaces of Los Angeles. First,

Los Angeles became home to many of the dispossessed Sonorans, whose substantial settlement north of the central plaza (see Fig. 5) caused the nascent
barrio to be derisively dubbed "Sonora Town" by Anglo Angelenos. Second,
the horrific violations of Mexican human rights in the northern counties
spurred a wave of Mexican social banditry in the north and south. Economic
interest, sometimes merely for survival, certainly underlay many of the raids
against cattle trains heading north to the mining camps and against an occasional mining settlement. However, many of these "primitive rebels" (Hobsbawm 1965) were compelled equally or more by a sense of cultural retribution
(Camarillo and Castillo 1973). This political motive was expressed by Tiburcio Vázquez, perhaps the most famous of these social bandits, who described
how "[a] spirit of hatred and revenge took possession of me. I had numerous
fights in defense of what I believed to be my rights and those of my country-
men. I believed we were being unjustly deprived of the social rights that be-
longed to us" (quoted in McWilliams 1976:60). Among the negative consequences of this social banditry for Mexican Angelenos was the "legitimate"
incentive it provided for anti-*mexicano* violence during the notoriously lawless
1850s and 1860s, when, as Carey McWilliams notes with dark irony: "The
practice of lynching Mexicans . . . became an outdoor sport in Southern California" (ibid.:60). Continuing with decreasing regularity until the end of the
century, the repressive violence against *mexicanos* in Los Angeles, often in conjunction with kangaroo-court proceedings, was a major aspect of general *mexicano* group consciousness. In contrast to the early period of status-conscious
differentiation between the elite Californios (*gente de razón* [educated people])
on one side, and the laboring *pobladores* and immigrant *mexicanos* on the other,
a growing consensus of opinion informed the collective Mexican-descent
population of their general subordination within an increasingly dominant
and hostile Anglo-American society:

> In the early years, the landholding Californios sided with the Anglo-
> Americans in condemning racial violence and banditry [even forming
> part of the first civic police force, the City Guards, in 1856]. But later,
> as the patterns of conflict became more fixed [and their own class and
> social status precipitously dropped], they rose to defend La Raza and
> condemned the racism of the Anglos. The division of the Mexican-
> American community into lawless and respectable elements gradually
> lessened as the Spanish-speaking discovered a common meeting
> ground in Mexican nationalism. (Griswold del Castillo 1979:105)

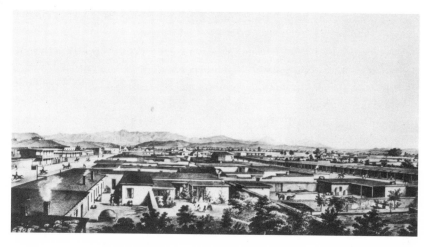

FIGURE 5.   A view of the Sonora Town adobe landscape, north from the Plaza area, in 1857. Courtesy of the Huntington Library, San Marino, California.

This emerging nationalist consciousness was also reactively fueled by a generalized anti-*mexicano* sentiment and a socioeconomic organization whose purposeful effects were ever less respectful of the social divisions that traditionally separated the elite and laboring classes.

An explicitly spatial manifestation of early "police" powers exercised against the working-class *mexicano* community came in the wake of the organized "revolt" of guerrilla bandit Juan Flores and the attendant marshaling of official and unofficial state forces against the nascent Sonora Town barrio.[1] In conscious retaliation against Anglo rule of the land, Flores and a band of followers took control of Mission San Juan Capistrano in 1857, using it as a launching point for their guerrilla raids throughout the southern counties. After a popular Anglo sheriff and two deputies were killed in an ambush by Flores' men, the fear of a broad *mexicano* uprising, coupled with the racial vengeance stirred up by the *Los Angeles Star* (Escobar 85–86), spurred Anglo leaders and their elite Californio allies to form a vigilante committee, which called on the notorious "El Monte Boys" to help quell the incipient rebellion. The El Monte Boys were led by several former Texas Rangers—a para–state police organization infamous in its home state as violently anti-Mexican—who had helped found El Monte as the first separate, all-white township in the region. Consequently, their activities as a quasi-police body may be

viewed through the twin critiques of a racially and spatially manifest antagonism to the local working-class *mexicano* population.

In the purported interest of community security during the peak of the Flores rebellion, the self-appointed vigilante committee declared martial law and
worked with the El Monte Boys to surround the working-class Sonora Town
barrio. Having cordoned off the residential zone, the vigilantes invaded barrio
homes in search of pro-Flores sympathizers. Without legal warrant or notice
of any kind, several persons were rounded up in a nocturnal raid (Griswold del
Castillo 1979: 105). Whether in fear or in solidarity, there was certainly some
support given by barrio residents to Flores' men. However, many of the *mexicano* residents arrested in the barrio and elsewhere during the anti-Flores campaign (some of whom were summarily shot or hung) were clearly unconnected
to the rebel leader. Their guilt lay in being poor and *mexicano* in an emerging
social order that needed their labor but feared and reviled their culture and
their potential collective mobilization along racial and class lines.

Of specific relevance to my thesis in this section, then, is the fact that this
momentary state of siege against the barrio marked a precursory model of
spatial containment and social control by police agents. This disciplinary
model would be recurrently exercised against public and private working-
class *mexicano* social space in Los Angeles during key moments of economic
or social crisis, and it would come to characterize the policing of the barrios,
particularly of their young men, as a matter of policy from the mid-1900s to
the present. Edward Escobar (1983: 96–108) provides graphic detail, culled
from primary documentation in the Anglo press, of counterinsurgent vigilante aggressions in the immediate postannexation period. In so doing, he
intimates the degree of terror experienced among working-class *mexicanos*
while he compellingly argues that the extent and form of retaliatory anti-
Mexican violence was strategically spectacular. That is to say, the spectacle of
violence, particularly in the form of public lynching, was not only entertain-
ing for some of the more malignly racist Anglos and classist Californios but
was, more importantly, a manifest strategy of psychological intimidation that
served to quell any future attempts to challenge Anglo-American rule. By all
accounts, it was a severely effective tactic that served to consolidate Anglo
rule against any lingering ideas of overt *mexicano* resistance and helped to secure Mexican socioeconomic decline as the groundwork for Anglo-capitalist
domination. The late 1800s thus spawned the earliest conditions for the genesis of the barrio residents' implicit social knowledge regarding the application
of a repressive law effect for the social control of barrio spaces.[2] Whether or
not one agrees with Escobar's hypothesis that the first wave of anti-*mexicano*

FIGURE 6. Anglo-American ascendancy in the built environment. Courtesy of the Huntington Library, San Marino, California.

vigilante violence and para–state "policing" was purposefully employed to economically and spatially displace the native *mexicano* population (1983:96–108), this violent period did conveniently precede the first concerted efforts of urban development to transform Los Angeles in anticipation of the coming landscape of Anglo-capitalist dominance.

THE LANDSCAPE EFFECT OF ANGLO URBAN LOS ANGELES

The symbolic force of the changing urban physiognomy in early Anglo Los Angeles is well stated in Robert Fogelson's study of the period: "Indeed, nowhere in southern California was the new order and new destiny promised by the conquerors in the 1840s more evident than in the emergence of Los Angeles as an [Anglo-] American town by the 1880s" (1993:23; see Fig. 6). Fogelson's broad characterization, while clear in delineating the lines of power in the transformation of Los Angeles, pales in tone next to the compelling description that Carey McWilliams offers on the same subject:

FIGURE 7.   Creeping bungalows on the edge of Sonora Town, late 1800s.
Courtesy of the Huntington Library, San Marino, California.

With the great influx of immigrants into Southern California in the
'eighties, the Hispano element was almost completely eclipsed. . . .
The typically Spanish appearance of the Southern California towns
changed overnight. With a truly awful swiftness of transition, they
became undeniably gringo villages [see Fig. 7]. As much as anything
else, the transition was symbolized by the disappearance of the adobes,
and the disappearance of the adobes symbolized the eclipse of the Hispano. (1976:64–65)

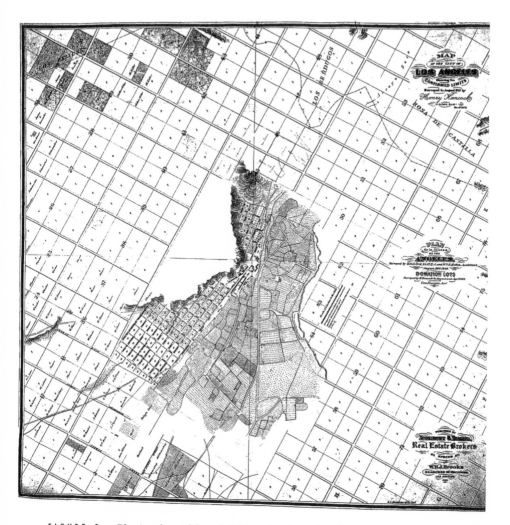

FIGURE 8.   Plotting the grid for subdivision; the Hancock real estate survey of 1857.
Courtesy of the Seaver Center for Western History Research, Los Angeles County
Museum of Natural History.

Among the infrastructural and administrative manifestations of the emerging
urban landscape of power were the reorganization of land-use patterns, transportation facilities, and water resources and their distribution, which collectively laid siege to the preceding *mexicano* organization and administration of
the community's public space. The changes in land use and administration
were particularly significant as both symbol and impetus for the restructur-

ing of the pueblo in its drastic succession by the Anglo township. The privatization of former pueblo common lands was the signal development in this regard, as it embodied both an economic transformation and a cultural conflict:

> The ayuntamiento not only administered the *ejidos* and *propios* (common and municipal lands), but also regulated the solares and suertes so as to prevent speculation. The Mexicans, who were not assessed for their property and considered it a livelihood, were satisfied with these arrangements. But the Americans, who paid taxes on their real estate and treated it as a commodity, objected to governmental restrictions on its exploitation. From their perspective, the thousands of acres the town inherited *[sic]* from the pueblo were more a liability than an asset. So long as the municipality held the land, the newcomers could not cultivate it, and the council could not derive taxes from it. The Mexican policy whereby the community retained control over the development of its land ran counter to both the American inclinations and their traditions. (Fogelson 1993:25)

Consequently, along with the privatization of domestic water distribution in the form of the Los Angeles Water Company, by 1885 the civic authorities had privatized tens of thousands of acres of formerly public, common lands (Fogelson 1993:39). While much has been made of the scale of loss and the unscrupulous mechanisms involved in the dispossession of private landholdings from the elite Californios, the livelihood and lifeways of many more landless *pobladores* were affected by the equally insidious privatization of the original *ejidos*, or common lands (Acuña 1984:6). This, too, was a form of deterritorialization. Even Mario Barrera, an astute and convincing critic of the historical imperialist landgrabbing of United States capitalism, betrays this crucial oversight when he observes that "while it was true that Californios were being displaced from the land, many Californios owned no land from which to be displaced" (1979:20). This originary urban development of the new American Common Council, which replaced the *mexicano ayuntamiento*, set a pattern for urban planning whereby private-sector interests were enabled by public-sector legislation, which Los Angeles public and quasi-public planning agencies would continue to enact into the present (Fogelson 1993:24).

In what would years later become the most densely populated and most spatially besieged area of the Chicano Eastside, Boyle Heights, laboring *mexicanos* experienced just such a displacement. If not as aggressive as the land-use incursions that would characterize twentieth-century urban developments east of the Los Angeles River, this initial restructuring of the original Paredón Blanco (White Bluff) area was nonetheless prophetic of the way in which exchange values would repeatedly dictate the evisceration of *mexicano* social space in Los Angeles. Until the late 1800s *pobladores* were using the bottomland between the river and the bluff for small-scale cultivation, with the higher ground serving as public pasture land. These settlers made up an ethnic majority until the 1880s. At that time, the area was renamed Boyle Heights—after Andrew Boyle, the first Anglo settler in the area—and subdivided as one of the original streetcar suburbs for the new upper class of postpueblo Los Angeles. Boyle's grandson recalled years later that this settlement marked the "colonization of the east side of the river" (Workman 1936: 183). Not surprisingly, very few Mexicans remained in the area after this originary gentrification (Acuña 1984: 5–6).

This suburban transformation of the *ejido* landscape was, however, surpassed in material form and symbolic resonance by the more intensive refashioning of the emerging urban core area around the old *mexicano* heart of the city near the plaza church. The condition of possibility and the active impetus for Los Angeles' urban and sub-urban transformations alike was the arrival of transcontinental railroad links in the 1870s and 1880s. In anticipation of the first trunk line from San Francisco, and of the intense real estate speculation that would surely be generated, Los Angeles and other Southern California towns began their first wave of physical makeovers with the plotting of outlying residential subdivisions and, of greatest consequence to emerging barrio social spaces, central urban redevelopment:

> By 1874 the "bubble of expectation" was full-blown. Picturesque cottages were torn down in Santa Barbara, Los Angeles, and San Diego to make way for the new buildings of the cities-to-be. Wharfs [sic], railway terminals, hotels, warehouses, and churches began to spring up in anticipation of the boom that everyone expected. . . . Old-Town Santa Barbara [the Pueblo Viejo barrio] was "bisected and torn down and almost entirely destroyed." Los Angeles . . . had, by 1876, undergone a similar transformation. (McWilliams 1976: 116)

In his study of this early urban renewal of barrio spaces, *Chicanos in a Changing Society*, Albert Camarillo cites one Californio resident's poignant reflection on the spatiocultural evisceration taking place during the 1870s and 1880s. While it refers to Santa Barbara, there is no doubt it can stand for Los Angeles, where the process was even more swift and complete: "Sometimes it does not seem Santa Barbara anymore—the new houses and strange people and hotels. Some of us have little to do now, and our town is no longer beautiful or gay. Even our houses are being pulled down, as you can see, and in a few years, I think, there will be no Spanish town" (1979:59). The pathos of this early barriological meditation clearly underscores the powerful affective element of grief that will recur henceforth in discourses of urban displacement by Chicanos. As the land-use patterns and built environment of the *mexicano* cultural landscape were being erased or marginalized from view during this initial period of Anglo-dominant urbanization, critical observations of these devastating processes began to appear in the Spanish-language press.

LA RAZA RESPONDE

Spanish-Language Press and the Discursive Space of Ethnicity

Editors of this era interrogated the symbolic cultural implications and practical infrastructural consequences of the Anglo-urban makeover. In 1877, a particularly indignant expression by José Rodríguez, editor of the weekly *El Joven*, adamantly protested the disregard of the City Council for the residents of the Sonora Town barrio. His critique of downtown urban designs made particular reference to the destruction of Californio historical place-memory situated in the plaza district. On this latter point, Richard Griswold del Castillo describes how Rodríguez

> was alarmed that the Anglo members of the Council had proposed destroying Pío Pico's house near the plaza. Pico's house, although in disrepair, held many memories for the Californios. In 1845 it had been the official capital of the province and had been the meeting place of Californio juntas during the 1850s. That the Anglos should regard this monument with such callousness disgusted Rodríguez. (1979:128)

That same year, the editors of *La Crónica* questioned the disparate allocation of infrastructural resources when they observed that "the 'barrio Latina' had inferior roads and public services. 'Why,' they asked, 'don't they give us the same services that the others have?'" (Griswold del Castillo 1979:128). In response to their own query, editors Pastor de Celis, Mariano J. Varela, and S. A. Cardona laid the blame squarely on the "discriminatory neglect of public officials" (ibid.). More significant for my discursive analysis of this emergent barriological critique was the editors' declaration of resistance to the erasure of collective social space. In calling for an organized response by the *mexicano* community, they made this poignant proclamation: "We still have a voice, tenacity and rights; we have not yet retired to the land of the dead" (May 16, 1877; quoted in Griswold del Castillo 1979: 128–129). This statement's integration of emotive sentiment with counterhegemonic expression would characterize much barriological discourse to follow. The identified "voice" both calls a community to political action in organizational defense of its rights and speaks the affective truth of its social reality in contestatory rhetorical form. Specifically, the language of the second clause—"we have not yet retired to the land of the dead"—draws upon one of the most recurring and potent motifs of critically deconstructive Chicano aesthetics: the equation of Chicano social structuration with a form of social death.[3] In the same period of this key editorial, many of the dispossessed Californio elites were committing their individual and collective testimonials to print and archives. Two separate and founding studies of this text-genre have been published, one by Genaro Padilla (1993) and the other by Rosaura Sánchez (1995). In Padilla's study of the genre, he makes note of the persistent figurations of death—social, symbolic, and literal—that pervaded the narration of the Californios' past memories and future prospects (16). Subsequent to this period, similar imagery would characterize expressions made under distinct but still dire social circumstances, as in many texts by Chicano and Chicana prisoners (Harlow 1991). More to the point of this study, however, these early discursive mediations of individual and social death would find corollary representation in the ubiquitous imagery of ghosts, specters, palimpsests, and other phantom presences that haunt contemporary Chicano narratives of urban deterritorialization. Such figurative images mark the present absences, or absent presences, of people, places, and histories that "development" so often obscures or disappears.

The critical editorial and testimonial intimations of social death could, of course, be quite literally substantiated, with reference to vigilante violence against *mexicanos*. Indeed, the Spanish-language press of the period played a significant role in mediating the community's implicit social knowledge of both legal and extralegal violations into a concrete *textual* form of cultural critique, thereby creating, along with the numerous testimonials of the dispossessed Californios, one of the historical and rhetorical antecedents of contemporary Chicano critical and counterhegemonic expressive production.[4] A representative counterdiscourse against the early law effects of Anglo Los Angeles is manifest in the outrage and irony directed against "los lynchamientos" in *Las Dos Repúblicas:* "That a civilized people . . . is converted into voluntary assassins deprecating the authorities . . . is really repugnant and a scandal. . . . Our race ["nuestra raza"] ought to open their eyes to the light of the truth and see what we can hope from the justice of our friendly cousins" [5] (quoted in Griswold del Castillo 1979:108). These and other editorial declarations of the Spanish-language press were being defensively and contestatively articulated in response to the coalescing landscape, law, and media effects of the Anglo power structure. Such explicit mediations of critical social knowledge in Raza newspapers proved "central to the psychological well-being of their readership" (Camarillo 1984:27) as well as to those who could not read but would still receive press-related information through informal networks of discussion. This is not to say that the various publications were of a single ideological voice. There was a broadly identifiable difference between the better-funded, longer-lived journals (such as *La Crónica* and *Las Dos Repúblicas*) published by—and expressing the generally accommodationist views of—the elite Californios, who cautiously clung to their dwindling legacy of public prestige and political influence, and the more poorly funded and shorter-lived newspapers (including *La Voz de la Justicia* and *El Eco de la Patria*) produced mainly by immigrant Mexicans, which more often articulated critical populist and nationalistic sentiments (Ríos-Bustamante and Castillo 1986:100).

In spite of their differences, the many publications that came and went in the late 1800s cumulatively and increasingly expressed positions of broad, if not uniform, community self-defense by critically evaluating the increasingly institutionalized practices—racial violence, land loss, job discrimination, legal injustices, political disenfranchisement—through which all *mexicanos* were being disempowered and made into second-class citizens. These interventions against the structural subordination of the Mexican community constitute the first sustained textual expressions of a barriological ethos directed against the specific instrumental practices or social consequences of barrioization. The consciousness of counterideological purpose was most evident in the common editorial stand taken against the misrepresentations of the dominant media effect, whereby Raza press

> editorial policy often included a pledge to fight for the dignity of all
> Hispano-Americans in the face of Anglo-American prejudice. This
> fight included a constant effort to alter the stereotypical portrait which
> Americans had of the Mexican character. These editors felt that this
> prejudicial attitude was often fostered by the American press, which

they brought under severe criticism for prolonging racial strife and misunderstanding in California. (Neri 1973 : 197)

In its self-conscious role as a medium of critical social information, the Spanish-language press promoted, if not invented, a major discursive resource—which also emerges in the collective discourse of the Californio testimonials studied by Rosaura Sánchez and by Genaro Padilla—for the articulation of a "new social space of ethnicity" (Sánchez 1995 : 303). Both in print and in oral usage, the self-appellation of "la raza" gained widespread currency in the late 1800s, representing the *mexicano* community's broad self-consciousness as a collectively and externally "Othered" cultural group, cognizant of their generalized social subordination within an alien but dominant Anglo social space, and by the early twentieth century, of their overwhelming proletarianization within a nascent industrial economy. Antonio Ríos-Bustamante and Pedro Castillo note that this appellation "emerged as the community's single most important linguistic symbol" (1986 : 100). Rosaura Sánchez echoes this point when she argues that the Californio testimonials constituted discursive

> spaces of collective identity. Here, for the first time in California we find wide-spread use of the construct of "la raza," . . . a construct that allows for an alliance of Latinos of different nationalities [i.e., native Californios, immigrant Mexicans, and a few Latin Americans] in similar situations . . . [where] in-group differences are blurred and they are all perceived as one and subject to the same racist violence. (1995 : 296–297)

She then goes on to conjoin the ideological text-practices of the critical, but essentially private, voices of the *testimonios* (mostly sequestered in the archives of Hubert Howe Bancroft) to the social effects produced by the more public text-practices of the early Spanish-language press, drawing usefully on Benedict Anderson's discussion of how discursively "imagined communities" influence the formation of nationalist consciousness:

> The articulation of ethnicity with language in the construction of an "imagined community" of "la raza" is further enabled by the publication of several Spanish-language newspapers from the 1850s to the 1870s in Los Angeles, San Francisco, and Santa Barbara. Especially crucial in Los Angeles were *El Clamor Público, La Crónica, Las Dos Repúblicas,* and *El Joven,* all dedicated to the defense of the community. (297)

However, the formation of Raza ethnic consciousness was not fostered just by literary textual practices, although these may make up its most identifiable (or documentable) discursive manifestations. The production of this emerging cognitive space was also informed by public festival or ceremonial events as well as through the activities of various practical and cultural self-help organizations that flowered in the second-city barrio zones during the same generative period.

LA ASISTENCIA: ENACTING PLACE THROUGH COMMUNITY-BASED NETWORKS

While not "texts" in the commonsense usage of chirographic documents, the practical and symbolic activities of organizations promoting Raza consciousness through public cultural spectacle entered into the textual contents of the Raza press, producing a symbiosis of discursive and enacted group self-consciousness. Identifying this conjunction, Richard Griswold del Castillo noted that the *mexicano* press gave regular and extensive coverage to Mexican patriotic celebrations, with editors essaying on the significance of nationalist symbolism and consciousness (1979:131). Similarly, a variety of barrio voluntary associations, cultural societies, and self-help organizations were established between 1850 and 1900, including various political and labor organizations, musical associations, fraternal orders, and a patriotic junta (which organized the Mexican national holiday celebrations).

On occasion, these groups engaged in symbolic spatial practices, as in the organization of *días patrias* (patriotic holiday celebrations) and related cultural events in public spaces of the city, most commonly in the Plaza area. Although he was referring to the early-twentieth-century barrio of Sacramento, Ernesto Galarza described his personal experience of the key symbolic function of such events as community-affirming spectacle. His observations would certainly hold true for the ritual psychological effects of similar events in the nascent Los Angeles barrio. Although all major public decisions affecting the barrio were "decided at City Hall or the County Court House," Galarza notes that

> [t]he one institution we had that gave the *colonia* some kind of image
> was the *Comisión Honorífica* . . . [which organized] the celebration of
> the Cinco de Mayo and the Sixteenth of September, the anniversaries
> of the battle of Puebla and the beginning of our War of Independence.
> These were the two events that stirred everyone in the *barrio*, for what

we were celebrating was not only the heroes of Mexico but also the feeling that we were still Mexicans ourselves. (1971:206)

Clearly, these public nationalistic celebrations were cherished occasions in which *mexicanismo* (Mexicanness), mediated through expressive cultural practices (music, dance, food, oratory, costuming, etc.), was directly, if momentarily, projected into a broader public sphere in the city, overlaying a strong collective persona upon the enforced anonymity that increasingly characterized the public identity of *la raza* in the Anglo-dominant city.

At other times, community organizations pursued more practical and long-term spatial interventions. For example, the mutual aid society La Sociedad Hispano-Americana, founded in Arizona but operating an affiliate network throughout the Southwest, initiated several projects of infrastructural development for the barrio community, proposing to build a charity hospital, petitioning the Common Council to build a Spanish-language school, and soliciting proposals from the community itself (through advertisements in the Spanish-language press) for development ideas (Griswold del Castillo 1979: 138). The community-defensive and identity-enhancing efforts of self-help and cultural organizations coincided with the ideological efforts of the press in expressing and constructing the emerging cognitive space of Raza ethnicity. Like the collective discourse of newspaper editorials and reporting, whose "importance grew in proportion to worsening social conditions" (Ríos-Bustamante and Castillo 1986:118), the various associations helped to develop "the symbolic identification of La Raza as a separate cultural entity" (Griswold del Castillo 1979:138). In the process, they underscored the counterhegemonic media effect of the Raza press by promoting *la raza* as a worthy and valuable, even contestatory, collective identity, in direct refutation of their increasing denigration as "greasers" in the racist imagination and media of mainstream Anglo society. The material and psychological effects of these emerging Raza-centric discourses and activities were essential to the survival of the *mexicano* community during the darkest years of overt racial violence and to its rejection of the perception "from above" that *mexicanos* were a disposable population occupying disposable space. Furthermore, the various participatory mechanisms of the voluntary and festival organizations, from membership to public-event production and attendance, offered empowering opportunities to barrio residents by structuring "small-scale networks of support in which Mexican leaders could emerge and serve their own community" (Ríos-Bustamante and Castillo 1986:123).

Along with these popular institutions and cultural associations, numerous mundane and truly "small-scale networks of support" formed the quotidian web of place-dependent, informal community self-help. These networks were made up of mutually beneficial exchanges of goods, services, and information that *la raza*, like other poor and working-class people, depended upon for their material survival and psychological well-being. These included such things as child care, lodging, cooking, job leads, home medical treatment *(curanderismo)*, midwifery, bartering for goods and services, moneylending, and miscellaneous practical or festive activities attendant upon bonds of friendship, *compadrazgo* (godparenting), or extended-family relations. While these goods, services, and information were of practical necessity, their circulation in the barrio carried with it an ethical component, or what might be called an "ethics of marginality" or even a "solidarity of the subaltern." Barrio-based networks of informal support brought their participants into a social compact in which personal obligation for repayment of services, goods, or information was more than a mere contractual agreement. Referring to the social milieu of an early-twentieth-century barrio in Sacramento, Ernesto Galarza aptly describes the functioning of this ethical component as it must have surely worked in other barrios:

> Beds and meals, if the newcomers had no money at all, were provided—in one way or another—on trust, until the new *chicano* found a job. On trust and not on credit, for trust was something between people who had plenty of nothing, and credit was between people who had something of plenty. It was not charity or social welfare but something my mother called *asistencia*, a helping given and received on trust, to be repaid because those who had given it were themselves in need of what they had given. *Chicanos* who had found work on farms or in railroad camps came back to pay us a few dollars for *asistencia* we had provided weeks or months before. (1971:201)

This practical and ethical nexus of *asistencia* was the circulatory medium for the social capital that helped keep the nascent barrios functioning against the odds of an often hostile urban environment. However, these intricately and intimately operative networks are not considered to be generative of any "real" value (i.e., exchange value) or, worse, not even recognized as existing when capitalist growth-driven decisions about urban development propose to displace residents from their laboriously constructed and spatially rooted networks (Logan and Molotch 1987:111–113). Though these socially vulnerable networks may appear to function invisibly, they are, recalling de Certeau, nonetheless effective in making habitable "places" out of dominant "spaces" and thus create a spatial practice of cultural resistance to total marginalization.

The early and multiple manifestations of barriological practice that emerged in the late 1800s would prove to be the historical precursors of the barriological ethos of contemporary Chicano and Chicana artists and activists who would similarly defend *la raza* against the dominant society's assault upon its social spaces. Well ahead of our own historical moment, however, the dialectic of barrioization and barriology would take several shaping turns as Los Angeles went through significant episodes of urban development in the early and mid–twentieth century. After an epochal set of speculative booms and busts in the late 1800s, spurred by the anticipation and then the arrival of direct transcontinental railroad links to Los Angeles, the promotion and development of the coming metropolis was passed from the hands of railroad executives to those of a self-selected group of local elites that included representatives from the major business and civic institutions of the day— most notably the self-designated "Colonel" (and later "General") Harrison Gray Otis, owner of the *Los Angeles Times*. This cadre of leading citizens undertook to set Los Angeles fully and irrevocably on its modern path. While the railroads had put Los Angeles and Southern California on the national map with their combined marketing of health, scenery, and real estate, the first civic boosters had a vision of the region's tremendous commercial and industrial future, and they set an epic growth machinery in motion to realize their dreams. In 1888, on the motion of Otis, the Chamber of Commerce was born, and it immediately proved itself to be the most ambitious entity of its kind in the country, "selling" the city to prospective tourists, settlers, investors, and industrialists in a manner and degree unmatched by any city in the world. Within three years of its formation, over 2 million pieces of literature promoting the personal and economic benefits of the region had been distributed throughout the United States (McWilliams 1976:129). In the process, the Chamber of Commerce set the standard for the wedding of urban development and promotional "imaging" that, in various forms, continues to characterize the peculiar fetishism and "imagineering" (in Disneyspeak) of the commodity known as "Los Angeles" (see Fig. 9).

Through its highly successful advertising efforts and development, the *Times*-led growth coalition—whose leadership passed in succession from Otis in the 1890s to his son-in-law Harry Chandler in the 1920s—willed modern Los Angeles into being. The first thirty years of the twentieth century witnessed a continuous industrial-economic expansion and tremendous demographic growth. From 1890 to 1930 the population increased from 50,000 to

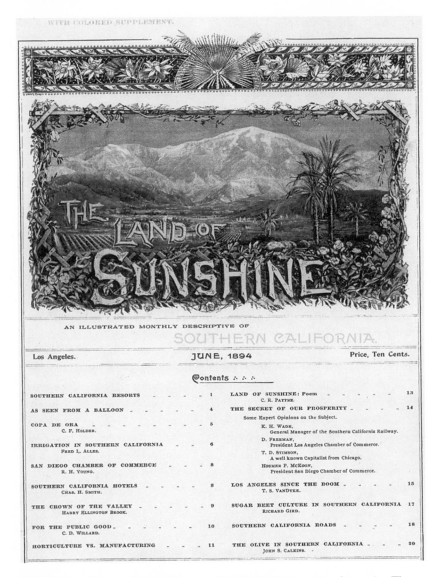

FIGURE 9.   Boosters also sang the region's praises in the promotional magazine *The Land of Sunshine*, edited from 1895 on by Charles Fletcher Lummis, the *Los Angeles Times* city editor and ex-officio cultural attaché to the Chamber of Commerce. Courtesy of Occidental College Special Collections.

1.2 million within the city limits, and from 101,000 to 2.2 million in the county. The *rate* of growth is equally stunning, as the population grew four-fold in the 1880s, doubled in the 1890s, and tripled in the years 1910–1930 (Fogelson 1993:77–78). These phenomenal transformations propelled Los Angeles solidly into the Anglo-dominant industrial future envisioned in the late 1800s by Otis and company. Instrumental to the twin explosions of population and production were the changes to the urban environment in key infrastructural categories that had previously defined the first metamorphosis of "American" Los Angeles: resource supply and allocation (again water, via the monumental Owens Valley Aqueduct completed in 1913, but now including oil and electrical energy); transportation facilities (improved roads and the equally monumental companion to the aqueduct, the artificial deep-water harbor at San Pedro); and land-use policies (through continued residential subdivision, but with the pioneering application of monofunctional zoning regulation). Once again, the impetus for these developments reflected the guiding hand of private-sector business interests, while their realization depended on public-sector financial and legislative support from various governmental bodies: federal allocations for the harbor and permission for the aqueduct right-of-way; local bond financing for the aqueduct; and city charter amendments for the series of zoning ordinances and the police powers of eminent domain to enforce them (Fogelson 1993).

The hierarchy of private-to-public influence, manifest from the very origins of postpueblo Los Angeles, was reenacted in the early twentieth century to an exponentially greater degree and the consequent profit of the Anglo ruling class. Similarly, the effects of this private-cum-public city-building proved especially damaging to the well-being of the growing *mexicano* community and their residential spaces. The conditions were set, then, for the next "modern" cycle of the barrioization-barriology dialectic.

STRUCTURING THE PUBLIC SPHERE AND THE COUNTER–PUBLIC SPHERE

Ethnicity, Zoning, and the Emerging Wonder City

As the Anglo-American population swelled to incredible volume, the *mexicano* community kept proportionate pace with this general growth. Even as *mexicanos* were overwhelmed in absolute quantity, their relative numbers rose from nearly 5 percent of the city's population in 1900 to about 15 percent by 1930. The low-to-high population estimates for *mexicanos* in this period range between 3,000 and 5,000 in 1900 and between 97,000 and 190,000 in 1930 (Camarillo 1984:34). However, the segregated residential patterns already established by the turn of the century guaranteed that the Anglo-American majority, dispersed among the outlying subdivisions, would have limited contact with the growing non-Anglo communities left to the central city. I say "non-Anglo communities," because, in fact, the downtown residential core radiating out from the heart of the city near the Plaza was heterogeneously made up of immigrant workers, most notably southern and eastern Europeans (Italians being the most numerous), Chinese, Japanese, African-Americans, Russian Molokans, Jews, and a smattering of other ethnic and national-origin groups. The tremendous labor needs fueled by metropolitan expansion drew great numbers of workers to Los Angeles, with the Plaza area serving as the principal point of entry, recruitment, and dispersal to all the compass points of the inner city. The dual immigration structure of affluent Anglo-Americans on one side and working-class and poor "ethnic" laborers on the other thus made class difference the most rigid sociospatial demarcator of the city at large (Sánchez 1993:77). Consequently, the various ethnic and national communities in the downtown core lived in relative, sometimes immediate, proximity to each other, producing conditions for cross-cultural contact and influence without, however, melting away their culturally distinct ethnic traditions and orientations.

As the largest of the central-city groups, most *mexicanos* were still clustered in their own barrios, but these were scattered in every direction from and including the original Plaza and Sonora Town area, moving increasingly east and northeast across the Los Angeles River during and after the 1920s. Continuing the trend of the late 1800s, immigrants were a growing proportion of the *mexicano* population in the city. By the early 1900s, foreign-born *mexicanos* outnumbered the native-born (Camarillo 1984:35). This ratio would only increase, with the depredations of the Mexican Revolution as the principal "push factor," until the determining reversal brought about by the effects of the Great Depression. As a result, the political, economic, and cultural patterns affecting *mexicano* community formation in the early twentieth century would be significantly influenced by immigrants with a strong orientation toward their *patria* (homeland) in Mexico.

As in the late 1800s, though, the dominant social structures within which community-building took place would grow increasingly unfavorable to both immigrant and native *mexicanos*. Until the 1920s, they were left largely to their own devices with respect to organizing their quotidian lifeways. Writing about the concurrent formation of the barrio in downtown Sacramento, but again resonating with processes in Los Angeles and other California cities, Ernesto Galarza describes precisely the "laissez-faire" attitude of the dominant culture toward the mundane exercises of culture within the "private" sanctum of the barrio: "There was no place in the public business of the city of Sacramento for the Mexican immigrants. We only rented a corner of the city and as long as we paid the rent on time everything else was decided at City Hall or the County Court House, where Mexicans went only when they were in trouble" (1971:206). Since *mexicanos* were needed as a reserve labor pool for service, construction, and production industries, and so long as their rent was paid, they were left alone in their residential spaces of reproduction. This relative live-and-let-live attitude would be significantly altered in the 1920s by the large-scale proselytizing activities of "Americanization" campaigns, whose significance to the social space of *mexicanos* will be discussed shortly. However, prior to this period, in one of the regular "spatial fixes" (Harvey 1993) that urbanizing capital requires for its continued growth, *mexicanos* living in the downtown core would be reminded of the ever disposable status of their communal living places within the organization of dominant urban space.

In response to the chaotic growth pains of the metropolis—characterized by tremendous population increases, unchecked physical expansion, social disorientation, and erratic variances in property values—civic leaders, revealing the influences of the progressive reform and City Beautiful movements that were prominent at the turn of century (Boyer 1983), felt they needed to intervene and bring order to the apparent disorder of urban morphology. In Los Angeles, zoning emerged as the principal institutional apparatus for realizing the civic leaders' vision of a rationally ordered metropolitan region. Furthermore, the city's built environment would help enact this positivist utopia, as it was conducive in its noble and organized form to moral edification and to a Protestant, middle-class standard of the much-invoked "good life," in cultural, social, and economic terms. The principal architectural signifier of this "progressive" vision, as of the general modernist refashioning of the early-twentieth-century metropolis, would be the new City Hall building, completed in 1928, whose rotunda proudly declared: "THE CITY CAME INTO BEING TO PRESERVE LIFE, IT EXISTS FOR THE GOOD LIFE." As "pioneers in the city zoning movement in the United States" (Glendinning 1941:181), and with the requisite application of police powers to enact the zoning commission's dictates, Los Angeles' municipal planners proceeded experimentally through a series of amended and increasingly variegated zoning ordinances beginning in 1908 and culminating in a comprehensive ordinance in 1925. In theory, this emergent form of government spatial regulation purported to "reform" the township's founding relationship of influence between private enterprise and public authority in urban development. In practice, however, the temerity of city planners, who "considered it essential to secure the support of the [private] developers" (Fogelson 1993: 254), guaranteed that private enterprise, the leading force in shaping the metropolis, would, in fact, be solidified by continued government support of private developers' interests. In a bold position statement, the Los Angeles Realty Board listed as one of their conditions of compliance with municipal planners that "the zoning power should be able to demonstrate that in addition to having relation to good morals, health, protection, and general welfare of the community, zoning has some relation to the general prosperity and to the general land values of the community as well" (quoted in Fogelson 1993:254).

This deepening symbiosis of "community" well-being and capitalist benefit was the precursor to subsequent formulas for urban redevelopment, both locally and nationally, as the public-sector good was always to be tempered by the private-sector bottom line. Zoning regulations consequently "sanctioned the patterns already imposed by private enterprise far more often than they shaped the cast of future development." Thus, already in the early twentieth century it was clear that "nothing in Los Angeles demonstrated the tenacity of private development [to mold the city in its own image and interests] as convincingly as the course of public planning" (ibid.:271).

The fate of the *mexicano* community's spaces and of their "good life" under these modernizing conditions was strongly determined by their always tenuous claim to urban place-rights (Acuña 1984:x; Sánchez 1993:78). In a legally defining court case in which a downtown industrial landowner challenged the powers of eminent domain in the city's first zoning ordinance, "public" municipal disposition was vindicated by the Supreme Court. In 1908, J. C. Hadacheck was required by the city to remove his brickyard from a residential-zoned district of downtown. Hadacheck's failed challenge to the city would prove to be only one of Los Angeles' many prescient achievements in the history of modern urban development practices. As city planner Mel Scott later noted, approvingly I should add, "Los Angeles paved the way for all cities and counties in the nation to exercise control over their growth and development by officially designating how privately owned land shall be used" (1942:20). Against such precedents, the slowly but steadily increasing homeowner class of the *mexicano* community, much less the majority renter population, could expect little recourse to defend their place-rights against the "public welfare" or "public good" determinations of the city planners and their judiciary allies. In fact, the major exercise of eminent-domain powers over *mexicano* residential place in this period, necessary to the expansion of the downtown commercial and business districts, was rationalized as being not only in the general public interest but for the specific welfare of the *mexicano* residents' health and safety (Ríos-Bustamante and Castillo 1986:113). This progressive-era claim was made with regard to the supposedly "pathological" conditions in the "Cholo" housing courts that were so often the subject of reformist discourse, which informed early Los Angeles urban planning via the City Council–appointed Housing Commission.

Following a 1906 visit by Jacob Riis, the most recognized national figure in the progressive reform movement, in which he observed that he had seen slum conditions "of greater area, but never any which were worse than those in Los Angeles" (quoted in Camarillo 1979:203), the Housing Commission was formed and empowered to eradicate the blight that soiled the spotless image of Los Angeles so carefully crafted by its boosters. As one history of the period pointedly described: "This commission took its job very seriously," destroying and evacuating over 450 units of "slum" housing; however, "better housing was not provided. So, Mexicans watched their barrios destroyed as they confronted the pain of total displacement" (Ríos-Bustamante and Castillo 1986:113). Whether this was a consciously racist exercise, as implied in Ríos-Bustamante and Castillo's characterization of it as "Mexican removal," or simply a neutral planning decision based on rational and humane motives, the end result of the Commission's actions made it very clear that "Los Angeles' urban planners gave priority to large economic interests and led government officials away from improving living conditions or investing in urban parks or recreation centers" (Sánchez 1993:82). An exceptionally vivid image of disfigured barrio space is cited by Ríos-Bustamante and Castillo, who describe how the major settlement house working with Mexican immigrants was forced to follow its displaced clientele eastward:

> Only by such a move could it hope to continue servicing the city's Spanish-speaking community. Originally built in 1901, near the Plaza just west of the Los Angeles River, the Brownson House was compelled to change with changing times. Mary J. Desmond, the head resident of that settlement house, recalled its very first days: "It was in a valley surrounded by pleasant homes and attractive gardens, but in

recent years the encroachment of commercial enterprises was so rapid
that the settlement house found itself entirely surrounded by factories and carried on its work beneath three huge towering gas tanks.
(1986:132)

The transparency of such landgrabbing led Albert Camarillo to identify this
specific instance of urban development as an "encroachment/displacement
phenomenon [that] would determine the course of barrioization for Los Angeles Chicanos for the next two decades and more" (1979:203). Indeed, this
structural dynamic, whose roots lay in the original refashioning of the proto-
urban township in the 1870s and 1880s, is a fundamental tenet of historical
consciousness among many barrio residents, even as it continues to be obscured within the dominant discourses of public-seeming urban revitalization. However, even within such shape-shifting, community-displacing parameters, *mexicanos* in the early twentieth century exercised a variety of
countervailing tactics of community-sustaining and -enhancing barriological
practice.

Raza Media and Marketplace Culture in the Central City

Evincing the continued importance of Raza discursive activity, and signaling
the increasing size and literacy of the community, the number of Raza publications grew steadily in number and variety during the first two decades of
the twentieth century. Given the immigrant dominance of the community,
news and commentary about the civil conflict in Mexico were regular features. Tied to this "homeland" orientation was Raza press coverage of various issues and debates pertinent to Mexican nationalist sentiment as expressed
in the United States (Should Mexicans become U.S. citizens? How to combat Anglo stereotypes and increase *mexicano* public image in the larger civic
sphere? etc.; Medeiros 1975). Also, considering the substantial proletarianization of the *mexicano* community, many publications gave significant coverage and editorial support to progressive and radical labor activism and anti-
capitalist agitation, most notably in *Regeneración*, published by Ricardo and
Flores Magón. Even with its strong internationalist orientation, *Regeneración*
gave critical attention to local problems of barrio community residents, such
as continuing racial violence, job discrimination, and judicial-system abuses
suffered by *mexicanos*. Similarly, a content analysis of *La Opinión*—the major
Raza journal (then and now)—during this period shows that, while less regu-

lar than the Mexican Revolution or other topics, significant attention was also given to "colonia solidarity," a category that included many issues that would fall under the barriological rubric, including urban development (Medeiros 1975). Perhaps the major topic under this heading was the contentious 1927 battle over the possible municipal incorporation of Belvedere, an unincorporated residential area immediately east of Boyle Heights. This area was emerging as the major zone of *mexicano*-cum-Chicano homeownership, with a rate of 44.8 percent compared to a rate of 18.6 percent for *mexicanos* within the city limits (Sánchez 1993:198). Interestingly, *La Opinión* argued for and defended the input and decision-making rights of the *mexicanos* in the district. At the same time, however, it took a staunchly nationalist position against *mexicanos* naturalizing as United States citizens in order to get more power as voters.

The Belvedere struggle was a practical barriological manifestation of resistance to the repeated attempts by business interests to transform this major Chicano residential community into a more upscale Anglo neighborhood. Evidence of Belvedere's significance as an emergent *Chicano* community is given by George Sánchez, who notes that by "1930, it had already emerged as the fifth largest area of Mexican settlement in the United States . . . . Family oriented and working class, Belvedere in many ways symbolized the future of East Los Angeles" (1993:198). Local growth interests had submitted several unsuccessful proposals to the county commissioners for the incorporation of this fast-developing barrio community. They hoped to squeeze out barrio homeowners through aggressive taxation and gentrify the area while real estate values were down in order to resell the properties "to middle-class Anglo Americans, forcing up the estate values in neighboring communities and making a tidy profit for real estate companies" (3). Such development would surely have weakened, if not wholly displaced, the growing *mexicano* presence in the area. But the transparent economic motives of Anglo-American gentrification were successfully thwarted by the local *mexicano* majority (both renters and property owners), giving clear evidence of their struggle to maintain control of their property and residential place-rights. The ability of this particular Chicano barrio to resist the imperatives of speculative developers was no minor accomplishment, given the reign of exchange-value directives shaping regional development. To any casual observer, the accumulative machinery of regional growth must have seemed nearly invincible, particularly when its path crossed *mexicano* communal spaces. However, the working-class *mexicano* residents of Belvedere revealed themselves to be more than casual or passive observers of this colonizing metropolitan impulse. Community knowledge of the city's imperious disregard for the recently erased downtown barrios and the continuing infrastructural neglect of the contiguous Eastside and northeast barrios must surely have influenced a consciousness of caution, if not outright distrust, regarding the motives of developers. More significantly, the successful "native" defense of Belvedere against this capitalist spatial transformation was a signal public and political articulation of residential place-rootedness by the now emerging "Mexican-American" or "Chicano" Raza of greater Los Angeles. This defense of social space clearly staked out a claim to place-rights *within* the United States.

The networks of public debate fueled by this and other community issues critically reported in the Raza press were in themselves significant components in the constitution of a *mexicano* "alternative public sphere" (Negt and Kluge 1988). In the central urban areas of greatest concentration and distribution of press publications, the very means of their dissemination and the interpersonal dynamics through which their contents were discussed were important manifestations of urban *mexicano* spatial praxis.

> In downtown's Main Street area, from First Street to the Plaza, people gathered informally to read local newspapers and argue perspectives. There were several bookstores in the area, and most of them offered a selection of Mexican as well as U.S. Spanish-language publications. Magazines and newspapers were usually distributed by people pushing carts along Main Street and throughout the Plaza area. . . . Often, workers would meet in poolhalls and billiard parlors spread along the northern sections of Main Street. It was there that they would read newspapers aloud and discuss points of interest. (Ríos-Bustamante and Castillo 1986:118–119)

Complementing the press-inspired discussions on the streets near the Plaza, popular commercial culture also contributed to the interpersonal enactment of public urban culture. Music producer and distributor Mauricio Calderón would regularly play the latest *corridos* (ballads) through a loudspeaker facing out from his store on Main Street (see Fig. 10), attracting groups of attentive listeners who would discuss among themselves the merits and contents of the latest recordings (Foster 1939).

In some cases, the *corrido* texts available on disc or broadside in Calderón's store were self-reflexive meditations on the vibrant public and aural space in

FIGURE 10.   Commercial landscape *de la raza*. Courtesy of El Pueblo de Los Angeles Historical Monument.

which they were being disseminated. Such is the case with the strange fatalistic verses—probably inspired by the conjunction of economic depression, millenarian proselytizing, and *mexicano* deportation of the period, all of which would have been especially manifest in the Plaza area—in the text of "El fin del mundo—música de la casita":

> Y a los de saco rajado
> y del pelo embadurnado
> también se los lleva el tren.
> Ya se acabó el palo blanco,
> ya no se les oirá el tranco
> por las calles de la Main.
> [And to those of split-tailed coat
> And of oiled hair
> The train will also take them.

The pale blond is out of the picture,
No longer will they hear the life on Main Street.]

. . . .

Y a los cuates papeleros
ese atajo de argüenderos
que nos gritan en la Main
Con todos sus papelotes
y sus raspados ganotes,
también se los lleva el tren.
[And to the pals, newsies,
That bunch of noise makers
That shout to us on Main Street
With all their big papers
And their scraped throats
Will also go to wreck.]
    (Quoted in Foster 1939: 122–123; original translation)

The active public culture intimated here and in the previous historical description was largely male-centered, since most of the residents, job seekers,
and other hábitués of the central area adjacent to and immediately north of
the Plaza were single men. Single women, married couples, and families were
increasingly concentrating in the growing Eastside barrios, particularly Belvedere, where homeownership was a more viable option (Sánchez 1993: 138).
However, the Plaza zone was not exclusively a male public sphere. Although
a slowly growing concentration of *mexicano* small businesses was emerging on
the Eastside, the business corridor running north and south of the Plaza remained the major enclave of mercantile, entertainment, and civic-festival activity for all Raza, young and old, male and female, immigrant and native-
born, until the 1940s (ibid.: 181). Residential dispersal of the community away
from the central business district did not diminish its connections to the historic heart of the Mexican city around the Plaza. Extended electric railway
connections to the Eastside and the concentration of industrial, construction,
and service employment in the central area kept otherwise scattered barrio
dwellers connected in a network tied to the traditional urban core (Ríos-
Bustamante and Castillo 1986: 129). Furthermore, the Plaza district did offer
the benefits of public urbanity to women who could avail themselves of it. For
most women, this meant transgressing the patriarchally constructed spatial
borders that kept many women away from the area, except in the sanctioned

contexts of commercial or festival occasions. But this was exactly the attraction of the area for many:

> "Here no one pays attention to how one goes about, how one lives," declared Elenita Arce, pleased at the greater freedoms allowed unmarried women. . . . Knowledge and use of effective birth control, for example, seemed concentrated in a small group of Mexican women living in these downtown communities. (Sánchez 1993:138)

With the eastward development of *mexicano* marketplace culture, however, specific sites of commercial activity catering to and run by women provided less culturally (patriarchally) transgressive but still empowering public spaces for congregation and women-centered discourses of daily life. For example, Vicki Ruiz has speculated on the appearance of Eastside barrio beauty parlors in the early twentieth century (as an epiphenomenon of the expanded commodification and promotion, via Hollywood imagery and print advertising, of personal grooming and style), claiming that "neighborhood beauty shops reinforced women's networks and became places where they could relax, exchange *chisme* (gossip), and enjoy the company of other women" (1993:117). Such public commercial women's spaces were specifically outside the purview and control of husbands, fathers, brothers, and other male figures of domestic patriarchal influence. They were also a more comfortable and creative alternative to the more regimented labor modes and spaces in the cannery and garment industries, which were a principal alternative or adjunct to work in the traditional domestic sphere.

The significance of the Main Street commercial and entertainment corridor, which traversed the Plaza, as a zone of *mexicano* public cultural identity and as a site of Otherness to the larger Anglo metropolis, cannot be underestimated. In the context of a growing ersatz "Spanish" cultural landscape— marked by such signal phenomena as the "Mission Revival" cult in architecture and home furnishings; the rash of Anglo-directed civic "fiestas," "fandangos," and "Mission Days" celebrations; and the touristic reification of a pseudo-Mexican marketplace culture in Olvera Street (which was the founding archetype, with an ethnic twist, for such manufactured "street environments" of today as Universal City Walk and Santa Monica's Third Street Promenade [see Fig. 11])—the real places of *mexicano* marketplace practices were sites of authentic cultural expression and reproduction.[6]

In the Plaza/Main Street commercial corridor, *mexicanos* could satisfy quotidian needs in a multisensory public sphere of *Mexicanidad* (Mexican-

FIGURE II. The original caption to this 1930 photograph reads: "A pretty Mexican girl is attendant at one of the many pottery marts on Olvera Street." Courtesy of Photograph Collection/Los Angeles Public Library.

ness). At the same time, this zone of public marketplace activity was the focal point for the progressive-era concerns of Anglo-Protestant reformers and like-minded citizens, fueling their fears of the moral and racial pollution of the new metropolis.

AQUÍ ESTAMOS Y NO NOS VAMOS

Attacking the "Mexican Problem": Repressive Pacification and Ideological Incorporation

Tied to the progressive-era fears of the corrupting influences of mass culture and its substantial "other half," that is, the ethnic immigrant constituency in the urban center, was a corollary fear of the political "mob" that that constituency also seemed to represent in the minds of business leaders and social reformers alike. Much of the founding impulse for late-nineteenth-century urban moral reform, whose discourses and practices underlay early-twentieth-century progressivism, was a conscious reaction against the perceived threat of political "anarchism" and related forms of radical labor activism. The many spectacular public manifestations of working-class unrest in the late nineteenth and early twentieth centuries (including strikes, pickets, rallies, marches, and violent confrontations with private and state police strikebreakers) indelibly impressed upon the collective mentality of the bourgeoisie and their increasingly suburban, middle-class functionaries the image and fear of "unruly masses" in public congregation as the great urban evil of the period (Boyer 1978; Weibe 1973). Given such precedent in the dominant cultural imagination, the use of the Plaza for *mexicano* (and other ethnic immigrant) labor organizing and political expressions—such as the efforts of the radical Partido Liberal Mexicano (PLM) organizers to rally support for the Magón brothers and other PLM leaders during their 1911 federal trial for violating United States neutrality laws—struck at the fears of Los Angeles' urban elites, who despised in equal doses the class and racial difference of Raza culture.

Perhaps the most spectacular spatial enactment of *mexicano* political culture in the Plaza, revealed negatively by the degree of violent police retaliation it prompted, was the Christmas riot of 1913. During a peaceful Christmas Day rally, principally attended by *mexicanos* and organized by the International Workers of the World to protest unemployment in the city, the police attempted to halt the event under the pretense that organizers had not secured the necessary permit. Refusing to disperse, the organizers brought the wrath of the waiting officers upon the crowd, and a full-blown riot ensued between police and citizens. Even after the riot subsided and the Plaza emptied, police carried out retributions in various *mexicano* public leisure spaces. Officers invaded Mexican restaurants, pool halls, and movie houses in search of suspected rioters (Escobar 1983:213–216). In spite of multiple witnesses attesting to the initial police provocation, many public officials called for measures to prevent "rabble-rousers" from instigating future unrest. Most fervent among these "leading" voices was Chief of Police Charles Sebastian. His call to legislatively restrict the right to free speech in public gathering places (ibid.:216–217), though not limited to the Plaza or its environs, was clearly meant to disable this political-cultural space in particular.

Against the reigning myth of *mexicano* "vagabond transience" (Ríos-Bustamante and Castillo 1986:136), such countermanifestations of place-identity as the grassroots defense of Belvedere and the enactment of cultural space and political activity in the central Plaza marketplace zones served public notice of the deepening urban place-rootedness of *mexicanos*. The contrast between a lingering hegemonic perception of *mexicano* impermanence and their actually increasing rootedness is revealed in Ríos-Bustamante and Castillo's description of an extensive report prepared by Dr. George Clements in 1929 for the Chamber of Commerce. In the report, they contest Clements' conclusion that the Mexican

> "comes to America primarily to sell his labor for American money so that he may return to Mexico and be a landed citizen." The utter absurdity of his claims, and the fact that many Mexicans in the United States raised families, bought homes, and sent their children to school did not stand in the way of widespread acceptance for the Clement paper. (1986:137)

If in the early twentieth century the growing commercial and cultural enactments of *mexicano* social space remained substantially outside the purview of the Anglo majority population, sheltered as they were in their early suburban cocoons, a decided shift in the dominant cultural attitude toward *mexicanos* was nonetheless emerging by the 1920s in the minds of a small but influential leadership class of urban reformers. The increasing public spatial practices of *la raza* collectively proclaimed *aquí estamos y no nos vamos* (here we are and we're not going away), thus fueling a proportionate increase in worried attentions and actions of the self-appointed guardians of middle-class, Anglo-American cultural propriety.

As Albert Camarillo suggests, when "the public began questioning the myth that Mexicans were here temporarily and would eventually return to Mexico . . . Anglos shift[ed] their focus to the 'Mexican problem.' Most of the early attentions after World War I took the form of efforts to Americanize the Mexicans" (1979:225). Americanization was considered a panacea for the perceived cultural maladjustment evidenced in *mexicano* practices of everyday life: personal hygiene, dietary traditions, religion, public use of Spanish, and patterns of household and family care. By changing these quotidian manifestations it was felt that the cultural differences at the root of *mexicano* alienation from mainstream "America" would be trained out of the culture. In theory, cultural reprogramming of *mexicanos* would make them more assimilable to the American civic body in their circumscribed role as complacent workers motivated by the Protestant capitalist work ethic. Consequently, Americanization efforts were considered a necessary strategic accommodation to the fact that *mexicanos* and their "problems" were not conveniently going to leave the city, as well as to the undeniable truth that they were essential to its continued economic and physical growth.

The ideology informing these reform programs clearly contained the seeds of an aggressive and broader cultural demonization that would follow the early Americanization efforts. Particularly under the intellectual leadership of Dr. Emory S. Bogardus of the University of Southern California, a cadre of leading Los Angeles social reformers and educators were infused with a proselytizing zeal and sense of mission in which they "saw their role as awakening the growing Anglo American population of Los Angeles to the social realities and dangers represented by poorer, ethnic newcomers to the region" (Sánchez 1993:97). Within the liberal paradigm of progressive reformism, these "realities and dangers" were understood as relatively benign ones of cultural difference, easily rooted out and replaced with proper "American" practices by training and education programs. But this clearly superficial analysis of the "Mexican problem" failed to identify, much less attempted to remedy, the institutional and structural inequities underlying the community's social subordination, thus largely dooming the reformers' efforts to failure (Camarillo 1979:226). Rather than provoking a necessary reconceptualization of the seeming unassimilability of *mexicanos*—and perhaps fueled by some frustration among the reform leaders themselves—Americanization campaigns would lend credence to much more malignant interpretations and scholarly claims of *mexicano* cultural pathology. The perceived failure of *mexicano* reorientation to the reformers' normative cultural values was easily translated to nativist stereotypes—which were gaining ever stronger currency in the period (Higham 1988:264–330)—of the innate Mexican propensity for violence, criminality, and general social malfeasance.

The arrest patterns of the city's police department contributed to this general perception of Mexican cultural deviance by criminalizing mundane patterns of community activity, especially among youth. Official police statistics for 1927 and 1928 showed that "one-fourth (24.5 percent) of all juveniles arrested for being idle and vagrant . . . were Mexican" ("Mexicans in California": 205). These apparently objective data offer no account of just how the police officers in the field defined "idle and vagrant" behavior. The "street-corner society" (Whyte 1943) of *mexicanos*, especially in the more crowded barrios, and the inevitable lulls in employment common in the seasonal labors in which many engaged, did not factor as social data. Such contextual concerns were of little importance to the positivist view of reformers and government officials who processed these numbers, focused as they were on the predictive value of the bare "facts." The California Fact-Finding Committee, whose 1930 report cited these statistics, was quite explicit in its socially interpretive use of police data: "Statistics of crime and delinquency of the Mexican element in the state in comparison with corresponding figures for the general population serve as an index of racial or national characteristic and also as an index of the adjustment or lack of adjustment of the Mexican to American customs and standards" ("Mexicans in California": 197). Since the resident Mexican community between 1925 and 1930 has been estimated at 7–15 percent of the total population of Los Angeles (Camarillo 1979:200; McWilliams 1976:316), there was clearly a significant degree of *statistical* delinquency on the part of Mexicans at this time, which was subsequently used as evidence of their inherent ethnic characteristics. This early collusion between statistical representation and cultural interpretation would continue to plague barrio residents, especially young men, in the decades to follow. It reached its first mass public crescendo during the 1940s, with the mainstream hysteria regarding the *pachucos/as,* or "zoot-suiters," as folk devils, which I will subsequently discuss.

Anticipating this discussion, however, it is worth citing at length from Ruth Tuck's ethnographic narration of the social production of Mexican youth deviancy during the early 1940s, since she deftly characterizes the sorts of contextual variables and cross-cultural misunderstandings that were almost certainly at work in the early statistical analyses.

It is certain . . . that the prejudices, conscious or unconscious, of law enforcement officers provide . . . [an] impetus to frequent arrest. . . . [They] certainly have no special equipment for the delicate business of handling second-generation youth. To such an officer, the youthful population of . . . [the *colonia*] is likely to appear as "jail bait."

If the arrest pattern of juveniles points to one moral, it is that the young Mexican-American leaves himself statistically unprotected by his habit of idling on street corners. The places at which arrests most commonly occur and the times at which they are made point up the picture vividly. Mike Maldonado and his pals are gathered at the corner of Sixth and Monticello, with no more criminal intent than that of "watching what is going on." If they are noisy, when the police car comes around at 9:30 P.M., they are "disturbing the peace." If they move a hundred feet in one direction or another, they are "loitering in the vicinity of a pool hall." . . . If they drift over to a municipal dance, their very appearance in a body may lead to further disturbance of the peace. The tragedy of juvenile misbehavior everywhere is its essential unplanned, undeliberated nature. . . . The boy of . . . [the] *colonia*, in following the village pattern of recreation set by his elders—that of idling and conversing on the streets—puts himself in further jeopardy. (1946:213–214)

While dominant authorities and social reformers may thus have been misreading the contextual circumstances and culturally specific uses of public space by *mexicanos* as signs of their maladjustment to American ways of life, a curious inverse phenomenon was also taking place: Hispanicizing aspects of the city's public memory in the semiotic form of the built environment and mass culture.

Although these two phenomena may not have been causally linked, they did tend toward a common effect: the neutralization or erasure of present, lived forms of expression, historical consciousness, and material iconography reflecting the city's actual Mexican legacy. This was effected, on the one hand, by the attempt to culturally deracinate *mexicanos*, and on the other, by the manufacture and promotion of a Spanish "fantasy heritage" for the region (McWilliams 1948:35). The latter was spectacularly expressed in the many "Days of the Dons" and "Mission Days" celebrations that flourished in the 1920s, theatrically enacted in the annual California "passion play" of *Ramona* in Hemet (in adjacent Riverside County), and architecturally manifest in the ubiquitous Mission Revival style. Conceived primarily as a ploy for promoting regional tourism and real estate development, this "orientalizing" (Said 1978) commodification of the fantasy heritage encoded in the popular imagination the idea that California's Mexican culture was "a quaint, but altogether disappearing element in Los Angeles culture" (Sánchez 1993:71), accessible only in the reified object-form of a pseudohistorical cultural landscape and iconography (see Fig. 12). The disarticulation and disempowerment of local, living *mexicano* cultural links to their past, and particularly to their historical resistance to colonization, "inflicted a particular kind of obscurity onto Mexican descendants of that era by appropriating and then commercializing their history" (ibid.).

To a careful and critical observer, of which there would have been many in the *mexicano* community, the hegemonic symbiosis of Americanization and Hispanicization must have been apparent. Carey McWilliams postulates as

FIGURE 12.   The fantasy heritage incarnate: "Dancers (descendants of the early dons) before old Avila home—Olvera St." [original caption by the Chamber of Commerce]. Courtesy of Photograph Collection/Los Angeles Public Library.

much about the critical awareness of barrio residents in early Anglo-dominant Santa Barbara with respect to the transparent hypocrisy of the Hispanophilic civic festival there:

> The 3,279 Mexicans who live in Santa Barbara are doubtless more bewildered by these annual Spanish hijinks than any other group in the community. For here is a [dominant Anglo] community that generously and lavishly supports the "Old Spanish Fiesta"—and the wealth of the *rancheros visitadores* is apparent for all to see—but which consistently rejects proposals to establish a low-cost housing project for its Mexican residents. (1976:82)

The ideological complementarity and hypocrisy of simultaneously attacking the "Mexican problem" while embracing the "Spanish romance" marked a signal moment in the dominant cultural placement of *mexicanos* in a material urban order and symbolic landscape of power. However, this hegemonic "moment" did not enter the designs of power, nor acquire its social meaning therein, sui generis. Instead, it recalls the originary period of *mexicano* historical severance and cultural neutralization in the 1870s and 1880s, when the founding structuration of the Anglo-American protometropolis was accomplished by the wholesale displacement of the architectural legacy, land-use practices, and politico-economic organization of the preceding pueblo social space.

As in the previous era, the administrative and spatial regime peaking in the late 1920s and early 1930s was built upon a concerted urban plan of physical displacement of *mexicanos* from the expanding downtown administrative and industrial districts, along with their corollary ideological and symbolic displacement from the historical and cultural geography of the city. Even as the Anglo city builders were ceremoniously crowning their achievement of modernist metropolitan urbanity with such material and spectacle achievements as the newly completed (1928) Art Deco City Hall building (made conspicuously outstanding as a public trophy building by its exemption from the 150-foot "earthquake-proofing" limit on construction height; see Fig. 13) and the 1932 hosting of the Olympic Games, the plans were already being laid for the next great incarnation of the metropolis in the post–World War II "supercity."

Just as the postpueblo, premetropolitan period laid the necessary groundwork for the epochal urban development that peaked in the 1920s, so this second period of metropolitan "wonder-city" growth planted the seeds for post–World War II "supercity" expansion. The first great traffic snarls of downtown Los Angeles, of a magnitude unmatched by most other cities until the 1950s, convinced the newly formed (1923) County Planning Commission of the high-priority need to devise and implement a master plan of highways for regional restructuring in the coming autopia (Scott 1942:23). With changes coming fast and furious on the horizon, *la raza* was in for another rough ride on the growth machine.

The Emerging Social Space of Mexican-American Identity in the 1930s

The *mexicano* community that would soon find itself in the path of the next epochal restructuring of urban space would be of a very different character than the one that staked out its vulnerable niches in the landscape of the late-nineteenth-century city and the early-twentieth-century metropolis. A predominately Mexican-*American* community would struggle under and against the disruptive impacts of the urban development in the successive stages of planning and construction of the postwar supercity. While Mexican Ameri-

FIGURE 13.   A sign on the landscape, 1929. Courtesy of Photograph Collection/Los Angeles Public Library.

cans would confront many of the constraining strategies of barrioization and exercise many of the contestative barriological tactics from the preceding periods, they would do so under a different rubric of political-ethnic identity and place-consciousness, compelled by the radical demographic and cultural impact of the Great Depression in the 1930s (Sánchez 1993:206).

The primary factor underlying this emergent identity formation was that approximately one-third of Los Angeles' *mexicano* population was forced, co-erced, or persuaded to return to Mexico in the 1930s. In the face of severe unemployment, the earlier reformist concerns about Americanizing Mexicans into their role as laborers gave way to the always-lurking nativist opinion that the solution for the new "Mexican problem" (Mexican laborers competing for jobs with Euro-American workers) was to get rid of as many Mexicans as possible. While actual forced deportations did not produce the majority of repatriations, they did set the tone of anxiety and felt antagonism that fueled the decisions of many "voluntary" returnees. Furthermore, part of the psychological strategy of deportation was the dramatic, almost staged performance of police-force invasion of *mexicano* public and private spaces. Most notably, on February 26, 1931, a highly publicized immigration raid of the Plaza district again revealed the great symbolism of the site for both *mexicanos* and the Anglo power structure. Four hundred people were detained by a joint force of immigration officials and local police that cordoned off the Plaza, but only seventeen (eleven *mexicanos*, five Chinese, and one Japanese) people were taken into custody (Sánchez 1993:214). Other less publicized incursions into the public spaces of the central-city and Eastside areas, as well as some intrusions into businesses and homes, also occurred. The cumulative message of these actions was to tell the immigrant majority (and many of the native-born as well) that they were not welcome, while signaling more insidiously that their public and private social spaces were, once more and in the last instance, little refuge against the exercise of authoritarian police force and intimidation. The *mexicano* community was thus served one of its intermittent spectacular notices of the repressive law effect.

The greatest demographic losses of the 1930s were registered among single men and young families, and these turned the ratio of immigrant to second-generation Raza on its head. This dramatic shift accelerated the demographic and cultural dominance of the native-born *mexicanos*-cum–Mexican Americans. Consequently, the decade witnessed a coalescence of social forces that marked an epochal shift in the social place-consciousness of the ascendant Mexican-American (native-born or raised) community. George Sánchez' narrative of this transitional moment merits extended citation.

The major outcome of repatriation was to silence the Mexican immigrant generation in Los Angeles and make them less visible. As construction on the new Union Train Terminal [monumentally designed in Mission Revival style] alongside the Placita in 1934 began, the presence of the Mexican immigrant community diminished further in the downtown area. Reminders of a vibrant Mexican immigrant life disappeared for the larger Anglo American population. The ethnic diversity which had in the past so profoundly marked the [central] city was now becoming more segmented as movement of Mexicans into East Los Angeles gained momentum. Increased residential segregation, decreasing inter-ethnic contact, and concerted efforts on the part of local officials to rid Los Angeles of its Mexican population resulted in Chicanos becoming an "invisible minority."

Nothing epitomized the redefined status of Mexicans in Los Angeles better than the movement to restore the Los Angeles Plaza area . . . [begun in 1928].

Ironically, restoration was completed at the very moment when thousands of Mexicans were being prodded to repatriate. The lesson was clear: Mexicans were to be assigned a place in the mythic past of Los Angeles—one that could be relegated to a quaint section of a city designed to delight tourists and antiquarians. Real Mexicans were out of sight and increasingly out of mind [see Fig. 14]. Physically further away from the center of power, Mexican immigrants remained close enough to provide the cheap labor essential to industry and agriculture. Repatriation removed many, but others continued their struggle for survival east of the river. *Their children, however, made it much harder for the Anglo American community to designate Mexicans as relics of the past. These young people, born and educated in the United States, demanded to be included in the city's future as Mexican Americans.* (1993 : 225–226; emphasis added)

Perhaps the most significant public organizational expression of this Mexican-American generation's reorientation to place-rights was their increased participation in U.S. labor-union activism (Sánchez 1993:228–229). While clearly related in class consciousness and organizational practice to *mexicano* labor activism in the previous decades, these struggles for workers' rights shifted the cultural-geographic orientation decidedly to the American national context and away from the Mexican international one. This "Americanization" process, unlike the progressive reformers' imposed programs, was self-effected by working-class Chicanos who were increasingly entering the city's expanding urban-industrial work force, albeit usually in the lowest unskilled rungs, even as they still provided a majority of the labor for the industrialization of agribusiness in the outlying county areas. In a number of differ-

FIGURE 14.   Painting of Olvera Street for a Chamber of Commerce display, 1930.
Courtesy of Photograph Collection/Los Angeles Public Library.

ent collective mobilizations, Chicano and Chicana workers earned important
work-place concessions in victory or learned valuable political lessons in defeat (Acuña 1988:220–231).

Materially, Chicanos were increasingly able to pursue homeownership,
sinking roots in Boyle Heights, Belvedere, Lincoln Heights, and the other
growing Eastside Chicano neighborhoods (see Fig. 15). The Raza population was thus beginning to construct the parameters of the East L.A. "super-
barrio"-to-be. The 1930s residential reorientation of Chicanos eastward
across the river continued the trend of intraurban migration given impetus
during the "Mexican removal" projects of the years 1910–1930. This emerging residential pattern was further consolidated by the emergence of a Mexican commercial district along First Street in Boyle Heights that rivaled and
would eventually displace the original Main Street district. However, the
rigid and divisive monoracial segregation of Chicanos and immigrant Mexicans would not be substantially achieved for another twenty years. With
new Anglo-American settlement increasingly concentrated in the blossoming
Westside subdivisions, the separation of the central from the western districts
was still more class based than racially determined. Although race-restrictive
covenants were widely employed to keep the "undesirable" poor and working

FIGURE 15.   Joe and Carmen Martínez in front of their home on 2nd Street, Boyle Heights, ca. late 1920s or early 1930s. Courtesy of Shades of L.A. Photograph Collection/ Los Angeles Public Library.

classes out of the Westside suburban WASP areas, the "other half" left to the central urban core remained, for now, ethnically diverse (Sánchez 1993:77).

The cultural variety of the inner city must be kept in mind in discussing this period of Los Angeles barrio formation, for even though East Los Angeles would in many respects emerge as the prototypical Chicano barrio of the United States, communities of Chicanos and Mexicans would establish significant barrio settlements in the entire residential circumference of downtown, often in company with other migrant ethnic communities, and usually as the largest of them in the polyglot zones. During the 1930s and early 1940s, therefore, conditions of relatively easy interethnic proximity and varying degrees of cultural contact and exchange best described the circumferential downtown barrios. As mentioned earlier, public transit allowed community networking to substitute for absolute residential clustering. With downtown serving as the hub of transit, work, and cultural entertainment for Chicanos and other working-class groups, a vital multicultural urban public sphere functioned in the Broadway theater district and the Main Street commercial and entertainment corridors through the 1940s. It was this centralized public culture that was severely affected by the emerging car-oriented urban plan. In spite of its functioning order, the dominant cultural planners would come to see only "blight," conveniently or coincidentally rationalizing their ideas to retake the area for their own "higher and better uses." The death of the electric-trolley mass-transit system and the triumph of the expressway super-city in the 1950s and 1960s would deal a crippling blow to the working-class urban multiculture existing downtown prior to the war.

The growing exercise of collective "voice, tenacity and rights" (to recall the language of *La Crónica*'s 1877 editorial declaration) expressed in American labor-union activism was repeated in numerous other Chicano organizational and cultural activities. These included a range of ideologically diverse, community-directed structures whose loosely collective momentum contin-ued the historical trajectory of *mexicano* voluntary associations, though now redirected to act through the American institutional public sphere, in the areas of educational reform, voting, electoral politics, and legal defense of civil rights (Acuña 1988:235). Among the more notable self-help groups of this period were the civil rights–oriented Congreso de Pueblos Que Hablan Español (Congress of Peoples Who Speak Spanish), the more accommoda-tionist (and predominately middle-class) League of United Latin American Citizens (LULAC), and the youth education–focused Mexican American Movement. The success of these and other Chicano organizational manifes-tations of civic place-rights was still circumscribed by the community's con-tinuing second-tier social placement within the Anglo-dominant urban order. Nonetheless, the sense of participation or membership in the larger Ameri-can polity and the perception of achievable economic security fueled a slowly growing hope, even optimism, among Chicanos that they might also partake of the American dream.

In contrast to those elements of transient "por mientras" (for the time being) place-consciousness (Galarza 1971:204) in the immigrant-dominant barrios of the first two decades of the twentieth century, the newly dominant Mexican-American generation of the 1930s was clearly staking its claims to locally rooted turf and place-rights. Along with the labor-activist expressions of rootedness, other less apparent but symbolically potent declarations of turf claims were also first noted in this period. Among these were the organiza-tional and expressive practices of a Chicano youth gang culture, born in the liminal transition from immigrant to native-born dominance. The first gang sets, or *clicas*, were formed in the 1920s and were flourishing in the 1930s (Moore 1978; Vigil 1988), marking a particularized, "American" manifesta-tion of local, defensive urban territoriality. The *clicas* were (and still are) an al-ternative public institutional structure within the already marginalized social spaces of *mexicano* culture in Los Angeles. Displaced from both the dominant culture of Anglo-Angelenos (as the already demonized "hoodlums" of developing social-scientific discourse and police imaginations) and the Mexican nationalist orientations of their parents, gangs and Chicano youth clubs (which are not synonymous) constituted a parallel public sphere and system of corporate identity within the marginal spaces they inhabited.

This liminality was simultaneously social, in the developing alienation of youth from the dominant cultural and familial ethnic spheres, and physical, insofar as it derived from the material geographic conditions in which the gang structure was manifesting itself. The spatiality of gang and club culture was literally signaled through the popular expressive practice of marking specific turf boundaries with their *placas* ("tagging," in contemporary usage). This practice was already in full bloom by the early 1930s (Romotsky and Romotsky 1976: 12; Sánchez-Tranquilino 1991: 55), and thus could certainly be pushed back to at least the 1920s for a point of origin. There are no ethnographies or other studies of this early period on tagging, as it would have been effectively invisible to barrio outsiders. However, contemporary studies of the expressive parameters and propositional functions of *plaqueasos* (tags) suggest possibilities for speculating on the likely significance of the practice in its formative period. Speaking broadly of the practice in the postfifties era, Marcos Sánchez-Tranquilino makes an explicit connection between the morphology of barrio spaces and the genesis of tagging:

> The space available to Chicano youth in the *barrios* (and housing projects in particular) for recreation and social interaction was severely restricted due to the carving up of these working-class neighborhoods by manufacturers and developers. *Placas* represented a system developed by Chicano youths by which they could divide what little space (territory) was left. Space as a limited resource was the territorial economy upon which their street culture was based.
>
> Operating on that level, *placas* were designed by them to serve as a public check of the abuse of power in the streets. *Barrio* calligraphy became an innovation developed by Chicano street youth culture to visually signal and monitor the social dynamics of power through coded symbology in the economy of restricted public space. To understand the socialization process of Chicano street culture is to understand the institution of *street social control* imposed, not by traditional authority, but rather by the youth who found it necessary to participate in it. (1991: 51–52; original emphasis)

The urban conditions outlined by Sánchez-Tranquilino for the postwar period also characterized the social and spatial conditions endemic to the central-city barrios of the years 1910–1940, when the expansion of the downtown administrative, industrial, and railroad zones severely exacerbated the shortage of decent residential spaces available to *mexicanos*. Then, as now, space was a limited resource, so that in all likelihood early *plaqueasos* were employed by the emerging Chicano youth groups for self-regulatory ends similar to those of contemporary *clicas*.

While the Mexican-American community was consolidating its new ethnopolitical consciousness and place-identity through official structures and unofficial practices, the dominant cultural leadership of Los Angeles was coordinating the apparatuses through which it would ideologically interpellate and materially locate this emerging community in a rebuilt landscape of power. Buttressing the authoritarian terrorism of forced or coerced "repatriations," the increasingly nativist scrutiny of the "Mexican problem" in academic and mass-media discourses gained a virulent momentum. Rodolfo Acuña notes that "during the 1930s, it became even more popular for Anglo-American educators and social scientists to blame the Mexican[s] for their failure to Americanize and progress in the utopia known as 'America' " (1988 : 235). The consequences of these supposedly objective discourses would prove brutally repressive to the Eastside community, particularly to its youth. A perverse sort of "applied research" was enacted in the public measures, intended to curb or remedy the growing "Mexican problem," that were increasingly taken by the conjoined forces of educational tracking, police antagonism, judiciary prejudice, and even vigilante violence. While these actions were directed particularly at Chicano youth, their cumulative effect, particularly via sensationalized mediation in the mainstream press, produced a generalized vilification of the Chicano working-class community. These social-scientific and pseudoscientific discourses of *mexicano* sociocultural pathology would come to be a fundamental category of evidence used to justify urban renewal as the social panacea for "blight" removal in the "infected" social spaces of the barrios. These discourses were supported by a cottage industry of committee reports and academic investigations, couched in the positivist rhetoric of clinical evaluation and made public spectacle in the press. This broad discursive-cum-institutional degradation of the growing Eastside Chicano community, not to mention the long prior history of working-class *mexicanos'* maligned other-ness to Anglo-Angeleno society, underlay the racialized assault they would spectacularly be subjected to during and after World War II.

From Military-Industrial Complex to Urban-Industrial Complex

TWO   *Promoting and Protesting the Supercity*

> *The power of place—the power of ordinary urban land-scapes to nurture citizens' public memory, to encompass shared time in the form of shared territory—remains untapped for most working people's neighborhoods in most American cities, and for most ethnic history and most women's history. The sense of civic identity that shared history can convey is missing. And even bitter experiences and fights communities have lost need to be remembered—so as not to diminish their importance.*
>
> —DOLORES HAYDEN, *The Power of Place*

> *When you operate in an overbuilt metropolis, you have to hack your way with a meat ax. I'm going to keep right on building. You do the best you can to stop it.*
>
> —ROBERT MOSES

BATTLE ON THE HOME FRONT

Moral Panic and Cultural Conflict during World War II

Describing the ideological context for the rising anti-Mexican sentiments of the early 1940s, Rodolfo Acuña noted that "the war-like propaganda conducted during the repatriation [campaigns of the 1930s] reinforced in the minds of many Anglos the stereotype that Mexican Americans were aliens.

FIGURE 16.   Zoot-Suit riots in downtown Los Angeles, June 1943. Courtesy of
Photograph Collection/Los Angeles Public Library.

The events of 1942 proved the extent of Anglo racism" (1988:254). The principal occurrence he goes on to recount is the mainstream media's demonization of Chicano youth in conjunction with the 1942 "Sleepy Lagoon" murder
trial of twenty-two members of the 38th Street Club. This major instance of
the ruling law and media effects was followed by the more generalized vilification of and violent aggression against Chicano youth (along with some
Black and Filipino youth) perpetrated by police and military personnel during
the infamous (and misnamed) "Zoot-Suit Riots" in 1943 (see Fig. 16). Both
events, and the corollary public hysteria about "gang wars" and "pachuco
crime waves" that they spawned, have been much commented on, then and
now, as shameful episodes of blatant institutional and individual racist assault
upon Chicanos (Acuña 1988:253–259; McWilliams 1948:227–243; Tuck
1946:212–217). What I want to distill from the ample historical record are
the spatialized discourses and spatializing practices directed against and contested by the Chicano community. I will thus be arguing that the events of
1942 and 1943 were signal moments in the continuing dialectic of oppressive
barrioization and contestative barriology.

Key tenets of the discursive-cum-spatial effect exercised against Chicanos in the war years are revealed in the "scholarly" testimony of E. Duran Ayers, head of the curiously named Foreign Relations Bureau of the Los Angeles Police Department, during the Sleepy Lagoon trial. Rodolfo Acuña conjectures that Ayers may not, in fact, have been the author of the report he read from and entered into testimony during the trial. Based on other published newspaper reports by Ayers, in which he appears to have shown some sympathy for the difficult social pressures that affected Eastside residents, Acuña wonders if he might have simply been the designated public spokesperson for policies and social interpretations of Eastside criminality drafted by higher-ranking officials (1984:17). Regardless of its precise authorship, Ayers' pseudoscholarly testimony was terribly derogatory toward the greater Mexican population. It identified a racially "innate desire to use a knife and let blood" (Acuña 1988:255)—as opposed to the more sedate violence of fisticuffs practiced by Anglo-Saxons—which supposedly originated in the sacrificial practices of their Aztec ancestors. The initial guilty verdicts rendered against the majority of the defendants seemed to give police officers official sanction to use exceptional means to curb these "innate" propensities of Chicanos. In this respect, Acuña concludes that the "Ayers report, which represented official law enforcement views, goes a long way in explaining the events around Sleepy Lagoon" (ibid.).

Bolstered by such official attitudes, specific preventive strategies—roadblocks, unwarranted searches, mass arrests, and the padding of statistical "gang files" with names of youth—entered the day-to-day repertoire of police and sheriff's officers' interactions with the residents of the Chicano barrios (Acuña 1988:255–256; McWilliams 1948:235–239). The intensified spatial vigilance and containment of the barrios were effective border-patrolling practices of particular strategic value to police agencies as Chicanos increasingly became automobile owners, with greater facility to move out of their barrios and potentially into the segregated enclaves of the Anglo-American majority. As troubling as this intraurban border enforcement was, its repressive effects would be further exacerbated by the more insidious police and military transgressions of public and private Chicano spaces that followed.

Fueled by the racist yellow journalism in the three major dailies—the Chandler-owned *Times* and the Hearst-syndicate *Daily Mirror* and *Herald Express*—fears of Chicano criminality amounted to a "moral panic" (Hebdige 1979:88) in the mainstream public imagination. Among the major newspapers, only the *Daily News* showed journalistic restraint in reporting the situation (Durán 1992:59). Responding to this media effect, and as members of its implicitly Anglo-American reading public, police agencies were no longer content to merely patrol the intracultural borders and monitor interzone transit. Increasingly, they turned to internal vigilance and aggression against the cordoned inner-city barrios and ghettoes. Joan Moore describes the effect of this transitional moment, noting that "until the 1940s, police policy for Hoyo Mara [an Eastside barrio] was to let a peculiar community go its peculiar way. Older [community] members recall that police harassment generally occurred only when gang members left their area" (1978:59). This period of relative security within the barrio would take a definitive turn around the "pachuco incidents" into the still current era of reciprocal antagonism (ibid.). Suspicion of the law became a key tenet of barrio implicit social knowledge, most clearly held by its youth, as illustrated in the comments of one East Los Angeles resident of the Maravilla housing projects. Recalling his post–World War II childhood, he notes: "How far back this fear and dread or how far back this fear goes or whatever it is, I don't know, but ever since I can remember, the cops meant something evil to Mexican kids" (ibid.:59–60).

A spectacular expression of this more aggressive, invasive, and substantially youth-directed policing occurred in June of 1943, when military servicemen, stationed just north of downtown in Chávez Ravine and following the lead of several off-duty police officers, invaded key public zones of Mexican youth congregation throughout Los Angeles County. The most recognized and probably most aggressive assaults, however, occurred in downtown and East Los Angeles. The vigilante military brigades further targeted the trolley lines, pool halls, sidewalks, and other public gathering places, where they beat and stripped young "Zoot-Suiters," sometimes shredding their clothes. Private homes were not always safe haven, and the physical assaults even involved sexual molestation and violation of some Chicanas.

Don't Spit on My Corner, Miguel Durán's memoir of this period, offers a rich experiential account of the public occurrences and of his intimately felt perspectives as an identified *pachuco* gang member. He notes that when the servicemen's riots broke out,

> all hell broke loose. Servicemen acted like vigilantes. They would roam up and down Spring, Main, Broadway and Hill Streets. In the beginning, they jumped any young person who looked Mexican or Black and dressed in drapes. Later, they went for anyone that was brown or black. White America cheered and the police stood by and watched the action. The servicemen got real brave, they got into taxi cabs and drove around barrios like Alpine, Temple, Califa and Macy,

looking for pachucos. Man, they spit on our corners! They were
treated like heroes by the Paddys. All of this was reported in those two
rags, the *Times* and the *Herald Express.* They wrote some inflammatory
stories about how the Zoot Suit hoodlums were going to be cleaned
out by servicemen and good riddance and all that shit! (1992 : 59) [1]

As Durán graphically recounts, these offensive actions by "our boys" were
inspired and supported by the conjoined effects of ideological and repressive
urban state apparatuses, as the military vigilantes were lauded by the press and
largely left to their actions by observing police and sheriff's departments officers. These latter agencies themselves "arrested over 600 Chicano youths
without cause and labeled the arrests 'preventive' action" (Acuña 1988 : 257).
Police even raided a Catholic welfare center to pick up some of its Chicano
clients. If not for the interventions of the Military Shore Patrol, the aggressions might have been worse. Although the servicemen were finally brought
under check, the years following the "riots" saw the police wage a continuing
battle against the young men and women of the Eastside who were categori-
cally figured as *pachuco* hoodlums. Describing this turn in police-Chicano
relations, McWilliams offered an example of the repressive interpellation of
Chicano youth in the case of a boy who was arrested forty-six times, without
once having a formal charge issued against him (1976 : 320).

   In spite of the transparent bias of the police arrests and racist vigilantism
of the servicemen, no significant reprisals were directed against the military
and police aggressors. The resolve of law enforcement agencies and certain
local officials to defend the servicemen's actions did not waver, even after the
public censure by Eleanor Roosevelt (Acuña 1988 : 258–259) and in the face
of pressure from the U.S. State Department, which feared straining hemi-
spheric Allied relations if Latin America got wind of an anti-Mexican race
prejudice. In fact, long-time Eastside activist Bert Corona recalls how Germany *did* attempt to represent this racial conflict to their propagandistic
advantage: "When the riots took place, the Nazis transmitted the news
throughout Latin America, broadcasting editorials to whip up resentment towards the United States" (Mena 1982 : 30). As a midcentury nadir in the application of official and unofficial state apparatuses against the public spaces
and public image of the Chicano community, the events of 1942 and 1943
served notice of just how vulnerably Chicanos were situated in the map of
power. Nevertheless, this sobering public message concretized the community's implicit social knowledge of their status vis-à-vis dominant institutions
of ideological and authoritarian power.

The Mantra of Urban Blight: Imagineering Expressway L.A.

Rhetorically related to the aggressions of press, police, and vigilante service-men against Chicanos and their community spaces were the equally repressive landscape effects of 1940s urban-planning discourses. Advocating highway construction, "slum clearance," and "higher-use" redevelopment of prime central-city property, urban-planning campaigns "took on the spirit of war-time propaganda, particularly aerial bombings," suggesting the urgent need for scorched-earth policies to raze the "infected" central-city neighborhoods as a check against their spreading to the better areas of the city (Klein 1990: 13). The specter of urban "blight," a term in discursive currency both locally and nationally since the late-nineteenth-century reformist "discovery" of the immigrant slums, returned with magnified intensity during the 1940s (see Fig. 17).

In this period "blight" emerged as the mantra of redevelopment boost-ers, who drew on the pseudoscientific rhetoric of professional planners self-designated as "surgeon generals" (Goodman 1971:67) in battle for the physical, economic, and moral health of the metropolitan body. Clearly, though, these collective representations by the regional growth coalitions were self-serving "strategic rituals" (Logan and Molotch 1987:154) meant to coordinate private economic and political interests with a public-seeming and apparently "value-free" concern for the greater metropolitan well-being. This was not necessarily bad faith or direct deception on the part of the urban elites, since in the context of the capitalist urbanism that framed their plan-ning decisions, the potential aggregate benefits of increasing growth and sur-plus accumulation (job development, increased tax revenues with rising real estate values, and the like) were considered to be a net good for the city as a whole, an attitude consonant with the entire history of postpueblo urban planning.

In a show of democratic spirit and public interest, the visionaries of the new Los Angeles offered their dreamworks for all to marvel at, and hopefully to quell any dissenting opinions by dint of seductive specular evidence of the wonders of the supercity to come. Practical example was made of the first major element in the emerging expressway metropolis: the Arroyo Seco Park-way. Pleasantly landscaped (for the moment, since the original garden-variety plants were soon asphyxiated by the automobile exhaust) and smoothly con-toured (for traffic topping off at around 40 miles per hour), the Parkway served as a full-scale, functional model of the highway advocates' techno-logical aesthetics. Complementing this working display were publicly dis-

BLIGHTED AREAS!

COMPARED WITH NON-BLIGHTED AREAS

WHAT THEY PAY IN TAXES

WHAT THEY COST **YOU**
For FIRE - POLICE - HEALTH - PARK SERVICES

NON-BLIGHTED AREA

BLIGHTED AREA

$ 4.25 $ 11.30
PER CAPITA **INCOME**

BLIGHTED AREA

NON-BLIGHTED AREA

$ 7.11 $ 3.67
PER CAPITA **OUTGO**

HOW THEY AFFECT HEALTH & CRIME

INCIDENCE   PER   10,000   PERSONS

	BLIGHTED AREA	NON-BLIGHTED AREA
FIRE ALARMS	256	·142
POLICE ARRESTS	350	100
CITATIONS	1240	370
JUVENILE DELINQUENCY	68	10
HEALTH SERVICE	356	54
COMMUNICABLE DISEASES	69	14
VENEREAL DISEASES	13	1
TUBERCULOSIS	705	91
CHILD HYGIENE	965	212
	4022 ◀ **LOOK** ▶	994

COMMUNITY   REDEVELOPMENT

FIGURE 17.   "You" versus "They": Rhetoric of the Other in blight discourse. Courtesy of Los Angeles City Planning Department.

seminated "photo-sketches of an orderly cityscape that bore no resemblance to what actually stood at the time" (Klein 1990:12), but that nonetheless prophesied a rebuilt modernist utopia in two dimensions.

The scale-model cityscape produced for visual consumption in the 1941 public exhibition of the Regional Master Plan projected the planners' visions

FIGURES 18 and 19. Strategic rituals of the freeway boosters. The Automobile Club's proposed motorway, 1937. Used with permission of the Automobile Club of Southern California.

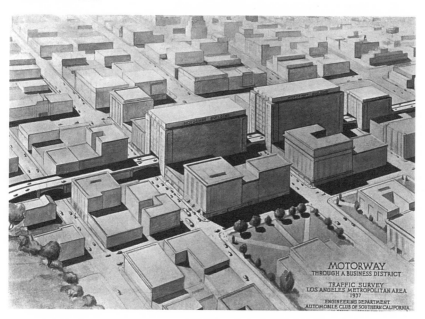

into three dimensions, likewise offering a completely rebuilt downtown. Accompanying this celebratory exhibit was the publication of Mel Scott's *Cities Are for People: The Los Angeles Region Plans for Living* in 1942. This text was widely disseminated and cited throughout the forties and was later revised and expanded into textbook form as *Metropolitan Los Angeles: One Community*. The 1942 publication is a gold mine of semiotica through which to analyze the technocratic mind-set and ideological worldview of the growth advocates. The cover shows an aerial photograph of a major traffic thoroughfare, which is linked to five cartoonlike figures through arterial projections leading straight to their hearts. The book felicitously plots the evolution of the city as an unending progression of technologically and legislatively facilitated improvements of the region, both in its urban and natural landscapes. The city is oddly figured as both an ever-expanding machine (of which its citizens are operative parts) and as an ever growing body. This biomechanical figuration and evolutionary narrative of the metropolitan area is literally framed by the signal technology of the region's next evolutionary stage: the stylized design of a freeway cloverleaf adorns both the front and back inside covers. The emphasis of the study, however, was not so much on the freeways to come as on the urban decay at hand, and Scott persistently invoked the mantra of blight in his pseudoscientific advocacy of surgical intervention.

Later promotional materials propagated the "imagineering" vision of the planners beyond the region, reminiscent of the turn-of-the-century marketing of the city under the auspices of the Chamber of Commerce and the All Year Society. Among these, the 1944 *Plans for Downtown Los Angeles' Four Pressing Needs* showed "virtually all of downtown north from Pershing Square gone and replaced, particularly Bunker Hill, already drawn as leveled, located west of an imaginary cloverleaf" (Klein 1990:6 n. 41). The wartime discourses and promotion of the expressway metropolis were more than innocent, if opportunistic, advertising. Los Angeles' freeway visionaries had been tellingly informed by the important contributions of Nazi Germany's national expressway system to its early military successes. The understated awe of Los Angeles freeway planners is detectable in a major document of the period that shows that the lessons were not lost on them:

> Germany's *reichsautobahnen*, an elaborate 1,330-mile system of express highways, expedited that country's early military successes in World War II. Attacks on Poland, the Low Countries, and France were delivered with such fury and suddenness that the world marveled. A complete system of parkways would not only assist in defense of Los Ange-

les from a military standpoint, but they would aid in the production of necessary war materials by reducing traffic's waste. (Los Angeles Department of City Planning 1941:8)

This technomilitaristic argument reached its national apogee in similar claims made by President Eisenhower's administration in support of the 1956 Defense Highway Act, the federal legislative catalyst that pushed the country irrevocably into the superhighway future. Furthermore, the faith in regional planning as the necessary form of urban-industrial organization was directly fueled by the war experience. The organization of production for wartime needs proved to be a dry run, under ideal autocratic and Keynesian conditions, of the very sort of centrally administered regional planning dreamt of by the city-building elite. In the war years, Southern California and the San Francisco Bay Area (like Seattle in the Northwest) were organized as centralized, functionally zoned, and coordinated regions of major industrial production. Describing the emergent regional growth coalition in the Bay Area, Chester Hartman noted that its business and government leaders "learned the value of concentration and regional planning for efficient economic organization" (1974:33), a lesson of tremendous profit. The incredible productivity exercised in support of the Allied triumph was taken as evidence of the professional planners' long-held faith in the effective and transformative power of rationalized land-use planning.

The homology of military and urban planning was made explicit in a major wartime report issued by the Los Angeles County Regional Planning Commission. "Freeways for the Region" (1943) is dedicated to William J. Fox,

"Colonel, United States Marine Corps [and] Chief Engineer of the Regional Planning Commission, who, through his active participation at the front is now helping to win the war, and who, after the war will help win the peace through his equally vigorous administration of such planning projects as this." (n.p.)

Driven by national emergency and fueled by government subsidy, Los Angeles enjoyed boom conditions of industrial growth and diversification (via Southern California's next great growth industry: defense contracting, particularly in aerospace technologies), labor immigration (both domestic and foreign), and real estate development (via the housing crunch for war workers). It was the best of times and the worst of times.

During the war, Chicanos and Chicanas served the Allied cause in the fields, in the factories, and on the fighting front, laboring under the illusion that patriotic duty would be rewarded with social acceptance and equal economic opportunity. Chicanos enlisted and died in combat at a rate greatly disproportionate to their percentage in the local and national population, and they became the most highly decorated of any national ethnic group (Morín 1963). Yet, on the wartime home front and in the experience of many returning veterans, the message was clear that Chicanos, and Mexicans who immigrated as contract laborers under the federal guest worker or Bracero Program initiated with Mexico in 1943, were still considered little more than a necessary but disposable and unappreciated work force. The obvious injustice and hypocrisy of this mainstream social attitude would fuel a much more critical assessment by many Chicanos of their real conditions of existence in American society, so while they continued to participate in the broader social system, many of them did so much more guardedly and with a well-grounded indignation.

Immediately after the war, the community would be given warning of the shape of things to come for their residential areas. In 1946, for example, county plans were drawn up to locate a juvenile detention center in Belvedere. While the plan was thwarted by Eastside community mobilization, it would not be the last attempt to put prisons in the barrio. The immediate postwar experience of unfulfilled promises and spatial incursions influenced the formation of postwar barrio organizations such as the American G.I. Forum and the more stridently activist Community Service Organization. Both of these drew on returning World War II veterans, who shared a sharpened sense of social contradiction in light of their heroic service to the war effort abroad followed by a return to second-class citizenship at home. With the help of such new organizations, as well as with the support of extensive grassroots community mobilization, Edward Roybal succeeded in winning a seat on the Los Angeles City Council, making him the first *mexicano* to hold public office in Los Angeles since the late 1800s. Not coincidentally, Roybal would be the most persistent, and at times only, voice of official dissent from the growth-machine interests that decisively guided city and regional development during the 1950s. Roybal's election was the clearest and most prominent public manifestation of the Los Angeles Chicano community's collective claim to political-cultural citizenship and urban place-rights in the period.

Attendant upon this moment of Eastside political consolidation, the fully coordinated assault of the landscape, law, and media effects against the barrios entered into its most disruptive period during the 1950s and 1960s. The degree of manifest aggression via this triad of dominating spatial practices led Rodolfo Acuña to aptly characterize it as a "state of siege." This coincidence of effects between barrio community empowerment and external disruption is precisely the sort of historical evidence that would later lead Dr. Ernesto Galarza to offer this pertinent estimation of social cause and effect: "As soon as the Chicano community begins to approach its political potential in East Los Angeles, the establishment will counter with the decimation of the barrio" (quoted in Muñoz 1973:5). This is precisely what would transpire in the 1950s in East Los Angeles. Since it is clear that the repressive ideological (media) and authoritarian (law) effects were fully functional in the 1940s, it only remained for the material spatial (landscape) effect to render its disfigurations upon the barrios in order to complete the repressive triad. The opportunity and means for realizing the downtown developers' transformative dreams was given to them through the support of the federal government. Legislative mechanisms and monumental subsidies for the "urban-industrial complex" (Goodman 1971:32) were made available via urban-renewal provisions introduced in the Federal Housing Act of 1949 and the previously mentioned Defense Highway Act of 1956. To get some sense of the economic scope of this urban-industrial complex, and thus to see how lucrative it is for those in its circuit, consider the following outlines of the national urban-growth machine:

> When all aspects are considered, metropolitan physical development accounts for perhaps one-fifth of the GNP and perhaps one-fourth of its growth since World War II. (Physical capital investment alone accounts for 16 percent of the GNP.) In relationship to these amounts, government tax expenditures on physical development amount to about 20 percent of the private capital invested. Direct government capital expenditures are also considerable. Currently, government at all levels accounts for nearly 27 percent of all construction as measured by value. Many of these government construction projects, such as roads, schools and other public facilities, and sewer and water systems, have a determining effect on where private physical investment goes. (Mollenkopf 1983:42–43)

Of particular appeal to growth interests was the nine-to-one ratio of federal-to-state subsidy for interstate highway construction. This deal made the federal program too good to pass up for ambitious local politicians, planners, and private developers (Wachs 1996:129–130).

LET THE SIEGE BEGIN: POSTWAR POLITICS OF SPACE

Barrio Disfigurement for "Higher and Better Use"

Just prior to and during the war years, working-class agitation had compelled the federal government to allocate funds for public housing, most significantly under the 1937 Wagner Act. However, private real estate and development interests, locally and nationally (especially through the coordinating efforts of the National Real Estate Board), consistently opposed such public works as anathema to their free-market practices and hinted at the "socialistic" precedent they would set. Nevertheless, because of wartime exigencies and in the interests of securing federal allocations for the construction industry, they grudgingly went along with the early projects. After the war, though, growth advocates lobbied with renewed fervor to implement their postponed private development schemes, initiating an agonistic battle with low-cost housing advocates (official agencies and inner-city residents) over the shape and direction of central-city development.

Building upon the Wagner Act, the 1949 Federal Housing Act retained in principle the major emphasis implied by its title and its legislative lineage: to increase the national stock of affordable housing. In practice, though, the influence of private commercial interests was decisively manifest in the crucial Title I provisions of the 1949 Act. While the national goal was set to construct 135,000 units of public housing, Title I introduced the place entrepreneurs' long-coveted category of federally subsidized, *private* "urban development." This signal provision tipped the scale of the New Deal and wartime social contract between capital and labor toward the urban bourgeoisie, opening the way for a paradigmatic shift in the practical consequences of the federal housing legislation. Don Parson notes this shift by describing how "slum clearance was no longer coupled with public housing but could have private housing, commercial or industrial uses, etc., as the final product" (1982:400). While the subsidized redevelopment of slum areas was to be "predominantly residential" in character, the vagueness of this proviso opened a privatizing wedge in the legislation that would be widened in subsequent amendments to the Act that allowed local redevelopment agencies to use 10 percent (1954) and later 30 percent (1960) of federal funds for commercial, nonresidential projects.

Even these figures are deceptive, underrepresenting the extent of actually practiced commercial development that occurred from the very start under the 1949 Act. This duplicity is described by Dennis Judd and Todd Swanstrom, who note that nationally, right from the beginning half or more of all funds were diverted away from low-income housing to commercial development. This was made possible by the way federal administrators interpreted the legislation. Any renewal project that allocated 51 percent or more of its funds to housing was designated by federal administrators as a "100 percent housing" project. By manipulating this definition, local authorities were able to allocate as much as two-thirds of their funds for commercial projects, despite the "predominantly residential" language in the legislation. (1994:138)

Furthermore, in the 1960 amendment to the Housing Act, the "predominantly residential" requirement was waived for projects involving expansions of universities, colleges, or hospitals, as was the requirement that urban-renewal projects contain a "substantial number of substandard dwellings" as a precondition for federal support (Parson 1982:405). These loosened parameters gave incentive to the recurring designs of White Memorial Hospital, affiliated with Loma Linda University, to gentrify their surrounding Boyle Heights community adjacent to the hospital. In 1962, they lobbied the City Planning Commission to approve 100 acres as an urban-renewal area, but were thwarted by the Committee for the Preservation of Boyle Heights (Acuña 1984:101).

During the administration of Mayor Fletcher Bowron, Los Angeles became the first major city to take advantage of the public-housing provisions of the 1949 Act, contracting with the federal government to construct 10,000 low-cost housing units, of which 3,300 were slated for the Elysian Heights Park jewel project (see Fig. 20). The location for this project was Chávez Ravine, a 315-acre site northeast of downtown. The Ravine was home to a sizable Chicano community (and a smaller Chinese population) complete with a church, elementary school, and small businesses (see Fig. 21). The barrios of Chávez Ravine were much maligned by reformers and coveted by developers as a major blighted district in the city. However, many observers who noted the structural deficiencies of the dwellings (the principal criterion for federal renewal project support) acknowledged that the barrio was possessed of the very "community values" so sought after by urban planners, including those commissioned to design the Elysian Park Heights project on the site (Hines 1982:130). And yet, since it was a sparsely settled area so close to downtown, the public-housing advocates could not help but make it the primary site for their grand plans.

Just as Elysian Park Heights was held up as an exemplar by housing ad-

61

EXHIBIT #13
Master Plan Chávez Ravine

CITY PLANNING COMMISSION   1948

Los Angeles, California

100   0   500   1000

OCCUPANT OWNED MULTIPLE HOUSING PLAN

Robert E. Alexander   Architect
Reginald D. Johnson   Consultant
Garrett Eckbo   Landscape Architect

6 STORY APARTMENT - 156 DWELLING UNITS
6 STORY APARTMENT - 108 DWELLING UNITS
HILLSIDE APARTMENT -   9 DWELLING UNITS
ROW TYPE APARTMENTS   5 DWELLING UNITS
ROW HOUSE
SMALL FAMILY RESIDENTIAL AREAS
SCHOOL
COMMERCIAL
CULTURAL CENTER

FIGURE 20.   Master plan for Chávez Ravine housing project, 1948. Designed by
Robert Alexander, Reginald Johnson, and Garrett Eckbo. Courtesy of the Los Angeles
City Planning Department.

vocates, it was cast as a bane by private-development, antihousing interests.
Apart from their free-market ideology, they objected to the entire public-
housing program for its goal of siting the projects throughout the city and
making them racially integrated (Parson 1982:400). A broad coalition of private real estate interests—given critical propagandistic support by the *Los Angeles Times,* which was a major downtown landowner—thus "began to wage
with increasing intensity an attack on the housing program as 'creeping so-

FIGURE 21. Chávez Ravine, 1935. Palo Verde School, *center right*. Courtesy of Bill Mason Collection.

cialism'—if not rampant communism" (Hines 1982:137). This assault on public housing followed a serendipitous course of public actions that culminated in the 1953 mayoral victory, after a malicious red-baiting campaign, of Norris Poulson, a front man for the *Times*-led growth coalition, over the incumbent Bowron (ibid.:138–140). Poulson immediately renegotiated the city's contract with the federal government, slashing half of the 10,000 public-housing units slated for construction. In the process, Chávez Ravine, cleared of all but a few holdouts, lay fallow while it awaited its fate. The victory of the anti-public-housing interests in Los Angeles had national repercussions, signaling once more the city's prescience in matters of urban development. As Don Parson makes powerfully clear, "The public housing war in Los Angeles . . . [was] an historic turning point which saw the total subsuming of the working class demand for public housing by the forces of urban redevelopment. . . . Following 1953, public housing construction in the U.S. fell drastically, with local contracts not even coming near the level of federal appropriations" (1982:402). Learning from Los Angeles, "such cities as Dallas, San Antonio, Houston, Seattle, Akron and Portland were able to sidestep federal housing projects" (ibid.) while still securing generous federal urban-renewal funds.

In 1957, the city essentially made a gift of Chávez Ravine to Walter O'Malley as part of an incentive package (which included oil rights on the property, the promise of $2 million in site improvements, and 200-year property tax–exempt status) to bring the Brooklyn Dodgers to Los Angeles. This publicly subsidized maneuver to bring the Dodgers to Southern California was yet another of Los Angeles' prefigurative growth strategies. The enticement offered to O'Malley by Los Angeles was the first instance of the now common lucrative packages not so much offered to as *demanded* by many professional sports franchises as incentive for their relocation in a particular metropolitan market.

In spite of vociferous protests against this landgrab, the contract was approved as a "public project" by electoral referendum, with the promise, ultimately unfulfilled, that O'Malley would construct some recreational space in the area (Acuña 1984:71). In retrospect, Mayor Poulson would describe the conflict over Chávez Ravine as "the hottest battle in California since the war with Mexico" (Parson 1982:403). In this ironically telling turn of phrase, he clearly identified the spatialized racial politics of this infamous "battle" that were abundantly clear to many Chicanos: Chávez Ravine was but another wrinkle in the continuing deterritorialization of *mexicanos* under the "manifest destiny"–cum–eminent domain of Anglo-American capitalism. The historian Kevin Starr, who at other times verges on boosterism, has described with great insight the significance of Chávez Ravine within the Chicano collective imagination: "the trauma of the removal of Latino families . . . was a representative drama. All Los Angeles, after all, had been seized from Mexico in 1846; and the sense of displacement felt by the evicted families remains an element in the Mexican imagination as it contemplates the lost Mexico north of the Rio Grande" (1997:M-6). In absolute terms, however, the cumulative impact of the freeways on the land-base and place-consciousness of Los Angeles Chicanos would far exceed that of Chávez Ravine in physical consequence, symbolic resonance, and expressive representation. By the 1980s, freeway construction had consumed 12 percent of the land in East Los Angeles while displacing approximately 10 percent of its residential population, thereby adding to the chronic shortage of decent and affordable housing on the Eastside (Acuña 1984:12; Pardo 1990a:101).

Popular lore among area residents posited that the tangle of freeways dissecting the Eastside was a strategic ploy by police agencies and civic leaders

FIGURE 22.   Tomorrowland L.A. A roof road designed by E. M. Khoury, published in *Motopia: A Study in the Evolution of Urban Space* (New York: Praeger Publishers, 1961). The original caption describes this as "a photograph of Los Angeles with the urban areas master-planned for the future in block bands knifing through the heart of the city . . . and tied in with the outside freeways. . . ."

to break up the territorial structure of the local gangs (Moore 1991 : 16). This conspiratorial intention is subject to verification and debate, but what can certainly be gleaned from such neighborhood folklore is the fact that in popular Chicano imaginative figurations of dominant urbanism, no other single element comes close to occupying the symbolic place of the freeways as a resonant symbol of the community's historical geography. Indeed, there appears to be a direct, though inverse, relation of symbolic investment between the boosters and builders of the expressway supercity on one side, and the community-based debunkers of the intruding freeways on the other. In fact, for several decades, until the great Bunker Hill corporate trophy-building constructions of the late 1970s and 1980s, the complex of freeways was, to many observers, the singular architectural and engineering monument of the city's contemporary public image. What the towering skyline is to Manhattan, the tangle of freeways is to Los Angeles. Along with the physical and social impacts of freeway construction, the sheer visual, ubiquitous presence and semiotic valences of the freeways have inspired equal and opposite measures of congratulation and condemnation.

"Tomorrow Is Another City": Monumental Rhetoric of the Expressway Metropolis [2]

From the booster side of the congratulatory/condemnatory dialectic, an aesthetic celebration of the urban freeways was present from their earliest construction, as in the 1941 observation that they "usually succeed in creating an environment of beauty over their locale, as witnessed by a flower-lined section of Los Angeles' Arroyo Seco Parkway" (Los Angeles Department of City Planning:8). This specular evaluation, however, was a fairly superficial description of the freeway's visual presence. An intimation of the freeway's informing semiotic resonances is suggested in the observation (from *California: A Guide to the Golden State*) that "building roadways can be as spectacular as erecting fortresses was in medieval times" (Hansen 1967: 165). While such hyperbole is endemic to the rhetoric of the tour-book genre, the statement still tellingly connotes the social power that is both practically and symbolically manifest in the material-aesthetic form of the freeway as an icon of powerful development interests for our time. When added to the companion observation that California's "Expressway System can justifiably be called one of the wonders of the modern world" (ibid.:164), the technocratic hubris is more fully revealed and consonant with a dominant mentality in the emerging expressway metropolis of the 1950s and 1960s. Lee Shippey's popular 1950 homage to Los Angeles, *The Los Angeles Book*, for example, anticipates a central image in Hansen's text when he notes that "'everlasting hills' are being torn down to enlarge the Civic Center and the freeway system" (106).

Such brash technocratic rhetoric, first significantly articulated in the late 1930s and early 1940s, gained increasing local and national currency throughout the cold war era, until it reached "a pinnacle of power and self-confidence in the 1960s, in the America of the New Frontier, the Great Society, Apollo on the moon" (Berman 1982:313). Specifically in Los Angeles, which was perceived nationally as the Mecca of this "expressway world," Reyner Banham's 1971 study, *Los Angeles: The Architecture of Four Ecologies*, became the academic codex of the freeway faithful. Although boosters of the expressway "supercity" had been proselytizing throughout the 1960s via regional promotional journalism—most notably in the American Automobile Association (AAA) organ *Westways* and the glossy *Los Angeles Magazine*—and cultivating the praises of national press attention, these representations were essentially saccharine products of the same propaganda machinery by which Southern California had always been discursively produced and sold to the public. Three notable instances of this national-press attention include centerpiece articles in *National Geographic* ("California's City of the Angels," by Robert de Roos and Thomas Nebbia) and *Fortune* ("Los Angeles: Prototype of Super-city," by Richard Austin Smith), and a special photographic color essay in *Life* magazine ("Los Angeles in a New Image," with photographs, including a foldout cover of the Hollywood Freeway at rush hour, by Ralph Crane and text by Charles Champlin).

However, the intellectual credentials of Banham, a noted architectural critic, offered the freeway faithful the elite cultural validation that their often lampooned urbanism had generally lacked. Placing the freeways in a world-historical trajectory, he codified them as the next great determining structures in metropolitan design. For Banham, the freeways conferred upon the city a "canonical and monumental form, much as the great streets of Sixtus V fixed Baroque Rome, or the *Grands Travaux* of Baron Haussmann fixed the Paris of *la belle epoque*" (1971:35; original emphasis). While he rightly chooses his canonical urban formations, he adduces them and their legacy in the post-urban landscape of Los Angeles with little or no critical consciousness, praising the lineage of metropolitan transit restructurings without consideration for the social contradictions that taint these epochal projects.

"In the spirit of high modernism" that links the transformation of mid-nineteenth-century Paris with urban renewal in mid-twentieth-century America (Harvey 1993:25–26), a legacy of monumental barbarism, particularly with regard to the wholesale eviscerations of certain poor and working-class quarters in the two urban time-spaces, underscores the symbolic and practical meanings of their related effects. Such materialist qualifications, however, never threaten to burst the bubble of Reyner Banham's autopian giddiness:

> One can most properly begin by learning the local language; and the language of design, architecture, and urbanism in Los Angeles is the language of movement. Mobility outweighs monumentality there to a unique degree . . . and the city will never be fully understood by those who cannot move fluently through its diffuse urban texture, cannot go with the flow of its unprecedented life. (1971:23)[3]

Notwithstanding his legitimate academic standing and his many insightful observations about Los Angeles' built landscape, Banham's interpretation of the freeways paints him as an erudite cruiser, enthralled by the very mirage of the Southern California good life that has always characterized the imagineered promotion of the city, particularly in the "happy days" of the 1950s and 1960s. Norman Klein has insightfully noted the inevitable biases and inherent blindness in the specular orientation of this autopian point of view. First, he cites Victor Gruen's observations from *The Heart of Our Cities, The Urban Crisis: Diagnosis and Cure:* "The city core of Los Angeles is not only small but void of true urban life as well" (quoted in Klein 1990:79). He then notes how Banham's autopianism echoes Gruen's assessment, particularly as it draws on Gruen's evidence that two-thirds of the downtown surface area was devoted to the car. Klein points out that in both cases, "Urban life was described without reference to communities, or neighborhood institutions. . . . [Instead], communities were defined [or rendered invisible] by the experience inside an automobile—essentially as a tourist driving through" (ibid.: 36 n. 43).

Neither Gruen nor Banham was unique or originary in his drive-through perspective on central Los Angeles. A specific and telling example of this automotive view of Chicano place in the heart of the city was expressed in 1958 by Dr. T. Gordon Reynolds, president of the College of Medical Evangelists—which was institutionally affiliated with White Memorial Hospital in Boyle Heights. In a letter written to Edward Roybal, then City Council representative for that district, Reynolds complained that he could not find adequate housing for himself and his employees near the hospital, stating this claim in support of designating the area an official urban-renewal zone. Without any reference to the opinions, interests, or needs of the many low-income area residents who would likely be displaced by renewal, he described the observable decline of the built environment. This emphasis was in line with the stated physical, as opposed to social, criteria for "blight" definition under federal urban-renewal legislation. In an interesting coincidence of perspective with the later observations of Gruen and Banham, Reynolds supports his argument in explicitly autopian, touristic terms, with reference to visiting freeway users: "Our new freeways will all pass this section and unless we redevelop this section *our visitors will enter our fair city receiving one of the most unfavorable impressions imaginable* as they pass through the ragged back-yard fences, the broken down garages and the sight of sagging kitchen doors" (quoted in Acuña 1984:66; emphasis added). Banham is also of an ideological mind with other precursory development boosters, whose "good life" plati-

tudes he echoes in his expressway reveries. In fact, booster discourse antici-
pated several of his key observations. Consider, for example, the clearly self-
serving praises of autopian mobility voiced five years before Banham by the
editors of *Westways* magazine: "By night or by day the city of Los Angeles
betrays a restless vitality, a rejection of stasis and a penchant for movement.
Its architecture, the curve and trajectory of its freeways betokens a shaping of
purpose" ("The Shaping of Purpose" 1965:36).

Another article in the same issue similarly prefigures Banham's joy-riding
identification of the city's unique, evolutionary metropolitan form: "Para-
doxically, the very freeways, which some critics point to as the reason and the
proof that Los Angeles is a scattered lot of self-seeking satellites, have become
the sinews of a supercity. The cynical winks and chuckles aside, no one who
has observed southern California for the past decade or so can seriously doubt
that Los Angeles . . . has come of age—economically, socially and *culturally*"
(Meyer 1965:27; original emphasis). This purported maturation of the "supercity" gestures obliquely to a recurring interpretive construct of modernizing Anglo Los Angeles in which the social spaces and cultural landscapes of
Chicanos and Mexicanos before them are central, in an antithetical manner,
to the reigning symbolic production of the city image.

In a range of hegemonic discourses, from touristic to academic, there
emerged a persistent trope, identified in such rhetorical figurations as "pueblo
to boomtown," "mission to metropolis," "ranchos to high-rises," and the like
(see Fig. 23).

Boyle Workman, in his recollections of the American "city that grew" out
of the Mexican township, benignly adduces this hegemonic conceit by inviting his "readers to relive with me those colorful, primitive days . . . as the
pueblo of 1250 people becomes the metropolis of 1,400,000" (1936:v).
Workman's figuring of the succession from old to new seems smooth and
mellow, almost in the manner of a natural evolution. However, the more ac-
curate disjuncture and abrupt transition between pueblo and metropolis is
intimated in the following representative statement from a major 1941 planning report: "The plaza was the social and business center for the town for
more than three generations, and on it fronted the architectural wonders of
their day. Then came progress" (Schuchardt 1941:240). This unproblematic
allusion to sudden "progress" identifies the culturally specific creative destruction of the built environment during the original thrust of Anglo urbanization in the late 1800s. It also insinuates the bellicose underpinnings of that
first spatial assault upon the preceding pueblo landscape described by the architectural historian Merry Ovnick: "In the flush of Manifest Destiny, the

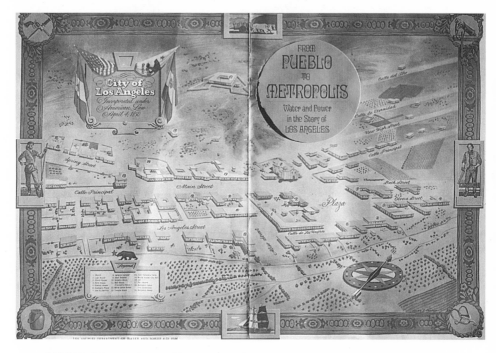

FIGURE 23.   "From Pueblo to Metropolis," a promotional booklet from the
Department of Water and Power. Courtesy of the Los Angeles Department of Water and
Power.

victor's culture was imposed on the land in the physical form of architecture"
(1994:57).

While it is a historical fact that the Mexican pueblo was succeeded by
the Anglo township and its subsequent urban metamorphoses, two dominant
ideological conceits are inscribed in the recurrent trope of postpueblo or an-
tipueblo modernization. In the first place, Los Angeles' "pueblo" past, particularly in its more romanticized representations, is severed from any relationship to its Chicano present. Simultaneously, the greater the difference
between the built environment of successive Anglo metropolises and that of
the prior and always inferiorized Mexican social spaces—not infrequently
by erasing more and more of the latter's material and cultural landscapes—
the more they express their material progress and cultural advancement. This
social-rhetorical construct is voiced with aggressive emphasis in the time-
space of the developing expressway metropolis by Mayor Norris Poulson, under whose administration Los Angeles was propelled into its space-age future:

I am convinced that *Los Angeles is destined to be one of the truly great cities of the world*, not only in size but in beauty, cultural attainment, commerce, industry, and all the elements it takes for true greatness. If you are not prepared to be part of this greatness, *if you want Los Angeles to revert to pueblo status*, if you want nothing changed, if you are wedded to the status quo . . . then my best advice to you is to prepare to settle elsewhere, because whatever you may do or what I might be able to do, we, singularly, or collectively, cannot stop the momentum which is thundering this city to greatness. (Quoted in Kovner 1959:1; emphasis added)

Poulson's argument that opposing the "thundering" momentum of urban development is both futile and regressive belies more than just the righteousness of the ruling growth interests that put him in office. If we recall Poulson's words describing the struggle over Chávez Ravine as the "hottest battle in California since the war with Mexico," the deep rhetorical structure of his preceding statement reveals its ideological inheritance from Anglo-American Manifest Destiny. Through this historical optic of ruling interests, all resistance was seen as reactionary: "to oppose them and their works was to oppose modernity itself, to fight history and progress, to be a Luddite, an escapist,

FIGURE 24. "Division of the Barrios and Chávez Ravine," a panel from *The Great Wall of Los Angeles*, Judith F. Baca, © 1983. Courtesy of the artist and Social and Public Art Resource Center.

afraid of life and adventure and change and growth" (Berman 1982:313). Furthermore, to stand in the way of this *destined* "beauty, cultural attainment, commerce, [and] industry" was to identify with the vanquished, and thus manifestly inferior, social spaces and cultural landscapes of the racial Other, in the Mexican, antimodern "pueblo status."

IN THE PATH OF THE JUGGERNAUT: EASTSIDERS RESPOND TO THE GROWTH MACHINE

In spite of Poulson's revealing biases, he was not off the mark in describing the nearly unrestrained engine of growth-oriented urban development set in motion in the 1950s. Yet his allusion to, and barely veiled contempt for, those who would dare contest this thundering urban destiny intimated the presence of concerted opposition to the plans of the downtown ruling elites. By the early 1950s, Eastside residents, now a Chicano majority, were mobilizing to defend their neighborhood turf-base and use values. The "battle against the bulldozers" of urban development and highway construction in the Eastside and central city was the principal rallying cry of Chicano community defensive spatial mobilizations in the 1950s and 1960s (Acuña 1984:48; Romo 1983:169). For example, in 1953, while the planners and developers were celebrating the much-heralded opening of the downtown interchange of the Hollywood and Pasadena Freeways—the first four-level freeway exchange in the country, commonly called "The Stack"—there were mass community rallies in Boyle Heights to protest disparate freeway impacts. In this period, City Council member Edward Roybal proved himself to be a major advocate for Eastsiders' place-rights. Often as a lone voice on the Council, Roybal raised regular objections to the policies of unrestrained urban development. In this capacity, he regularly clashed with the downtown elites. Most notably, Rodolfo Acuña has identified Roybal's persistent conflicts "with the *Los Angeles Times*, not only over the issues of rent control, the scapegoating of Mexican youth and police brutality, but also over freeway construction, urban renewal and public housing" (1996:45).

In a corollary effect, the fresh wounds of the multiple spatial assaults upon the barrios were engraved as implicit social knowledge in the popular imagination of Los Angeles Chicanos. The signal evisceration of Chávez Ravine, followed in the 1960s by the equally monumental erasure of the Bunker Hill neighborhood's polyglot cultural landscape,[4] would be regularly evoked by community members, through various media, both as indignant reminders of

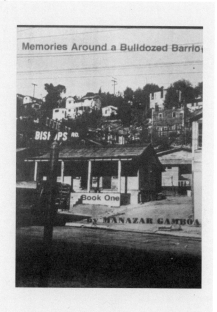

Cover photograph shows a street sign that reads "Bishops Rd.," the name of the street where Manazar Gamboa lived from birth to age 16.

The cover photograph was taken on August 7, 1951, by the Los Angeles Housing Authority in an effort to document slum conditions in Los Angeles. However, the Los Angeles Housing Authority neglected to say that by the time this photograph was taken, the houses had been abandoned because its residents had been coerced into evacuating their homes.

Cover Design: Manazar Gamboa

FIGURE 25.   Inside front page and cover design for Manazar Gamboa's self-published elegy to his lost community in Chávez Ravine. Courtesy of the author.

past injustice and as cautionary evidence against present and future manipulations (see Figs. 24 and 25).

On the journalistic front, repeated allusions to community place-violations appeared in the critical editorial and reportorial interventions of the weekly *Eastside Sun*, quite often in the words of its crusading publisher Joseph Eli Kovner. Kovner was a Jewish-American liberal whose persistent advocacy for Eastsider place-rights recalled the once-significant Jewish presence in Boyle Heights and signaled his strong, if "somewhat paternalistic and flamboyant," identification with the now majority Chicano population of the area (Acuña 1984:274). The *Sun* also provided a public forum for Chicanos to voice concerns in defense of their community's social space and place-identity.

The patterned degradation of a residential area's image in the greater public imagination is a key factor in justifying its "renewal" (Gans 1962:308). This and other examples of the material efficacy of "collective representations . . . projected by growth coalitions" leads the urban semiologist Mark

Gottdeiner to argue that investigations of such social representations "must connect symbols with social interests and the use of images as tools in specific forums" (1986:208–209). Conscious of the material force of dominant representations, Eastsiders defended their community against its mainstream vilification as a socially blighted zone in specific rebuttal to the "'outside' image of East Los Angeles as poor, crime ridden and politically powerless . . . [that] was used to justify 'dumping' everything no other community wanted in East L.A." (Pardo 1990a:288–289). Among the most fervent defenders of the Eastside against such external denigration by the media as well as by repressive state agents was Ralph Guzmán. During the 1950s, Guzmán was persistent and indignant in his editorial criticisms of the mainstream press and the police demonization of the Eastside community, particularly of its youth. His writing against police abuse and criminal youth and broader Eastside stereotyping was consistent with his advocacy role in the East Los Angeles–based Community Service Organization, where he was in charge of its civil rights committee. His corrective and contestatory discourse is summed up well by the title of one of his many editorial interventions, "Let's Get the Story Straight," which debunks the exaggeration and racism of the *Los Angeles Times* for reporting on a supposed wave of Eastside crime and gangland warfare, and for its attendant influence on police interactions with Eastsiders. Guzmán's corrective critiques of mainstream press degradations of the Eastside is captured well by his pointed rebuttal in the very next issue of the *Sun* (June 25, 1953), when, in no uncertain terms, he accuses the *Times* of using East Los Angeles crime copy to sell newspapers. The late 1800s Anglo press and popular public ascriptions of banditry to *mexicanos*, the "Mexican problem" of the 1920s and 1930s, and the precedent yellow journalism of the mainstream dailies during the "Zoot-Suit Riots" and Sleepy Lagoon trials of the early 1940s thus recurred in the "happy days" of the 1950s.

With respect to the continuing spatial assaults upon the Eastside, in the 1960s and early 1970s columnist Arturo Montoya would replace Kovner as the most consistent critic of downtown public and private development interests. Similar positions were evident in the reporting on community place-struggles by Mario Hernández and Eddie Pardo, in various letters to the editor from neighborhood residents, and in the published articles and interviews with Chicano professionals variously involved in urban-planning issues. Examples of residents' letters and professional articles reveal how both broad social critique and insider community descriptions were tactically deployed by Eastsiders to interpret their spatial structuration and argue for their community place-rights. First, in a published copy of a letter addressed to Sargent

Shriver, then director of the federal Office of Economic Opportunity's Community Action Program, Isabel Medrano and N. Sterlink complain that

> in cities such as Los Angeles, elements in power and influence begin looking for land that can become available in single tracts and at negligible prices. These elements are instantly attracted to city parks and recreational areas and especially . . . from low-income minority areas and it is these areas that suffer the most serious land expropriations. Those expropriations, of course, eventually lead to the so called "asphalt jungles" and to continually more crowded living conditions that in turn induce, augment and perpetuate many of the evils associated with poverty. (1965)

While Medrano and Sterlink deconstruct the rapacious and socially disabling impacts of external growth interests, community planner Raúl Escobedo focuses internally to identify the sustaining, if vulnerable, place-bound mechanisms of community life. In "Life Style within the Boyle Heights Community," he offers his observations on the use-value orientations and culture-defining practices of Eastside residents. Relatedly, in the rhetorically titled "Is Boyle Heights Worth Saving?" Escobedo notes the symbiosis of economic necessity and affective links to local place that make Boyle Heights a valuable social resource for its low-income residents: "It has many characteristics of neighborhood cohesiveness, and many residents are socially, emotionally and historically tied to the area. To a great majority of the residents—long-term residents, recent arrivals, young couples, senior citizens, homeowners and renters alike—this area is their only economic alternative" (1974:A-10). Escobedo goes on to intimate the experientially felt legacy of the Chicano community's epic spatial expropriations, some of which (freeway construction) he lived firsthand, in noting that the "emotional scars of Bunker Hill and Chávez Ravine are not easily erased. And the social disruption and physical displacement caused by four major freeways is still considered recent history by many long-term community residents" (ibid.:A-1).

With unflagging persistence, and often colored by rhetorical bursts of indignation, the various contributors to the *Eastside Sun* collectively narrated and interpreted the continuing saga of urban "landgrabs" in the Eastside, and to a lesser degree citywide, exposing the private-cum-public good driving urban renewal and criticizing the complicity of key public officials in the process. Unfortunately, many of the more substantial community mobilizations reported and supported by the *Sun* were limited or defeated in their efforts to check the spatial state of siege; they gained scattered concessions but failed to stop the major displacements and social disruptions of urban renewal and freeway construction. If the *Eastside Sun* largely documented the marginality from effective decision-making or decision-influencing power of the largely poor and working-class barrio residents, the textual record it offered still served a significant discursive function for its time, and for our own as well. Speaking of the *Sun*, as well as of *The Belvedere Citizen* (a second, though generally more conservative, Eastside weekly), the historian Rodolfo Acuña identifies the counterhegemonic lessons that can be culled from them.

> Countless forgotten battles are relived on the pages of the two bulletin boards. The siege of the Eastside and the responses of its citizens come alive. Congressman Edward R. Roybal shines through the articles as a champion in the fight against urban renewal. . . . Their articles serve to refresh the memories of area residents and to document their struggles for the modern researcher. They provide history that cannot be gleaned out of the major dailies or government records. (1984:274)

If former Mayor Poulson was maliciously correct in positing the monumental efficacy of the supercity growth machinery, Acuña's evaluation of the Eastside weeklies suggests that positive uses can subsequently be made of the knowledge they convey about those communities "in the path of the 'juggernaut'," to use Kovner's expressive figure (*Eastside Sun*, January 3, 1957). This future use of past knowledge strategically informs Acuña's own barriological historiography. In his monograph *A Community under Siege: A Chronicle of Chicanos East of the Los Angeles River, 1945–1975*, from which the previous citation is drawn, he states that his intention in producing the chronicle "is not merely to revive memories. It is to identify and clarify the issues that have shaped the Eastside so that the community will be able to withstand the sieges that will inevitably come" (1984:274). This deployment of historico-geographic knowledge, very often informed by personal experience, has been a fundamental tenet in the socio-aesthetical expressive practices of Chicanas and Chicanos who document and contest the sociospatial subordination of their communities.

Just as the various spatial assaults upon the Eastside in the 1950s were a flash point of community protest and defensive mobilizations, so they were again in the late 1960s and early 1970s. During this second broad period of the battle against the bulldozers, coincident with the urban Chicano civil rights move-

DEAR FRIEND:

We of the United Neighbors to Save the Beaudry-Temple Community are
seeking your support to help us fight City Hall!

Our small neighborhood which lies between 1st. and Temple Street
and between Beaudry Street and the Harbor Freeway, is threatened by the
Bank of America and the lack of interest shown by our elected and appointed officials.

FIGURE 26.   Detail of a flyer by the United Neighbors to Save the Beaudry-Temple
Community, early 1970s. Part of the accompanying text reads: "[T]he Bank of America is
seeking a zone change so that they can construct a nine-story Computer Center Complex,
with parking for 1300 cars, on the 10 acres where our neighborhood is now situated. Some
of us were forced out of Chávez Ravine—only to be evicted from Bunker Hill." Courtesy
of Rosalío Muñoz Collection.

ment, the lessons learned or transmitted about earlier community-turf battles
helped some barrio residents to defend their place-rights. Don Parson notes,
for example, that "Chicano grassroots actions in the early '70s stopped, froze
or limited urban renewal plans in Latino areas: Temple-Beaudry project,
clearance plans for Lincoln Heights and Monterey Hills were recast to do
housing rehabilitation only" (1982:408).

Among barriological activists, the Chicano movement ethos of tactical alliance and joint action was promoted as a direct counterprocess to the specific spatial assaults of urban development. The various conflagrations that
erupted in the most aggrieved neighborhoods from the mid-1960s forward
were unmistakable, if sometimes inchoate, cries of accumulated and collective

frustration with this spectrum of social deprivations affecting the barrios and ghettoes. The shortage of decent, affordable housing, in particular, was consistently identified as a major cause of civil unrest (Mohl 1993 : 141). In many cases, freeway incursions compelled direct defensive mobilizations (Frieden and Sagalyn 1989 : 45; Mohl 1993 : 136–139). These urban grassroots uprisings were merely the most public and spectacular articulations of rage by inner-city residents against the metropolitan growth machine. The Watts rebellion in 1965 and the Eastside conflagrations following the 1970 police-force assault against Chicano antiwar demonstrators were demonstrative social texts of the popularly and often aggressively expressed indignation of inner-city residents. In these variously organized and spontaneous critical public manifestations, it becomes clear how "'structural constraints' force as well 'conjunctural opportunities'" (Harlow 1991 : 161). Such a relationship of contending forces is described by the community activist Guillermo Flores, with reference to its manifestation during the Chicano movement in the early 1970s:

> I think the existence of the community is very important for the sense
> of collectivity which comes through Chicanos living together and
> maintaining their culture. When developers come and try to disperse
> people it breaks up that cohesiveness. Of course it can also serve to
> unify various barrios that were at each other's throats before, by bring-
> ing them together for the first time to fight a common enemy. . . . For
> the time being, I think the struggle to maintain the physical existence
> of the community has acted to solidify the spirit of the barrio and
> increased the determination to make it a real Chicano community.
> (Quoted in Barrera and Vialpando 1974 : 26)

What Flores is identifying, of course, is the historically recurring dialectic between external spatial assault and internal social organization of Chicano urban barrios. Speaking more broadly of the same period, Manuel Castells characterized this dialectic as the "old chant of the urban condition: the transformation of the space of exclusion into the space of freedom," in which the oppressed residential zone of the inner-city neighborhood might serve the "community as the material basis of social organization, cultural identity, and political power" (1983 : 67).

While Flores voices this characteristic Chicano movement ethos, he also wisely indicates the uncertain and tactical nature of this process in his cautionary proviso "for the time being." Positive and empowering effects of barriological activity and community cohesion do not uniformly or necessarily characterize life in the barrios. If they are operative in given historical moments and milieus, such positive effects are never secure, since the compelling forces of capitalist development and state planning continue to operate in ways that are often damaging to the vulnerably situated social spaces of the barrio. Understanding the tenuous nature of community defensive practices, many barriological activists in this period brought historically based spatial knowledge to bear upon practical organizational mobilizations. Their goal was to support and instruct grassroots community efforts against the disparate impacts of urban development. The 1974 monograph *Action Research in Defense of the Barrio*, produced by the *Aztlán* journal publications group at UCLA, was a significant intervention of this sort. In their introduction, editors Mario Barrera and Geralda Vialpando clearly stated their intention of providing tactical information for barrio defense projects.

> This pamphlet is a report to the Chicano community on a set of processes that are going on throughout the urban Southwest. The effect of these processes is to fragment and dislocate the barrios that exist in and around the metropolitan areas, displacing the Chicano population and acting as a source of disruption and instability in the community. . . .
>
> By calling attention to this situation, and by presenting some information on Chicano counter-efforts, we hope to stimulate the formation of barrio defense projects in other areas that are being similarly affected. (1974:1)

Among the projects treated in this report was the work of the East/Northeast Committee to Stop Home Destruction, based in the Lincoln Heights area of Los Angeles. The pertinent information was gathered by interviewing one of its principal organizers, Rosalío Muñoz. Throughout the interview, it becomes clear that Muñoz' own barriological interventions in place-politics and urban planning applied historical critique to grassroots and public institutional activism. In his influential role as an organizer and barrio organic intellectual, Muñoz exercised the proactive documentary function that the historian Rodolfo Acuña later intended for his chronicle of East Los Angeles, which was to "identify and clarify the issues that have shaped the Eastside, so that the community will be able to withstand the sieges that will inevitably come" (1984:274). Recalling the Californio editorial interventions against the earliest postpueblo reconstructions, Muñoz' journalistic work, published in the *Eastside Sun, La Gente* (a UCLA Chicano student newspaper), and the *Community Defender*, deconstructed the community-displacing effects of dominant urban planning.

An important example of Muñoz' discursive activism is the 1973 essay "Our Moving Barrio: Why?" in which he addressed the most recent thrust of Chicano deterritorialization. Responding to drafts of the new city and county Master Plans (they were made final in 1974), the essay took direct aim at the prospects of a new wave of urban renewal in the Eastside. In the Master Plan rhetoric that called for "recycling the inner city," Muñoz saw a thinly veiled effort by the "political economic elite" to forestall the "imminence of Chicano political strength and domination in the heart of one of the largest metropolitan areas of the world" (1973:5). Linking past effects to present concerns, he argues that "this is at least the third effort to carry out the strategy of removing the Mexican population. The first two were relatively successful. The first was around the turn of the century when Los Angeles was changing from a village town to a small city. . . . The second wave came during the forties and fifties" (ibid.). In the full text, Muñoz describes the upheavals of initial Civic Center development, downtown industrial expansion, Union Station and additional railroad yard construction, freeway building, and federal urban-renewal and housing projects (most significantly the notorious battle over Chávez Ravine); in other words, many of the signal or trophy constructions of Los Angeles' twentieth-century dominant spatial odyssey from boomtown to wonder city and into the supercity future. In his periodization, the 1960s and early 1970s (encompassing the administrative regime of mayor Sam Yorty) were the "third phase," in which he found himself writing and acting. For Muñoz, this phase's monumental transformation was shaped by the "Bunker Hill Urban Renewal Project [see Fig. 27] which destroyed the last barrios immediately next to downtown" and engraved its creative-destructive achievement on the landscape in the built form of the new Music Center complex, the headquarters building of the Department of Water and Power (see Fig. 28), and the first generation of trophy-building skyscrapers and upscale residential complexes of the recentered financial district.

Muñoz was certainly not unique for journalistically criticizing the continuing disparate impacts of urban development. I single him out here, however, because his critique of the high-rising cultural and financial citadel includes an image that portrays its specific *representational* effect, thus attacking its symbolic signifying power as an architectural "text." Calling it a "Tower of Phallic Babelism" (1973:5), he metaphorically underscores its power-laden

FIGURE 27. Courtesy of Seaver Center for Western History Research, Los Angeles County Museum of Natural History.

FIGURE 28. Los Angeles Civic Center Complex, ca. 1970s. Department of Water and Power (*left*, ringed by water); Music Center (*middle*); City Hall (*far right*). Courtesy of Los Angeles Community Redevelopment Agency.

FIGURE 29.   The transformation of Bunker Hill in the early 1970s. Courtesy of Los Angeles Community Redevelopment Agency.

meaning. Like the builders of the biblical tower, the architects and planners of Bunker Hill signed their monumental self-image on the landscape for all to see (see Fig. 29).

The inflated self-importance signaled in this architectural text was not unique to Bunker Hill developers. It was commensurate with the reigning self-importance shared by engineers, planners, scientists, and assorted technocrats who were collectively realizing the mega-projects of the 1960s and early 1970s—including superhighways, supercities, and supraterrestrial explorations.[5] The ethos of this "best and brightest" professional cohort was aptly characterized in my previous citation from Marshall Berman, in which he observed that the brave new world they were fashioning was presented "as the only possible modern world: to oppose them and their works was to oppose modernity itself" (1982:313). Against such reigning attitudes, Muñoz' disparaging image of Bunker Hill development may also intimate a sedimented fantasy of the vanquished: that this monumental construction might, as in the biblical parable of Babel, also someday crumble under the weight of its own hubristic designs.

In the 1950s and 1960s, varying declarations of the imperious supergrowth mentality were regularly addressed to Los Angeles citizens, Chicanos and

others, who dared to oppose the emerging acropolis on Bunker Hill and beyond (Parson 1993). Former Mayor Poulson's brash statement regarding the
city's thundering destiny (cited earlier) is only the most audacious of such
expressed attitudes. Muñoz' socially symbolic deconstruction of the latest
"Mexican removal" project is demonstratively historical and in fact "brushes
history against the grain" (Benjamin 1968:259) as it situates contemporary
urban restructuring within a recurring cycle of Chicano neighborhood displacements. As such, his chronotopic deconstruction of hegemonic urban
planning, like that of other barriological observers and activists who preceded
and would follow him, offers clear evidence and orientations to fuel the present and future struggles of barrio residents.

AGAINST THE DOCUMENTS OF BARBARISM: REVISIONARY NARRATIVES OF *LA CIUDAD DE LOS ANGELES*

While sharing a critical historical ethos with Muñoz' pointed expository
documentation, the poet and journalist Victor Valle employs a more fully
developed figurative discourse to offer an alternative story to the evolutionary
and celebratory narratives of Anglo city-making. The latter were identified
earlier in their recurring manifestations from propagandistic city promotion
to celebratory historiography to Poulson's discursive demagoguery. Although
his work is not allied with specific grassroots defensive mobilizations, as was
Muñoz', Valle's critical discourse is influenced by his intimate social experience of place-violations. This personal orientation is expressed in the poem
"Cuervos," in which he relates the specific and disabling intrusions of the
freeway as the mechanism of hegemonic urban planning in his home milieu.

> I lived in one of the first
> suburbs to spring up
> along el Río San Gabriel;
> our backyard a hand that touched
> a still wild river,
> home for paloma, coyote, carrizales,
> the green smell of moss
> outside my window.
> Later, we were barricaded
> by boulevards, freeways,
> clouds of high octane smoke
> and a ceaseless roar. (1991:14)

Valle's imagery recalls and reinvigorates a poetics of Romanticism, in which an agonistic contrast of natural and technological elements produces a critique of the place-deforming urbanism that invades his childhood milieu. However, I would stress that this Romantic "structure of feeling" (Williams 1977) is not exercised by Valle to fix his familial Chicano milieu in the realm of the "natural" as if his childhood home were a site of pure felicity, even if it may be partly recollected that way by the poet or perceived as such by the reader. Rather, I would argue that the criticism of specific technologies of dominant urbanism is made to defend the memory of a place not primarily because it is *natural*, but because it is *native* to the poet (Williams 1973: 138). This is to say that Valle intimates a *social* critique of the urban designs that destroyed a socially enacted—not innate or purely natural—place (his "home") whose significance is constituted in the relationship between a specific quasi-rural environment and the lived uses to which it was put—including play, aesthetic appreciation, and perhaps even for sustenance and medicinal applications of the flora—by him and others living in the area.

Valle's figural deployment of ecological devastations to posit a social critique is more explicit and historically informed in his counterepic poem "Los Angeles." A stinging rebuttal to the celebratory histories of "American" westward expansion, Valle's revisionary narrative describes, at one point, the morphology of the landscape following the arrival of the "pioneer" Anglo settlers:

> And beyond Sonora-town,
> the settling of lomas began,
> bridges over rivers that flooded
> to Maravilla, El Hoyo, El Sereno
>   now no ciénagas or muddy rivers
> instead dead cement
> over alluvial paths
> This was one stroke across the map,
> recent impulse to unfurl a destiny
> from ocean to ocean (1991:52)

In an earlier version of this text, published in 1982, Valle gave added emphasis to the transformation of the pueblo milieu, opening this section with the lines: "And the random / eating of Lomas began around Sonora town . . ." (1982:24). The "impulse" of Anglo settlement is thus more aggressively debunked as a ravenous consumption of original social spaces and landscapes.

Subverting the positivist rhetoric of "progress" that colors the hegemonic historiography of Anglo Los Angeles, Valle casts the city's modern settlement as another phase of this nation's imperial Manifest Destiny. The component terms in the image of "dead cement" figuratively conjoin, on one side, the knowledge of physical and social death that was suffered by native residents (including the originary devastation of indigenous American inhabitants by Spanish colonization) and, on the other, the identification of subsequent urban infrastructural development. The specific development was the rerouting and cementing of the Los Angeles River, as well as several of its tributaries and other rivers, by the U.S. Army Corps of Engineers.

However, the allusion can be read broadly as a chronotopic synecdoche for the city's successive urban modernizations that constitute the "thundering [manifest] destiny" so aptly identified by Mayor Poulson. Valle, in fact, compresses the trajectory of capitalist-compelled spatial restructurings into a litany of resonant allusions that describe the unacknowledged costs exacted on the land and the people by the lauded achievements of the city builders,

> a new landed gentry,
> the Huntingtons, the Crockers, the Bixbys
> who broke ground with rails, barbed wire and aqueducts,
> placed an ocean at the foot of a city,
> and its workers under a Coronel's boot.
> He erected his fortress over two dead Wobblies
> the way a wasp deposits her eggs
> on its stung, moribund host,
> and thereafter bequeathed to his protogés [sic]
> Command of the Words.
> With these they abducted a river,
> subdivided a desert,
> walled families with velocities. (1991:59)

This thickly layered section takes precise aim at some of the leading speculators ("the new landed gentry"), signal technologies ("rails, barbed wire and aqueducts") and determining infrastructural developments (the artificial port, theft of Owens Valley water, real estate subdivision, and the freeway system) that irrevocably transformed the city and region into a modern landscape of power. In so doing, Valle offers a trenchant illustration of the observation made by Walter Benjamin in the seventh of his "Theses on the Philosophy of History":

Whoever has emerged victorious participates to this day in the trium-
phal procession in which the present rulers step over those who are
lying prostrate. According to traditional practice the spoils are carried
along in the procession. They are called cultural treasures, and a historical materialist views them with cautious detachment. For without
exception the cultural treasures he surveys have an origin which he
cannot contemplate without horror. They owe their existence not only
to the efforts of the great minds and talents who have created them,
but also to the anonymous toil of their contemporaries. There is no
document of civilization which is not at the same time a document of
barbarism. And just as such a document is not free of barbarism, barbarism taints also the manner in which it was transmitted from one
owner to another. A historical materialist therefore dissociates himself
from it as far as possible. He regards it as his task to brush history
against the grain. (1968: 258–259)

Valle's text intervenes in the historical-materialist mode identified by Benjamin through its subversion of the monumental, even reverential aura surrounding the great men and great developments that gave rise to modern Los
Angeles.[6] Three of the developments Valle alludes to have indeed been epic
in scale, ranking as the largest of their kind in the world—the Owens Valley aqueduct, the human-made port at San Pedro ("at the foot of the city"),
and the Huntington-owned interurban railroad system (now defunct) (Davis
1990: 113)—and have been touted by boosters as concrete manifestations
(thus "documents" in built form) of the region's technologically enabled evolution from mission era to modernity. Valle clearly rubs this celebratory tele-
ology of Los Angeles' history "against the grain" of its self-promoting hubris,
identifying the underlying circumstances of conquest and appropriation upon
which much of the region's storied growth depended. One example suggests
a typical rhetoric of hegemonic historical representation: "The spectacular
transition of a little Mexican pueblo, with its huddle of sun-baked adobes,
into one of the world's great cities within so brief a span of time [1850–1950],
still entrances the imagination. Hardly less remarkable are the more recent
changes" (Hylen 1981: 1). Against such dominant historical narratives of urban and cultural progress, Valle brings the oppressive shadow tale out into the
light.

   This critical exposition is most strongly exercised in the invective censure
he directs against the founding actions and legacy of the "Colonel," Valle's

oblique figure for the self-designated "General" of early Los Angeles: Harrison Gray Otis. Here, Valle mirrors one of Benjamin's central metaphoric motifs ("in which the present rulers step over those lying prostrate") by detailing how the creation of the modern metropolis was substantially predicated on the victory of the Otis-led Merchants and Manufacturers Association over the city's organized labor movement. More aggressive, even, than the imaging of the "rulers" by Benjamin, Los Angeles' early ruling elite placed its "workers under a Colonel's boot." The deadly efficacy of Otis and his cohort is rendered by Valle in monstrous imagery, as the Colonel nurtures his present and future power by sucking the very life-force from the working class, "the way a wasp deposits her eggs / on its stung, moribund host." By itself, this representation of decimated labor unionism serves a counterideological function by inveighing against the historical power of local capital. Valle's critique, however, delves deeper into the form and function of Otis' ruling mechanisms. Although in the final instance direct police repression broke the back of labor and allowed Otis to erect "his fortress over two dead Wobblies,"[7] the continued political control over the region's growth depended equally, if not more, on the hegemonic exercise of power. This effect was, of course, manifest in Otis' consolidation of the *Los Angeles Times* as the leading newspaper in the region, and its institutional role as a power broker in subsequent local and regional growth coalitions was, in Valle's critical narration, "bequeathed to his protogés *[sic]*" as "Command of the Words."

This phrase may support some exegesis of biblical connotation. The capitalized orthography of the term "Words" as well as its implicit ascription of activism and power in the poem invite comparison with the term "Word" as it appears in the Gospel of John: 1. In that section of the New Testament, although it is used in the singular as a metaphor for Jesus, the Word is tied to God's originary powers in construction and ordering of the cosmos. The Word is, in fact, the very medium for realizing the designs of His creative will. ("In the beginning was the Word: / the Word was with God / and the Word was God. / He was with God in the beginning. / Through him all things came into being, / not one thing came into being / except through him" [John 1:1-3]). Given this biblical figuration of the enacting power of the Word, it seems a reasonable inference that Valle's use of "Words" connotes something of the messianic, genesis drive that compelled many of the early modern boosters (led by Charles Fletcher Lummis, who was employed by Otis) and builders of Los Angeles. Norman Klein has described the prevailing rhetoric of this period's "boosterish language" as something like a cross between the Apostles and a salesman's handbook, as if a deal had been cut with God about how to promote real estate. Like many adventurous businessmen of the day, these market managers claimed to be possessed by the evangelical spirit. But they were selling something even grander than leather-tooled editions of the Good Book. They were selling the City on the Hill as prime real estate. (1997:27)

Certainly, this early cadre's forceful promotional discourses and machinery (their "Words") marketed "Southern California as the promised land of a millenarian Anglo-Saxon racial odyssey" (Davis 1990:20) and helped to set in motion the great waves of Anglo-American in-migration necessary to realize Otis and company's speculative visions. In a sense, therefore, Los Angeles' turn-of-the-century urbanization could be said to have been specifically willed into being through Otis' exercised "Command of the Words" via his leadership in the Chamber of Commerce, as well as his ownership of the *Los Angeles Times*, which in the dawn of the modern city *was with* Otis and *was* Otis.

The urbanizing power of the Times-Mirror corporation has of course had a tangible material basis in its substantial real estate holdings, particularly in the central-city area. However, intimately tied to the power of its spatial capital (a function of the landscape effect) has been the influential force of its discursive capital (the media effect). As the dominant media apparatus in the city's modern history, the *Los Angeles Times* has regularly marshaled its journalistic and editorial powers to influence urban-development planning in ways that would profit its own class and propertied interests and those of allied individuals and institutions with which it has variously entered into growth coalitions. For example, the role of the *Times* in sabotaging the city's public-housing plans in the 1950s was previously noted in the discussion of Chávez Ravine. Its aggressive editorial support for Norris Poulson helped secure his victory over incumbent Mayor Bowron and signed the death warrant for the dispossessed Chávez Ravine barrios.

Valle is well informed of these and other interventions of the *Los Angeles Times*. At this writing, he is a professor of journalism at California Polytechnic University, San Luis Obispo campus, and he was a former *Times* reporter. In these capacities he has been well positioned to observe and interpret the ideological trends of the *Times* on issues of urban development, as well as regarding specific coverage of Latino communities in the region. In fact, in a book-length study of Latino Los Angeles that he is currently cowriting with the political scientist Rudy Torres—*Latino Metropolis*—Valle directly confronts the politics of journalistic representation by the *Times* in relation to urban development and inner-city, working-class Latino and Black residents. Valle and Torres argue that the *Los Angeles Times*' propositional reporting and editorializing in support of the Community Redevelopment Agency facilitated the conversion of public funds into private wealth, as ultra-upscale development mightily benefited downtown property owners (including the Times corporation) at the direct expense of public infrastructural and community service needs in South Central Los Angeles. The same deconstructive vision that Valle exercises in his Los Angeles counterepic is applied in the present "postindustrial" moment, as he and Torres reveal how the raising of Bunker Hill's corporate acropolis simultaneously fueled the razing of Black and Latino inner-city community spaces.

By correlating Valle's discursive activity as a poet and as an academic-journalistic investigator, I wish to explicitly locate him within the trajectory of aesthetic and critical expressive discourses long practiced by the Raza press and more recently by Raza scholars, writers, and artists who articulate and defend community interests and history. Indeed, it is a practical discursive legacy that Valle is cognizant of, as revealed in the following collective text to which he contributed: "Since the conquest of California, this city's cultural chauvinism has suppressed the participation of Chicano poets and journalists who were consequently forced to publish their works in scores of Spanish-language newspapers" (Los Angeles Latino Writers Association 1982:3). This citation is from the editorial introduction to the barriological literary and artistic anthology *201: Homenaje a la Ciudad de Los Angeles*, a monograph produced by the Los Angeles Latino Writers Workshop (alternately known as the Los Angeles Barrio Writers Workshop) and the affiliated *Chismearte* journal collective. As a guiding member of the Writers Workshop and a founding editor of *Chismearte*, Valle brought a powerful intellectual-historical perspective to this group of writers and artists. In *201*, Valle's editorial activities and his contribution of the original version of his Los Angeles counter-epic poem ("Ciudad de Los Angeles") jointly demonstrated his impulse to textually reinscribe the displaced histories and social spaces of Latino Los Angeles. In so doing, Valle and his fellow editors and the *201* contributors collectively employed institutional and discursive strategies that have historically been deployed to barriological effect by Raza cultural activists.

At an institutional level, the members of the Latino Writers Workshop came together in the same spirit of self-help that has characterized many community-based associations, and they specifically "represented the first attempt by Latino writers in L.A. to organize themselves" (Los Angeles Latino Writers Association 1982:3). Not coincidentally, one of the original writers who helped to bring the workshop into being was Ron Arias, whose 1975 novel *The Road to Tamazunchale* will be substantially treated in Chapter 4. In the discursive realm, *201* distilled many of the same counterideological tactics discussed above regarding the earliest testimonial expressions of the displaced Californios and their various Raza-press successors. The principal tactic involved the subversion of hegemonic representations that have conspired or conduced to discursively dispossess Los Angeles Latinos of their place in the city's cultural history, parallel to their geographic deterritorialization. The introduction to the anthology[8] relates the centrality of this corrective impulse both to the formation of the writers' group and to the publication of *201:*

> The commemoration of the Los Angeles Bicentennial became a driving force in the development of the Workshop. Certainly a bicentennial celebration in this city without a just tribute to its Spanish-speaking people would have been a commemoration of faceless suburbs, Hollywood fantasies, California Club's Sunday lunches, and would have been little more than a celebration of the elite culture imported by Belair opulence. The cultural heritage of this city's more than two million Spanish-speaking people who have stubbornly thrived like the nopal of our desert hillsides, can no longer be ignored. (Los Angeles Latino Writers Association 1982:3)

Adducing a native claim to territorial and cultural primacy in the image of the indigenous cactus, this metaphor of rootedness and persistence in place introduces the underlying purpose of the publication to both re-site in social space and re-cite in discursive space the Chicano community's historical and present realities. This social-textual declaration evokes one of the persistent and underlying impulses of all barriological praxis: to inscribe the individual and collective identities of *la raza* in a sphere of "counter-public" (Crawford 1995:4) cultural citizenship. This impulse is shaped simultaneously by dynamics of denial and affirmation. Denial is manifest in the multiform critiques of cultural Otherness and public invisibility that is socially imposed upon Chicanos. This attitude is captured by Harry Gamboa, a multimedia avant-garde artist and contributor to *201*, who laconically notes that "Chicanos are . . . viewed as a phantom culture. We're like a rumor in this country" (Norte 1983:12).

Such hegemonic denials of Chicano cultural presence are precisely the object of contestatory *affirmation*, as expressed in the closing lines of the introduction to *201*, which recalls institutional, popular cultural, and textual expressions of the barriological attitude "aquí estamos y no nos vamos." The manner in which *201* offers public testimony to the stubborn persistence of Chicanos to stake their claim to the city brings us back full circle to the link between this recent generation of Raza cultural activists and the collective, counterideological expressions of the proto-Chicano generation of Californios who originally exercised a declamatory and reclamatory project in their testimonial declarations and editorial activity one hundred years earlier. In terms that could equally apply to the collective discursive proposition of the *201* contributors, Rosaura Sánchez describes how

> several among the Californios who are acutely aware of the lack of self-representation see the need to reconstruct the past from their own vantage point if the collectivity and its history are to survive textually and if they are to envision a future. The effect of this reconstruction of the past and the construction of an ethnic identity, the "imagined community" of *la raza*, is thus twofold: historical and political. (1995:271)

Similar desires clearly motivated the textual discourses of Victor Valle and his colleagues. They are also infused in various recollective narrations by other contributors to *201*. For example, Luis Rodríguez' "La Veintinueve" and Enrique Hank López' "Overkill at the Silver Dollar," which speak of the tragic events surrounding the 1970 Chicano Moratorium rally in East Los Angeles, are particularly forthright and indignant in their reconstructive and revisionary impulses. This is not surprising, since this infamous case of police intervention (both covert and overt) against a legal public gathering was immediately canonized in the Chicano political imagination as the next signal instance of the historically repressive legacy of the law effect. At this point in history, the siege mentality evidenced by police and sheriff's officers confirmed a popular perception of them as no less than an occupying army. The particularly emotional significance of this latest police incursion against barrio space and public congregation was fueled by the fact that the police agents responsible for inciting the violent melee at Belvedere Park and for the killing of reporter Rubén Salazar at the Silver Dollar Cafe were officially absolved of fault for their actions.

The original version of Valle's Los Angeles counterepic is joined by Juan Gómez-Quiñones' historical poem "Canto al trabajador" and Jesús Mena's interview of community activist and labor organizer Bert Corona ("Testimonio de Bert Corona: Struggle Is the Ultimate Teacher") to offer longer views of historical presence and struggles for place-rights that have helped construct the social space of ethnicity among working-class barrio residents. Clearly echoing the 1877 collective editorial declaration of Pastor de Celis, Mariano J. Varela, and S. A. Cardona, Victor Valle and the rest of the contributors to *201* also asserted their place and voice to express the fact that "we still have a voice, tenacity and rights; we have not yet retired to the land of the dead." Responding against the hegemonic erasure of Chicano culture so aptly represented by Harry Gamboa, the members of the Los Angeles Barrio Writers Workshop and contributors to *201* render its rumors as truth and its phantoms as flesh through their collective declarations of Chicano presence in their second city: Nuestra Señora la Reina de Los Angeles de Porciúncula.

"Phantoms in Urban Exile"

THREE *Critical Soundings from Los Angeles'
Expressway Generation*

*In Los Angeles there is an impression that the fluidity
of the environment and the absence of physical elements
which anchor to the past are exciting and disturbing.
Many descriptions of the scene by established residents,
young or old, were accompanied by the ghosts of what used
to be there. Changes, such as those wrought by the freeway system, have left scars on the mental image.*
— KEVIN LYNCH, *The Image of the City*

*The distinctive sign of nineteenth-century urbanism was
the boulevard, a medium for bringing explosive material
and human forces together; the hallmark of twentieth-
century urbanism has been the highway, a means for putting them asunder.*
— MARSHALL BERMAN, *All That Is Solid Melts into Air*

Cutting a broad swath through the central-city barrios, the juggernaut of Los
Angeles' postwar redevelopment effected its devastations upon a wide cross
section of the Chicano community. For many contemporary writers and artists who grew up in the path or in the shadow of this voracious growth engine,
lived experience provided the raw material that they would later transmute
into compelling barriological expressions. Like the range of discourses treated
in Chapter 2—including critical journalism, activist scholarship, and revi-

FIGURE 30. East Los Angeles Interchange, 1962. Courtesy of California Department of Transportation.

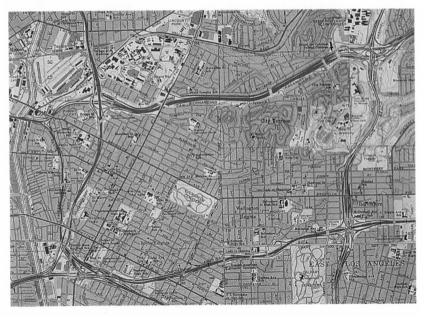

FIGURE 31. Geography of the expressway generation, greater East Los Angeles. Courtesy of United States Geological Survey.

sionist historical narratives—the creative forms and thematic contents of texts produced in the 1980s and 1990s also serve to "identify and clarify the issues that . . . [have] shaped" Raza urban social space and consciousness (Acuña 1984:274). In sharp contrast, therefore, to the glib pronouncements of freeway boosters and urban developers, who promoted their projects as monuments to Southern California's celebrated "good life" (if not as its very conditions of possibility[1]), a counterdiscourse has emerged among a generation of contestatory Raza writers, informed by their cognizance of the many neighborhoods razed for the achievement of the city's "modern marvel" (Parson 1993). Among the notable examples discussed in this chapter are works by author Helena María Viramontes, lyricists Willie Herrón and Jesús Velo of the rock band Los Illegals, poet and author Gil Cuadros, playwright and performance artist Luis Alfaro, and poet Gloria Alvarez.

These writers—and many other Raza artists whose work cannot be taken up here—exercise a specific modernist social-geographic aesthetic, described by Marshall Berman, which was engendered within and against the repressive effects of contemporary urbanism. This critical expressive ethos, was "at once more personal and more political . . . [and one] in which modern men and women could confront the new physical and social structures that had grown up around them. In this new modernism, the gigantic engines and systems of postwar construction played a central symbolic role" (1982:310; see Fig. 32). Berman here describes an experientially based and affectively compelled discourse of artistic "back talk," or backlash, against the material and psychological ravages of the contemporary metropolis. This expressive impulse is commensurate with the exigencies of life in an imperious urban-growth machine such as Los Angeles. As it has historically been demonstrated to many Chicanos that they "are not in a position to effectively claim that their neighborhood, as used by them, is . . . useful for attracting capital," they have consequently been forced to "make a more 'emotional,' a less 'public-regarding' . . . case for their rights to their homes and shops" (Logan and Molotch 1987:135–136). This affective case for place-rights can be made through any number of publicly expressive activities, as presented in the opening chapters. However, it is particularly germane to the thematic and formal structures of the works discussed here, in which the deeply *felt*, and often suffered, experience of urban deterritorialization has figured so prominently.

I have purposefully drawn the first part of this chapter's title, "Phantoms in Urban Exile," from the work of Harry Gamboa, whose talent for laconic characterization of social truths was seen at the end of Chapter 2. This specific phrase was taken from the subject heading for his series of ten con-

FIGURE 32.   From *The Visual Environment of East Los Angeles* (Los Angeles: Barrio Planners, 1973). Courtesy of Barrio Planners, Inc.

cise Internet texts—each not more than a paragraph or two—posted to CHICLE, the Chicano Literature and Culture Internet discussion group, in late 1995 and 1996, and later published in *Aztlán: A Journal of Chicano Studies.* Gamboa's spectral image is important for its pithy evocation of Chicano cultural invisibility and social death, tropes that characterize his critical absurdist imagination much as they have haunted the social-geographic consciousness of Raza writers since the mid-1800s.[2] Although the "Phantoms" series is more recent than the other texts I will treat in this chapter, the first of Gamboa's published postings serves as an appropriate text to retrospectively introduce this period of Chicano and Chicana writing. Its very title, "Man under the Asphalt," gestures toward a ghastly consequence of the city's equally monumental and barbaric freeway system. The first two lines of text substantiate this critical innuendo: "I've heard rumors that the freeways in L.A. are the concrete ribbons of a package that will never be opened before exodus. The asphalt coating of billions of square feet is the icing on the multiple social layers of a dysfunctional environment" (Gamboa 1997:197). It is precisely this dysfunctional urban milieu—produced not only by freeway constructions but by the range of infrastructural redevelopments constituting the brave new expressway world of Los Angeles—that the expressway generation of barriological writers take it upon themselves to document and deconstruct in their various narrative modes.

ROOT DESTRUCTION: HELENA MARÍA VIRAMONTES' "NEIGHBORS"

Helena María Viramontes, a native of East Los Angeles, participates in this expressive trajectory of social-geographic narration in her 1985 collection *The Moths and Other Stories.* In broad terms, the stories in her collection describe the multiple and intersecting constraints of race- and class-based oppression that threaten the cultural cohesion, physical safety, and psychological integrity of Latino communities, whether at the local level of individuals and families in California barrios or at the global level of citizens and nations in Latin America. Viramontes also narrates socially gendered experiences of women within the masculinist context of their own Latino communities, an element of intracultural place-consciousness that will be discussed more fully in the next chapter with regard to the spatialized poetics of Lorna Dee Cervantes. This broad variety of themes suggests Viramontes' range of concerns as a politically engaged artist with a broad, pan-American perspective as well as a focused concern for the pressing social issues affecting her home geography in East Los Angeles. However, her political engagement is not merely a function of literary representation. She has contributed to the grassroots Latino cultural infrastructure of Los Angeles as an early member of the Los Angeles Latino Writers Association, which she joined in 1978, and as a founder of Southern California Latino Writers and Filmmakers in 1989. Relatedly, in collaboration with professor María Herrera-Sobek and others, she has co-organized several important university conferences on Chicana literary and cultural criticism. In both her community-based and university-based institutional activities, Viramontes has participated variously as creative writer, critic, administrator, and editor. Aspects of each of these functions coalesced in her contributions to *201/Two Hundred and One: Homenaje a la ciudad de Los*

Angeles, which was discussed at the end of Chapter 2. The contestatory intervention of *201* in the field of cultural discourse about Los Angeles was identified by its editorial common cause with the ideological-aesthetic programs of other barriological publications from the period such as *Con Safos* and *Chismearte*, which similarly evinced "the importance of the barrio in this city's literary tradition" (Los Angeles Latino Writers Association 1982:4). As the literary editor of *201*, Viramontes influenced the formal and ideological parameters of this landmark barriological document and played an important role in offsetting some of the masculinist tendencies of her co-editors (Viramontes, personal interview 1994).

In such creative company and historical context, and because of a deeply felt identification with her barrio, Viramontes' writing could not help but meditate on multiple aspects of that simultaneously intimate and public social space. In particular, Viramontes' story "Neighbors" is a somber reflection on her East Los Angeles home geography, setting forth a tense dialectic of utopian and dystopian associations with the narrated social space. The plot in "Neighbors" revolves around the experiences of Aura and Fierro, *anciano* (senior citizen) neighbors of an unspecified barrio on the Eastside. Like the common plot of land on which their two houses sit, the two *ancianos* share a common lot in life. Their mutual solitude, increasing and painful physical disabilities, and sense of imminent death connects them in a quiet bond of suffering and solidarity. Two significant and interwoven narrative scenarios irrevocably alter the fragile security of their mutual routines. First, the mysterious appearance of an unnamed woman who moves in with Fierro sparks an almost magical life force and sense of *gusto* (pleasure) in Fierro's pained existence. As Aura observes the woman's effect on Fierro, she too feels a re-kindled will-to-pleasure, only to have it destroyed by the second scenario. In this one, Aura asks some young neighbors, the "Bixby Boys," who are hanging out in front of her house, to lower their music. When they mockingly refuse her request, her long-brewing frustration with this and other intrusive street activities pushes her to call the police, whose violent zeal in handling the matter sets in motion a tragic escalation of retribution between Aura and the young men.

Narrated through these two scenarios, Aura's sense of entrapment and felt threat raises fundamental issues regarding the dissolution of a communitarian ethos under the killing effects of the barrio's contemporary social-geographic subordination, both through the social ennui produced by the deindustrialization of the barrio in the late 1970s and the precedent disfigurement of East Los Angeles' physical landscape by the infrastructural developments of postwar urban restructuring. Viramontes notes of Aura, and we can extend the statement to Fierro as well, that "[p]eople of her age died off only to leave their grandchildren with little knowledge of struggle" (1985:102). The root social causes and terrible personal consequences of this broken chain of communitarian knowledge and place-memory inform the critical narrative of "Neighbors." Through such narrative mediations, Viramontes continues the line of historical geographic critique discussed in previous chapters, although transmitting her critique through the compelling affective register of tragedy.

Broken Bonds of Community: Aura's Monadic Experience

In the opening paragraph of "Neighbors," Viramontes introduces us to Aura and her barrio neighborhood with a chilling characterization of individual and collective social death.

> Aura Rodríguez always stayed within her perimeters, both personal
> and otherwise, and expected the same of her neighbors. She was quite
> aware that the neighborhood had slowly metamorphosed into a
> graveyard. . . . She shared the same streets and corner stores and mid-
> nights with . . . tough-minded young men who threw empty beer cans
> into her yard; but once within her own solitude, surrounded by a tall
> wrought-iron fence, she belonged to a different time. Like those who
> barricaded themselves against an incomprehensible generation, Aura
> had resigned herself to live with the caution and silence of an appari-
> tion, as she had lived for the past seventy-three years, asking no ques-
> tions, assured of no want, no deep-hearted yearning other than to live
> out the remainder of her years without hurting anyone, including her-
> self. (1985:102)

Aura's very name suggests she is perhaps more a phantasmic than a corporeal body, and thus a sort of living-dead entity. The *American Heritage Dictionary of the English Language* defines *aura* as "1. An invisible breath or emanation. 2. A distinctive air or quality that characterizes a person or thing . . . 3. A soft breeze. 4. Pathology. A sensation, as of a cold breeze, preceding the onset of certain nervous disorders." The pathological meaning of *aura* as a premoni- tory sensation, like a cold breeze anticipating a nervous disorder, foreshadows Aura's imminent breakdown under the aggravated and aggravating conditions of her multiple social, physical, and psychological containments. It may also be a clue to Viramontes' use of Aura as a metonymic figure for the disintegration of her neighborhood, in which the dysfunctions of the larger barrio community are reflected on her mind and body. A specific literary allusion to *Aura*, Carlos Fuentes' ghostly novella, may also be at play here. Viramontes has stated that various Latin American authors influenced her own formal literary style (1989:37). If Fuentes was not among them, then it is an eerie coincidence that his ghost story is set in the darkly ambiented home of an old woman, in the center of Mexico City, which has been walled in by modern constructions. As Señora Llorente tells a young visitor: "Es que estoy acostumbrada a las tinieblas. . . . Es que nos amurallaron, señor Montero, nos han quitado la luz" ["It's that I'm used to the darkness. . . . It's that they have walled us in, Mr. Montero, they've taken away the light" (my translation)] (1986:29).

In Section 4 of "Neighbors," Viramontes describes Aura's pained and atrophying body, as we see her shuffling about the solitary rooms of her home.

> By the evening she had tried almost everything to rid herself of the pain and her lips parched with bitterness. Miserable and cornered, she began cursing her body. . . . She began to hate. . . . She hated the way her fingers distorted her hand so that she could not even grasp a glass of water. But most of all she hated the laughter and the loud music which came from the boys who stood around the candied-apple red Impala with the tape deck on full blast. They laughed and drank and threw beer cans in her yard while she burned with fever. . . .
>
> "Go home," she pleaded, leaning against a porch pillar, her legs folding under her. "Go home. Go home."
>
> "We *are* home!" Rubén said while opening another malt liquor. The others began to laugh. . . . [S]he slipped and fell and they continued to laugh. (1985:107–108; original emphasis)

The mocking laughter of the young men exhausts her patience to the point that she disregards a fundamental tenet of barrio implicit social knowledge: "It was their laughter at her inability to even stand on her own two feet that made her call the police" (108).[3]

From a nonbarriological perspective, the recourse to police intervention may seem unproblematic. And yet, such a view contradicts implicit social knowledge regarding historical barrio-police relations in Los Angeles, as has been repeatedly illustrated throughout this study. If her physical pain and emotional humiliation cause her, in this moment, to forget the wisdom of the barrio with regard to the exercise of the dominant law effect, the actions of the police reconfirm, for her and the reader, the often calculated excesses of this repressive state apparatus: "Her feeling of revenge had overcome her pain momentarily, but when the police arrived, she fully realized her mistake. The five cars zeroed in on their target, halting like tanks in a cartoon. The police jumped out in military formation, ready for combat" (108). Clouded by vengeance, Aura believed that she could turn to the police "to get some kindness" from her neighbors. But their quasimilitary police assault on the Bixby Boys unmistakably reawakens her barriological consciousness, as she witnesses the chilling pursuit of one of the boys.

> [H]e ran towards the door, and for a moment Aura was sure he wanted to kill her. It was not until he lunged for the door that she was able to see the desperation and confusion, the fear in his eyes, and he screamed at the top of his lungs while pounding on her door, the *vowels* of the one word melting into a howl, he screamed to her, "Pleeeeeeease." . . . [H]is howl was abruptly silenced by a dull thud. (109; original emphasis)

Quite contrary to the resolution Aura had hoped for, there will be no kindness forthcoming from her assaulted neighbors: "[S]he remembered the last thing Rubén yelled as the patrol cars drove off. . . . 'We'll get you,' he said. 'You'll see'" (109).

If Aura misread the roles of victim and victimizer between her neighbors and the police, she was compelled to call the police in the first place by the mocking disdain of the young men toward her pleas for silence. The "incomprehensible generation" is equally uncomprehending of Aura's physical pain and, more important, of any possible communitarian relationship to her. In traditional Mexican cultural terms, *les falta respeto:* "she refused to be mocked by these little men who knew nothing of life and respect" (108). The young men's disregard represents more than their simple selfishness or unconcern. It evidences two tendential forms of community disarticulation that are either aggravated or compelled by recent negative trends in the social and economic reorganization of East Los Angeles.

On the one hand, if we take the Bixby Boys to be a gang clique, then their disregard for Aura and their other neighbors represents a disturbing trend toward increasing tensions between gang and nongang residents of the Eastside. Joan Moore's longitudinal research in this area suggests a downward spiral of relations: "What evidence we have indicates that the cliques of the 1950s were more closely integrated with the conventional barrio structures and norms. The cliques of the 1970s appear more remote, and faced more disapproval and more efforts at control" (1991:69). She goes on to note that though some gang members attempted to work within consensual community norms with respect to the common social space shared by barrio dwellers, others "made no pretense at neighborhood altruism: they were quite aware that they intimidated neighbors" (ibid.:71). The blade cuts both ways, of course, since a growing number of gang members in Moore's study felt that "neighbors were hostile to their clique. Even though a majority continued to feel that neighbors were either neutral or favorably inclined, an increased proportion in both neighborhoods recognized sharp conflicts" (ibid.:70).

The increasing breakdown of consensual norms about how to coexist in the barrio gestures toward the second trend figured in the Bixby Boys' mocking disdain for Aura. Here I refer to the disintegrating chain of intergenerational communication, already noted in Viramontes' opening observation that Aura's "generation died off only to leave their grandchildren with little knowledge of struggle" (1985:102). These twin dysfunctional tendencies in the East Los Angeles community—of gang to nongang relations and of cross-generational exchanges of experiential knowledge—are, in no small part, a disabling effect of the contemporary reorganization of social space in Los Angeles, described by Mike Davis as "the brutalization of inner-city neighborhoods and the increasing South Africanization of its spatial relations" (1990:227–228).

Along with such exacerbated conditions of the contemporary Eastside, "Neighbors" intimates, at a more sedimented level, the numbing consequences of recent demographic changes and post-Fordist economic transformations upon the working-class barrios. In the late 1970s and 1980s, the large-scale influx of Central Americans fleeing the ravages of civil war in their homelands "coincided with local economic restructuring . . . to drastically constrict the job opportunities available to Chicanos in the area" (McCarthy and Valdez 1986:40). The economic factor having the single greatest impact was the "almost Detroit-like decline of traditional, highly unionized heavy industry" (Soja, Morales, and Wolff 1984:211ff) upon which many Chicanos and Blacks in the east and south-central industrial corridor of the city had depended for their well-being:

> As the Los Angeles economy in the 1970s was 'unplugged' from the American industrial heartland . . . non-Anglo workers have borne the brunt of adaptation and sacrifice. The 1978–1982 wave of factory closings in the wake of Japanese import penetration and recession . . . shut-

tered ten of the twelve largest non-aerospace plants in Southern California and displaced 75,000 blue-collar workers. (Davis 1990:304)

The net effect of this "unplugging" was a dramatic rise in the unemployment, underemployment, and displacement of many Chicano and Black workers into various forms of unorganized and low-wage industrial labor or service-sector employment (Soja 1989:201), conditions still reigning at the end of the 1990s. These economic conditions are obliquely manifested through the conspicuous absence of materially sustaining—much less spiritually generative—labor in "Neighbors."

In reality, the dispiriting inactivity produced by mass unemployment or downward economic mobility is especially acute among young Chicanos, particularly men. The socially generated ennui in this sector of the community is clearly revealed in the disheartened public-space activities of "the children gathered near her [Aura's] home in small groups to drink, to lose themselves in the abyss of defeat, to find temporary solace among each other" (Viramontes 1985:102). The conspicuous absence of any sustaining labor or productive activity and the resulting ennui described by Viramontes intimate, in sedimented fashion, the consequences of urban economic restructuring in the Eastside community. Furthermore, in a cyclical chain of effects, repressive police containment is increasingly used today to quell—even as it effectively deepens—the growing disaffection of barrio residents, especially among the young people displaced from traditional avenues of socioeconomic security and mobility. Subsequently, the economic and police brutalizations of the barrio, scenically represented by Viramontes, act as conjoined social forces that influence the anticommunitarian disrespect shown to Aura by the "tough-minded young men." When she pleads for them to "go home," they correctly point out that they already *are* home!" While their reply mocks Aura's plea, it also illustrates how many young barrio residents have already hit a dead end near the beginning of their life road. In this respect, the "candied-apple red Impala" is significantly immobile. Its positive symbolism as a prized icon in barrio lowrider subculture can only be enacted in a mobile, *flâneur*-like display of style. Instead of cruising the boulevard, the young men are merely standing around the totemic vehicle. Since cruising is a strongly male-centered and male-controlled expressive province (Plascencia 1983; Stone 1990), the impotency of the totemic Impala symbolizes the social emasculation of Chicano activity and identity.

Viramontes' words and scenes point out the near impossibility of escape from residential containment and social death-in-life for residents of the contemporary barrio. The broader social restraints imposed on the young men and the community at large are subsequently mirrored in "the geograph[ies] closest in" (Rich 1986:212) to Aura's personal experience. Specifically, I have already noted the pain and atrophy that make Aura a suffering captive of her own flesh and blood: "Miserable and cornered, she began cursing her body" (Viramontes 1985:107). The syntax of this quoted sentence suggests that she is "cornered" both in her body and her home. The captive immobility of her aging body contrasts sharply with remembered images of dancing from her youth. One night, during the mystery woman's stay with Fierro, "a faint nasal melody playing against a rusty needle . . . penetrated her [Aura's] darkness and she cocked her head to listen. . . . [She] tried to remember why the song seemed so familiar. The Hallmark dance floor. She remembered the Hallmark dance floor and smiled" (109). Against the earlier description of Aura's "lips . . . parched with bitterness" (107), the smile sparked by remembered youth is cathartic. The mystery woman revives a sound of life and pleasure for Fierro and Aura, similar to the "song of life" that will be seen to figure so prominently in *The Road to Tamazunchale*. Fierro's recorded music interrupts and, symbolically and literally, contests the aural dominance of other, more disturbing street sounds in Aura's environment: barking dogs, police sirens, the neighbor boys' tape deck. In the interim between the violent police scene and the realization of the Bixby Boys' promised revenge (a few days), Aura is briefly transfixed and imaginatively transported by Fierro's music. The invitation to experience the expressive freedom and pleasure of movement in dance, whether remembered (in Aura's recollections of youth) or revived (in the unnamed woman's sensual dance and Fierro's visual pleasure), sparks a flash of imagined or felt release from atrophying bodies and pained spirits in both Aura and Fierro.

For Aura, the voyeuristic pleasure resuscitates her long-frustrated desire for physical release and creative mobility: "Aura was in the mood to dance, to loosen her inhibitions from the tight confines of shoes and explore a barefoot freedom she had never explored in her wakeful hours" (110). This description suggests the severity of her personal, and likely gendered, repression of expressive desire, which reigns during all "her wakeful hours." The exercise of her intimate desires is thus left to the time and place of her reveries and dreams. However, the significance of Aura's dreaming time-space must not be underestimated as a merely *private* escape from repressively *real* social contingencies, nor as a purely "compensatory reaction against public situations, but rather [as] a way of reading those situations, of thinking and mapping them, of intervening in them, albeit in a very different form from the abstract reflections of traditional philosophy or politics" (Fredric Jameson, quoted in Flores and Yúdice 1993:208). Viewed in this way, Aura's imaginative desires are significant, if implicit or intuitive, ways of "reading" her "public" situation as a woman constrained by the daily obligations and abnegations expected of a woman within a traditional working-class *mexicano* cultural milieu. Aura's physical and social constraints compel the dream-bound realization of her desires. Her knowledge of these constraints, after a lifetime of experiencing them, lets her return from her mnemonic interlude at the Hallmark Ballroom without remorse: "[S]he awoke to stare at her feet, to let reality slowly sink in, and she was thankful and quite satisfied simply to be able to walk" (110).

But this morning soon provides a ruder awakening than most. This time, the impossibility of "barefoot freedom" provokes an emergent bitterness, experienced physically: "she felt weak and uneasy." At first, she mistakenly "attributed the hollowness of her stomach to the medication she had taken throughout those endless nights" (110), but she soon confronts the true source of her nausea ,when she sees the woman "standing barefoot on the porch, tossing bread crumbs to the pigeons while her bracelets clinked with her every toss, Aura knew it was not the medication" (111). The unsettling effect of the unnamed woman has to do with her unorthodox physical and psychological characterization, which allow her an eccentric freedom unavailable to Aura. The physical attributes of the woman—whose description brings to mind a street person or bag lady—represent a grotesque embodied critique (in the manner described by Mikhail Bakhtin [1984]) of socially prescribed femininity. She is unfeminine, even antifeminine, and unconstrained by reigning definitions of what a woman's body or a woman's proper conduct "should be," as revealed by the completely self-assured manner in which she first appeared in the neighborhood, "unmoved by the taunts and stares" (Viramontes 1985:103) of the residents. In spite of, or because of, her socially transgressive body—most notably her overpowering odor—she is unconcerned with people's dismissive responses. Her "barefoot freedom," both physical and attitudinal, implicitly cast Aura's abnegated experience into sharp relief.

While Aura "always stayed within her perimeters, both personal and otherwise" (102), the mysterious woman literally overflows her own body and personal-space boundaries (her malodorous scent signifies both of these excesses) in a radical disengagement from social propriety. Her ability to enliven

Fierro from his degenerating condition, her easy, sensuous physical expressiveness and related characteristics constitute her as a figure of fecund vitality within the otherwise deathly ambience of the story. Her life force provokes Aura's long-stifled will-to-pleasure into wakeful desires. Once resigned to a life of "asking no questions, assured of no want, no deep-hearted yearning" (102), Aura has a qualitative change of heart toward the end of the story, admitting her long-frustrated "wants."

Lacking the physical mobility of the other woman, Aura turns to a very specific expressive domain to exercise her creative will-to-life: "Since the rainfall had soaked the soil, she could not pass up the opportunity to weed out her garden, and even though her movements were sluggish, she prepared herself for a day's work" (111). Aura's horticultural labor is the single affirming and productive activity in her otherwise repressed existence. In this expressive capacity her garden serves as a vital space of retreat, a function the social geographer J. B. Jackson has identified more broadly: "The garden is where we impart to others our knowledge of a family tradition, and where we can briefly withdraw from the perplexities of the outside world; it is where we plant a seed which we hope will someday flower into a more beautiful landscape, and a more harmonious community" (1980:35).

Such a familial legacy is specifically gendered in Aura's garden work, which clearly expresses her desire to connect with a community of women. It brings her out of the shadowy confines of her house into a symbolic matrilineal lineage, since "[s]ome of her bushes . . . [had] begun as cuttings from her mother's garden" (Viramontes 1985:111). Here, Viramontes recalls Alice Walker's "womanist" articulation of "mothers' gardens" as a metaphor for the ways in which African-American women experience and mediate their generational legacy, marking a Chicana womanist inheritance in the signifying space of Aura's garden. Elsewhere, Viramontes has noted the conscious identification with African American "womanism" as a thematic model in her own work: "Once I discovered the Black woman writers—[Alice] Walker, [Toni] Morrison, [Gwendolyn] Brooks, [Ntozake] Shange . . .—womanism as a subject matter seemed sanctioned, illuminating, innovative, honest, the best in recent fiction I've seen in a long time" (1989:37). In a similar vein, Bettina Aptheker has expanded on Walker's formulation to understand the significance of gardening and other practices (quilting, recipes, letter writing, etc.) of women's everyday domestic culture as specific manifestations of "women's standpoint." In her suggestively titled study, *Tapestries of Life: Women's Work, Women's Consciousness, and the Meaning of Daily Experience*, she defines the "meaning of daily experience" as the patterns women create and the meanings women invent each day and over time as a result of their labors and in the context of their subordinated status to men. . . . *The point is to suggest a way of knowing from the meanings women give to their labors.* The search for dailiness is a method of work that allows us to take the patterns women create and the meanings women invent and learn from them. (1989:39; emphasis added)

Through the identified and organic links of Aura's plantings to her mother's garden, Aura feels rooted in a continuum of maternal descent that offers some mooring against her present dystopian milieu. Because of these felt and reproduced links, what Aura sees as she steps outdoors and confronts the promised vengeance of the Bixby Boys marks her deep and final alienation from even this residual community:

She bit her fist in disbelief. Most of the graffiti was sprayed on her front porch with black paint, but some of it was written with excrement. As she slowly stepped down, she inspected the windows, steps, walkways, pillars, all defaced with placas, symbols, vulgarities. She rushed over to the chayote vine and made a feeble attempt to replant it, but everything, her flowers, chayotes, gardenias, rose bushes, were uprooted and cast aside. . . . She had spent years guiding and pruning and nurturing them until they blossomed their gratitude. She tried unsuccessfully to restore them, the thorns scratching her face, her bare hands bleeding. (Viramontes 1985:111)

This complete and "radical" (recalling the Latin etymology of the term) destruction, unearthing the very roots of her garden, severs Aura's link to a collective womanist past.

Aura's futile attempts to salvage the garden seem to provoke her final capitulation, manifested as a resignation-unto-death. "'I'm so glad,' she thought, fighting back the tears as the mutilated bushes began shriveling under the morning sun, 'I'm so glad I'm going to die soon'" (112). While the deforestation of Aura's matrilineal garden and home space severs her from a specific cultural continuum and community of women, a broader and equally devastating uprooting is effected upon the greater barrio and its historical-cultural landscape. This aggressive deterritorialization is produced at the level of city planning under the recurring guise of urban modernization. As with so many other barriological expressions, the telling (anti-)monument of these hegemonic spatial practices is the ubiquitous freeway system cutting through the barrio.

Geographies of Things Past: Personal Memory as Place History

If the opening characterization of Aura describes her "aware[ness] that the neighborhood had slowly metamorphosed into a graveyard" (102), the narrative around Fierro reveals one of its compelling external causes. His individual effort to retain a memory of his son's death and of the neighborhood's topographical transformations calls attention to the larger processes affecting the barrio's historical and material deformation. Fierro's will-to-memory is also a metaphor for Viramontes' own authorial struggle to discursively render the consequences of East Los Angeles' social-geographic subordination into usable, transmittable community knowledge through the medium of her fiction.

The importance of Fierro's memory function is immediately suggested as he is introduced to the reader in the context of his most intimate recollection of loss. His first substantial characterization opens with an omniscient narrative flashback to his son's murder.

> Dressed in his Saturday sharpest, Chuy finished the last of his beer
> behind the Paramount Theater before meeting Laura in the balcony,
> "the dark side." When he threw the *tall dog* into a huge trash bin, three
> men jumped the alley wall and attacked him. As they struck at him, he
> managed to grab a 2 by 4 which was holding the trash lid open, but it
> was no match for the switchblade which ripped through his chest.
> (104; original emphasis)

However, Fierro's encroaching senility threatens this memory and others he still retains of the neighborhood. In fact, speculations on his mental fortitude are a significant topic of neighborhood gossip. The focal point of people's discussions concerns Fierro's communications with the ghost of his son, Chuy, who died at the age of nineteen. Although opinions vary regarding what to make of Fierro's dialogues with the dead son, there is consensus "on one thing: Fierro was strangely touched" (104). While his neighbors cannot agree on the existence of Chuy's ghost, there is no doubt that for Fierro the past coexists in the time and space of the present, and that the crucial role of memory for Fierro's well-being is what fuels his persistent mnemonic exercises.

Viramontes emphasizes the deeply personal memorial labors of Fierro by endowing a casual-seeming activity with a resolutely critical and mnemonic function: "Years and years later . . . [Fierro] sat on Aura's porch, whittling a cane for himself and murmuring to his son" (104). It is not incidental that Fierro is whittling a cane, nor that he is accompanied in his labor by Aura in hers, "as she watered her beloved rose bushes, chinaberry trees, and gardenias" (104). The wood he is crafting is the same two-by-four plank used by Chuy in his futile self-defense years earlier. Fierro had pried it loose from his dead son's fingers and stored it away, until "years later, as his legs grew as feeble as his mind, he took the 2 by 4 from his closet" (104) and began his craft. The dual function of the cane is to support equally his faltering legs and his faltering memory. Fierro's practical, creative project is equated to Aura's gardening. Their mundane labors expressively cultivate a sustaining link to the past, in Fierro's memory of Chuy and in Aura's connection to her mother's garden. A gendered division of traditional skills (woodcrafting for men, gardening for women) produces objects (cane, plants) that are material correlatives of personal history evoked or recalled in the present.

As a practical exercise, Fierro's cane-making sustains the memory of his son against the forgetfulness of debilitating old age. As a symbolic one, it is a synecdoche of the larger battle in which hegemonic practices threaten to erase collective past knowledge from the mind of the barrio community by erasing its very material landscape. Consequently, one source of the desperation coloring "Neighbors" is the imminent, if not already achieved, victory of this hegemonic erasure effect. Under the crushing sociospatial conditions mediated in the story, communitarian or personal-historical knowledge is shared only between Fierro and Aura, rather than being passed on to succeeding generations: "He alone was allowed to sit on her porch swing as he whittled. With sad sagging eyes and whiskey breath he described for hours his mother's face and the scent of wine grapes just before harvest. He often cried afterwards and returned home in quiet shame, closing his door discretely" (105).[4] The years of "sharing the same front gate," as well as their common moments of resonant productive labors and personal memories, produce a "silent bond between the two [that] sprouted and grew firmer and deeper with time" (105). The persistent "root" metaphor of horticulture is clearly evoked in the "sprouted" bond between the two *ancianos*, further confirming Viramontes' articulation of the organic and sustaining, but threatened, potential of communitarian culture. The pathos of "Neighbors" consequently lies in the fact that the memory seeds are not sown enough or fall on the infertile soil of an uncomprehending younger generation. Fierro's agonistic memory practices

resist the erasure of personal and collective community history by the hegemonic deforestation (material and spiritual) of barrio social space.

I noted above the doubly sustaining function of Fierro's cane as a physical
prop to his feeble legs and a material correlative of his personal memory.
Fierro uses it, therefore, to both physically traverse the space of his present
neighborhood and to mnemonically traverse the palimpsestic traces of its historic built environment. We are told, for example, that "[w]ith the help of his
cane, Fierro walked home from the Senior Citizen Center Luncheon" (105).
In describing this trajectory, Viramontes narrates an itinerary of remembered
spaces, laden with Fierro's intimate meanings as well as broader community
meanings. At the apex of his journey home, Fierro reaches a freeway overpass
and disrupts traffic as he crosses the on-ramp at one end. The truckers waiting
for him to cross show no sympathy for his labored movement, assaulting him
with their horns. Fierro curses the "cabrones" (roughly, "sons of bitches")
and then tries to escape the sonorous assault of the freeway by shutting off his
hearing aid, "so that the sounds in his head were not the sirens or motors or
horns, but the sounds of a seashell pressed tightly against his ear" (105).

Like the Bixby Boys' loud music and mocking laughter fueling Aura's desperation, the freeway's cacophonous activity provokes a similar anxiety in
Fierro. As he pauses, distraught, on the overpass, a passing neighbor's concerned inquiry provides the occasion for us to see the disfiguration that has
been made of Fierro's past and its devastating effects on his spirits.

> The woman shouted over her grocery bag and into his ear. He
> remembered to turn on his hearing aid, and when he did, he heard
> her ask, "Are you all right?"
> "Heartaches," he said finally, shaking his head. "Incurable. It's a
> cancer that lays dormant only to surprise you when you least expect it."
> "What could it be?" the young woman asked. . . .
> "Memories," Fierro said. (106)

Fierro's moment of silent respite is interrupted by the woman's questions.
When he turns his hearing aid back on, the re-admitted sounds of the freeway
push forth the contents of his pained memory.

> He heard the sirens again, the swift traffic whirling by beneath him.
> He was suddenly amazed how things had changed and how easy it
> would be to forget that there were once quiet hills here, hills that he

roamed in until they were flattened into vacant lots where dirt paths became streets and houses became homes. (106)

Fierro's recollection of a rural landscape, with its symptomatic opposition of natural and urban "prospects," may appear to reproduce the elegiac pastoral ideology of Euro-American romanticism or preromantic landscape art and literature. Certainly the use of naturalistic imagery as a critique of urbanization marks a partial similarity between the structure of Fierro's memories and that of such canonical Western aesthetic figurations. However, a closer examination reveals the distinct experiential and phenomenological conditions influencing the two country/city expressions.

For example, in the British landscape and romantic traditions studied by Raymond Williams in *The Country and the City*, writers often articulated their critical naturalism at a distance (by class privilege and/or by literal geographic location) from the central urban proletarian areas most affected by early industrial capitalism, whose physical, social, and spiritual upheavals were a major object of their critique. Furthermore, many of the "green" landscapes rendered in figural opposition to the degraded urban geographies were often more "cultural" (by cultivation) than "natural." They were often the gardens, "Arcades," arboretums, and other privatized idylls of domesticated "nature" to which the older landed and emerging monied classes retreated as refuge from the urban industrial centers. Ironically, a "civilizing" effect was ascribed to such cultivated "natural" spaces in conscious or unconscious opposition to the "wild" masses, classes, and perceived nonculture of the cities.

Conversely, Fierro's palimpsestic preurban landscape is not located at a class or spatial distance from the increasingly degraded urban geography. It is, precisely, that once "natural" space at first refigured and then disfigured by successive modernizations. In this respect, Fierro's memories do recall a central critical tenet in the British tradition of "nature" poetics, in which the most astute meditations on the loss or deformation of "country" by "city" recognize that what is being lost is, "for any particular man, the loss of a specifically human and historical landscape, in which the source of feeling is not really that it is 'natural' but that it is 'native'" (Williams 1973:138). The difference remains, however, that even with the most critically astute poets, the meditations are often exercised in retreat from those very "human and historical landscapes" under siege by capitalist modernization. With reference to John Clare's poetry, for example, Williams notes that, even as the poet critically meditates on the disruptive consequences wrought upon the social space of country laborers by the privatizing enclosures of common lands, "It is from . . . [the] actual village, where a community lives under pressure, that the poet *withdraws* to the quiet of nature, where he can speak for his own and others' humanity" (ibid.: 140; emphasis added).

In contrast, Fierro's elegiac meditations are firmly rooted and expressed from *within* a threatened geography where his community still lives under the external pressure of its continuing sociospatial deformation. From this inside location, therefore, Fierro specifically identifies the human and institutional agents of his neighborhood's degradation.

> [T]he government letter arrived and everyone was forced to uproot, one by one, leaving behind rows and rows of wooden houses that creaked with swollen age. He remembered realizing, as he watched the carelessness with which the company men tore into the shabby homes with clawing efficiency, that it was easy for them to demolish some twenty, thirty, forty years of memories within a matter of months. As if that weren't enough, huge pits were dug up to make sure that no roots were left. The endless freeway paved over his sacred ruins, his secrets, his graves, his fertile soil in which all memories were seeded and waiting for the right time to flower, and he could do nothing. (Viramontes 1985: 106)

Walter Benjamin's characterization of counterdominant historical consciousness is appropriate to Fierro's memory function here, "as it flashes up to him in a moment of danger" (1968: 257). His memory does not call upon abstract figurations of "city" displacing "country." Instead, it is akin to the materialist experiential consciousness of the grassroots community-defensive organization, the Mothers of East Los Angeles, for whom the "freeways that cut through communities and disrupted neighborhoods are now a concrete reminder of shared injustice, of the vulnerability of the community" (Pardo 1990b: 5). Fierro's memory identifies both the planners ("government letter") and the executors ("company men") of his neighborhood's uprooting, thus bearing witness in the manner of a testimonial recollection to its social destruction. The purposeful nature of this violation was revealed by the way "huge pits were dug to make sure no roots were left" (Viramontes 1985: 106). There would be no chances taken in severing the physically inscribed genealogy of his community's social space.

Fierro is deeply wounded by the evisceration of his community topogra-

FIGURE 33. "... to be sure no roots were left...." Interchange of Interstates 5 and 10 under construction in downtown and East Los Angeles. Courtesy of California Department of Transportation.

phy, but while he concedes the irreversibility of objective material effects, he still responds against their subjective memorial consequences. With the community's social space made infertile by the freeway, his own mind becomes the seeding ground of personal memory-cum–popular history. Consequently, Fierro's mind becomes the next geography threatened with erasure and deformation: "his greatest fear in life, greater than his fear of death or of not receiving his social security check, was that he would forget so much that he would not know whether it was like that in the first place, or whether he had made it up, or whether he had made it up so well that he began to believe it was true" (106). While this particular threat does not necessarily reside in specific hegemonic practices, it is analogous to the actual social devastations his memory documents. His will-to-remember the disfigured landscapes and their layered histories is, like Aura's womanist horticultural labors (before their disablement), a conjunctural practice produced within but directed against the psychosocial effects of contemporary barrioization.

The implicit critical consciousness compelling Fierro's remembrances contests the alienation that threatens to sever him from the contents of his own memory. Consequently, he engages himself in an interior dialogue, reported by the narrator, in which he tells himself, "here was where the Paramount Theater stood, and over there I bought snow cones for the kids, here was where Chuy was stabbed, over there the citrus orchards grew" (106). The rhetorical structure of Fierro's mnemonic orientations reveals a place-consciousness supporting Michel de Certeau's contention "that the places people live in are like the presences of diverse absences. What can be seen designates what is no longer there: 'you *see*, here there used to be . . . ,' but it can no longer be seen. Demonstratives indicate the invisible identities of the visible" (108; original emphasis). I would further interpret the form and function of Fierro's mental exercise through Fredric Jameson's definition of "cognitive mapping." Drawn from Kevin Lynch's famous study, *The Image of the City*, Jameson's concept identifies a practice of psychospatial "disalienation" by contemporary city dwellers that "involves the practical reconquest of a sense of place, and the construction or reconstruction of an articulated ensemble which can be retained in memory and which the individual subject can map and re-map along the moments of mobile, alternative trajectories" (1988:51). This practice is applicable to Fierro, with one important specification. Jameson refers to the "reconquest of a sense of place" within a materially extant geography. The spatial coordinates of this geography are present to the physical senses of the mapping individual. For Fierro, the physical erasure of coordinates and landmarks that made up his devastated neighborhood ensure that his sense of place, as an "articulated ensemble," can *only* be retained and traversed in memory. Having recourse and reference to a purely recollected geography, Fierro's memory not only marks the key features, it forms their very phenomenological substance.

Viramontes' narration of Fierro's memory struggles extends her meditation, introduced through Aura's experience, on the possibility of retaining and passing on personal and historical knowledge as a practice of a community-nurturing ethos. However, the tragic inertia of the story suggests a bleak prospect for such use to be made of Fierro's or Aura's knowledge. Although Fierro fears, and has begun to feel, the inexorable pressures of disfigurement encroaching on his mental maps, they are still substantially present to him throughout the narrative. But his death in the end claims his memory along with his body. He welcomes death (recall Aura's similar resignation) as a release from the "heartaches" of his memory, which literally "crush his chest" (Viramontes 1985:116). The grief of the mysterious woman, a helpless witness to his final convulsions, sends her wailing out of Fierro's house toward Aura's porch. At this same moment, Aura, who is cowering in her living room in fear of the Bixby Boys, holds a gun pointed at her front door. This ominous turn of events is a further sign of Aura's uprooting from a womanist continuum. Replacing the now useless tools of her garden practice, she is forced to take up, with clear revulsion, a resonantly male tool in the form of her grandfather's old revolver. When she dug it out of the deepest recesses of her cellar, "she examined it like the foreign object that it was" and in a telling juxtaposition of gender-signifying objects "placed the gun in her apron pocket" (112). The story closes on this ominous scenario. Uncertain fates await Aura and the woman, with implications that one or both may soon meet with a tragic death. The mysterious woman's demise would destroy the only regenerative force in the story. We are thus left with a nearly total devastation of the principal characters, of the personal or community spaces they inhabit, and of the memories that reside in their minds or in their homes. This bleak prospect signals the myriad social pressures working against the lived and articulated "power of place—the power of ordinary urban landscapes to nurture citizens' public memory, to encompass shared time in the form of shared territory," (Hayden 1995:9) in aggrieved urban neighborhoods like that of Aura and Fierro. The tremendous pressures that barrioization can impose on Chicano social spaces are thus shown in their most dire consequences for individuals as well as for the residential community more broadly. This radical disabling of communitarian place and ethos leaves the reader to extract such lessons or impulses to action as may be compelled by the moving and disorienting power of Viramontes' tragic text.

While this may seem to offer little if any positive potential, the importance of memorial place-consciousness must be seen in all its possible manifestations. Consequently, as noted by the architectural historian Dolores Hayden, "even bitter experiences and fights communities have lost need to be remembered—so as not to diminish their importance" (1995:11). If Viramontes offers us an intimate fiction for consideration as tragic lesson, the machinations of exchange-driven urban development offer recurring support for the importance of Hayden's admonition. As one dramatic example, the recent community response to the projected plans for a professional football stadium to be built adjacent to Dodger Stadium in Chávez Ravine prompted the *Los Angeles Times* columnist Frank del Olmo to note that "as far as many Latinos are concerned, the possible sale [since realized] of the Dodgers baseball team is just the latest twist in the Battle of Palo Verde [a displaced Chávez Ravine barrio]" (del Olmo 1997:M-5). The possibility, acknowledged by many informed observers, that Dodgers owner Peter O'Malley was playing hardball to "pressure the community activists and elected officials who opposed his football expansion plans to back down" led del Olmo to positively acknowledge the critical historical rage and "grief responses" (Fried) expressed by many former residents, "Not just as sad memories, but as words of warning" (del Olmo 1997:M-5). So, too, can we read the intimate revelations in "Neighbors."

LOS ILLEGALS' LYRICAL DECLAMATIONS

The themes of topographical evisceration, social death, psychological disfigurement, and intracommunity aggressions articulated in Viramontes' dystopian narrative are given parallel expression in the same period in the declamatory lyrics of *Internal Exile*, the 1983 album by the Eastside rock band Los Illegals. On this LP, the band lashed out at the powerful urban interests that "rip out our houses / just to build a freeway." This imagery, underscored by a frenzied "agit-pop" melodic line, is just one detail in their broad lyrical deconstruction of the city's "landscape of power" (Zukin 1991). While Viramontes' characters tragically lament the evisceration of their community spaces and communitarian ethos, Los Illegals rage directly against the depredations of the urban-growth machinery and its supporting agents who work through ideological and repressive state apparatuses (Althusser 1971)—most notably metropolitan growth coalitions, the allied police-judicial system, and the mainstream media—to socially marginalize and spatially contain the Chicano (and now greater Latino) working-class residents of Los Angeles (Acuña 1984; Moore 1978:15–17).

In the political climate of the late 1970s and early 1980s (not unlike that of the 1990s)—when the band was formed and most actively performing—a racialized aggression was being directed against immigrants and native Latinos alike as part of the government- and media-fueled hysteria regarding the "lost control" of our international border with Mexico (Cockcroft 1986; Fernández and Pedroza n.d.). By their own declaration, the bandmembers—consisting, at the time of the recording, of Willie Herrón, Jesús Velo, Bill Reyes, Manuel Valdez, and Antonio Valdez—came together "with the intention of providing a palatable and relevant statement," against this regressive public discourse (Los Illegals n.d.). Thus the band's name, which consciously inverted the negative connotations popularly associated with "illegal aliens," seemed "an obvious choice, and a musical commentary was formed on a slice of a life which up until now has been shoved into a darkened corner of the American psyche" (ibid.).

Within their broad commentary on Latino experience, significant attention is paid to the politics of place and space in the barrios. In fact, Los Illegals specifically identify the repressive triumvirate of landscape, law, and media effects that have been historically exercised against Los Angeles' Raza communities, decrying their conjoined deployment in "putting us down." The oppressive triad is most forcefully rendered in the lyrics to "We Don't Need a Tan." The opening and closing refrain does not mince words in naming the conservative political and police state-of-rule constraining the barrios: "Policía nos mandan, nos mandan / Derechistas nos mandan, nos mandan" (The police order us around / The conservatives order us around). Having named the law effect, the lyrics take on the other heads of the urban hydra, the landscape and media effects:

> We've got our own sector,
> where they keep us away
> rip out our houses
> just to build a freeway
> the media burns us
> they rip out our pride
> they stereotype us
> like in Boulevard Nights.
> (Herrón and Velo 1983)

The collusion of repressive effects is depicted through parallel ascription in the stanza, as urban reconstruction of Chicano place and Hollywood interpellation of Chicano identity produce simultaneous eviscerations: ripping out "our houses" along with "our pride."

Los Illegals' denunciatory rage recalls Marshall Berman's characterization of a critical modernist poetics "at once more personal and more political . . . , in which modern men and women could confront the new physical and social structures that had grown up around them" (1982 : 310), which I alluded to in opening this chapter. With Allen Ginsberg's agonistic poetics in "Howl" as his exemplar, Berman had in mind an aesthetic of discursive backlash or back talk against the physical and psychological ravages of the modern metropolis. This socioaesthetic impulse drives the lyrics to "Rampage," as Los Illegals

decry both the material devastations of urban development and its intimate
consequences on a youthful generation.

> Tangled in a battlefield—Of mortar and steel
> Wasting rows of innocence—Destroyed that's for real
>
> Unexpected sounds of thunder—Shatter expectations
> will we make it thru the night? Or see a revelation?
> (Herrón 1983b)

Beyond documenting their community's ravaged social geography, Los Illegals stress the intentionality of powerful development interests by personify-
ing the agents of this destructive reconstruction.

In his poetic "Howl" against the growth machinery of New York, Allen
Ginsberg cast his metropolitan nemesis as Moloch, the nefarious Old Testament deity whose bloodlust demanded youthful sacrifices. For Los Illegals,
similar offerings are demanded by their antagonist, whose name is drawn
from a specific technology of urban destruction/construction:

> Take the children in your arms—Help them to be strong
>
> Cause Jack Hammer's in his suit—He's ordering intrusion
> Cultured few stand up—Don't wait for the conclusion!

Though clothed in professional attire, Jack Hammer—like Ginsberg's Moloch, whom Berman equates with the monumental New York City planner
Robert Moses[5]—is exposed in his invasive and destructive capacity. Extra-
polating beyond this single figure, Los Illegals inveigh against a generalized
enemy:

> They charge us from the left—They charge us from the right
> Drive you on your head—till the red turns into white
>
> Damn the idiots—they know just what they're doing
> All our lives are at stake—save yourself from ruin
>
> Tangled in a battlefield—Of mortar and steel
> I am witness to a lifestyle—being destroyed it's for real!

Although these nefarious social agents are rendered anonymously, the effects
of their ubiquitous assaults, like military campaigns, clearly place the Eastside

"community under siege," in the phrase used by the historian Rodolfo Acuña to characterize the growth machinery's impacts on the postwar barrios. Los Illegals' imagery of indignation and warning is spurred by the willful actions of the anonymous invaders, who "know just what they're doing."[6]

By bearing "witness to a lifestyle—being destroyed," Los Illegals' critical lyrical activity falls squarely in the trajectory of contestatory discourses established by their ethnic and textual precursors a century earlier, which bore original witness to the destructive machinations of hegemonic planning. To wit, Rosaura Sánchez' analysis of the Californio *testimonios* identifies their precedent critical spatial epistemologies as well as the homology of the Californios' structural subordination to that of late-twentieth-century Chicanos, both of which lend support to my argument of precursory comparison. Regarding the former, she notes that "the appropriation and domination of social space is the crucial problematic for the Californios, who by the time they are narrating their testimonials no longer occupy dominant social spaces or actively produce them" (1995:45). Indicating the structural continuity between Raza social spaces then and now, Sánchez cites historical studies that reveal how "their descendants, the Chicanos, continue to face a number of social problems and contradictions that first came to the fore in the nineteenth century with invasion and modernization, that is, with conquest . . . and the definitive inclusion of the territory within capitalism" (ibid.: 268). In their declamatory mode, therefore, Los Illegals echo both the early-modern soundings of their deterritorialized nineteenth-century precursors and the high-modernist invectives of their immediate generational and countercultural predecessors. Drawing strength from both discursive (af)filiations, Los Illegals' lyrics are urgent counterexpressions to the positivist platitudes of the metropolitan growth machinery, as they identify the nexus of repressive apparatuses and effects that produce a social cordon around the barrios and set the low limits of possibility for many of their residents.

Like Viramontes, however, Los Illegals do not shy away from casting their critical gaze at the internal ravages of a community eating away at itself under the pressures of life in the second-city cordoned zones. Willie Herrón, principal lyricist and vocalist for the band, gives unflinching accounts of the internecine gang violence by which a small but significant element of barrio youth were self-destructing in the late 1970s, a peak period of violence in the Eastside. As was true of all Los Illegals' lyrics, this particular thematic strain was informed by the bandmembers' intimate experiences of social conditions in their community. In 1972, Herrón's younger brother nearly died from stab wounds he suffered in a brutal assault by antagonistic gang members. This incident, and his general awareness of the state of brown-on-brown warfare, was tremendously influential in Herrón's multiple artistic practices. Long before making this a subject of his lyrical declamations in the album recordings of "Not Another Homicide" and "Secret Society Man," Herrón had dealt with his brother's assault in literary and graphic expressions.

An immediate expressive response was rendered in Herrón's famous mural "The Wall That Cracked Open," painted in 1972 in the same City Terrace alley where the assault occurred. That same year, Herrón contributed an integrated word and image text to the Eastside cultural journal *Regeneración*, several issues of which he helped to edit with Harry Gamboa and other activist artists who would go on to make up the core membership of the avant-garde artists' collaborative Asco. Herrón's text combined a pen-and-ink image of Herrón's badly bruised brother—strapped onto a stretcher, cradled in an ominously torn hand, and set behind a fragment of Herrón's alley mural—with an adjacent dramatic dialogue of two *vatos* (dudes) planning their revenge attack against the guy who jumped the brother of one of the speakers ("Ese Vato Va Marchar" [That Dude's Gonna Die]).

These early creative expressions of rage intimate Herrón's deep visceral feelings of grief and vengeance for the devastating injury done to his brother. By the time the experience was transmuted into his lyrical narrative, he had transcended the purely personal cathartic impulse in order to advocate an end to the barrio warfare in the lyrics to "Not Another Homicide." However, in making his plea to "stop this senseless killing," Herrón does not lay unequivocal blame on youthful gangbangers. Instead, in "Secret Society Man," he brings to light the limited life chances and circumscribed sphere of action in the postindustrial barrio that compel many young Chicanos to take up such nihilistic pursuits:

> He had a name and reputation
> a territory to defend
> without a job, no recommendations
> just to score, deal and pretend
>
> Real tough, real strong
> needs attention to get along
> no education, recreation
> needs a chance for full control
>
> . . . .

and each day there's no tomorrow
just to smoke, drink, steal and hide

Far more explicitly than Viramontes, if in minimal narrative form, Herrón identifies a conjunction of social effects that, like a social cordon around the barrio, set the limits of mobility for many of its residents. These external social limits reproduce a racial-spatial formation as an integral effect of Los Angeles' landscape of power.

QUEER AZTLÁN:
INTERROGATING THE INTIMATE GEOGRAPHY OF *LA RAZA*

While Los Illegals' broad critical perspective mediates the general parameters of Latino Los Angeles' racial-spatial formation, writer Gil Cuadros manifests a more personalized but no less conflictual social-geographic consciousness. In his vignette "My Aztlán: White Place," Cuadros introduces us to the City Terrace milieu of his youth as a site of creeping malaise and social death. Recalling the "graveyard" metamorphosis of Aura's neighborhood, Cuadros renders his original home site in chiaroscuro tones and with a multisensory ambience of decay: "Black spray paint letters fuse into unlit alleys. Parked cars are tombstones. The air is sewer-scented" (1994a:54). Within this noirish milieu, Cuadros' palimpsestic vision recalls the site of his family's razed house: "I was born below this freeway, in a house with a picket fence now plowed under. It was the same street my uncle and Tia lived on. . . . I've been here before, time after time, told my mother where our old house would be buried, near the call box, under the fast lane" (ibid.:54). Cuadros evokes the persistent motifs of evisceration, burial, and social death common to much critical Chicano urban place-narrative. At the same time, he pushes his figurative critical inquiry beyond a purely intercultural interrogation of dominant urban designs. This broad critique is certainly present, but it is complicated by the additional *intra*cultural interrogation of his "home" location, based on his problematic experiences, as a gay Chicano, of simultaneous inclusion and exclusion within that ethnic space. He further intimates conditions of neighborhood self-destruction in the cryptic hieroglyphs of gang *plaqueasos*, or territorial graffiti tagging. More substantial, however, is Cuadros' interrogative addition of gay experience to the social coordinates of race and place (both undergirded by class) that predominate in Chicano critical discourses of social geography. With this accretion, Cuadros severely questions the assumed (if often circumscribed) security of "home"-place mooring and ethnic cultural identification. Whether considered a historically existent or mythical site, Aztlán is definitively *not* a "white place." Consequently, the oxymoronic conceit of the vignette's title immediately clues the reader to the complex renderings of place and subjectivity that Cuadros will take up.

At first we see the speaker on a freeway, drunk and speeding toward East Los Angeles, in flight from the white gay club scene on the Westside: "Hours in Rage, Revolver, Motherlode and Mickey's have made me wish for my childhood home" (1994a:53). His intercultural alienation is revealed through the described difference of "those West Hollywood bar types—blond hair, blue eyes. . . . Their fingers are pale compared to my darker skin. They run them down my neck, under my lapel. They ask where I'm from, disappointed at my answer, as if *they* are the natives" (ibid.:53; original emphasis). The narrator's understated indignation toward the Anglo usurpation of place-primacy ("as if *they* are the natives") resonates with the cultural claims of regional territorial primacy in the nationalist concept of Aztlán, the mythical Chicano homeland encompassing the greater U.S. Southwest. This conception of a lost indigenous geography, and the accompanying sense of violated place-rights stretching back in time and forward to contemporary Los Angeles, is particularized in Cuadros' specific account of the physical home-site his family lost to freeway construction.

His mythical consciousness and life experience identify coincident, if phenomenologically distinct, forms of deterritorialization: "I imagine the house still intact, buried under dirt and asphalt, dust and neglect. Hidden under a modern city, this is my Aztlán, a glimpse of my ancient home, my family" (ibid.:55). And yet, in this narrative moment resonant with a nationalist barriological ethos—in its correlation of mythical indigenous place-identification with historical urban development—Cuadros complicates the purported security of the ethnic topos. Unable to claim the certainty of communal affiliation, he reveals a crack in the protective shell of his kin-group location: "All it takes is a well-chosen phrase to cave in: Mom, why did you burn my hands with the iron and say it was an accident? tattoo my arms with the car's cigarette lighter? make me wish your wish, that I was never born?" (ibid.). Here, Cuadros scrutinizes the comfort of an unassailable nationalist place-identity from his simultaneously "native" but "aberrant" position as a gay barrio Chicano, thus revealing that his family home, his Raza microcommunity and personal Aztlán, is a severely compromised utopia.

In his poem "There Are Places You Don't Walk Alone at Night," Cuadros extends this meditation on internally compromised social spaces beyond his family's home and onto the streets of East Los Angeles. Recalling the harassment he experienced in his youth in such areas as "Whittier Blvd., Beverly, Atlantic, / over by Johnson's Market, / or the projects on Brooklyn" (1994b: 112), Cuadros specifies that it was not a random threat of physical harm that he had to beware of, but the particular aggressions directed against him for being identifiably gay.

> The cholos . . .
>
> . . . .
>
> They'd cuff me from behind,
> their hands lingering on my neck, saying
> "Come here faggot, kiss me."
> Their shoes made me crawl,
> black mirrors, pointed tips,
> Imperials that my lips fell upon
> and leather soles
> that brushed the hair out of my face
> nearly blinding me. (1994b: 112)

His difference as a gay child in a heterosocial and masculinist barrio culture marks his vulnerability within a familial and ethnic social space that might have served, under "straight" circumstances, as a haven against a hostile outside world. The speaker is rendered doubly displaced: by his alienation from the white Westside gay community for being Chicano, and by his victimization in the Eastside barrio community for being gay. Cuadros' multivalent interrogations of social space exemplify a progressive thematic current in critical Chicano spatial narrative. In this current, the deconstructive gaze commonly applied to externally dominant social forces and agents is now simultaneously directed against oppressive elements within the ethnic social space, such as normative heterosexuality and patriarchal authority, which also compromise the community topos' claim to security and integrity.[7]

The playwright and poet Luis Alfaro—a 1997 recipient of a MacArthur Foundation "genius" fellowship—contributes to this progressive direction in Chicano urban place-narrative. Like Cuadros, he mediates his experience of double displacement, noting that neither the white gay nor the straight Chicano communities can wholly embrace his multiple identifications.

> The Mexicans only want me
> when they want me to

talk about Mexico.
But what about
Mexican Queers in L.A.?

The queers only want me
when they need
to add color,
add spice,
like *salsa picante*
on the side.
                    (1994:235; original emphasis)

Alfaro is careful here, as throughout his work, not to comparatively rank his identification and (af)filiation with the social differences of being gay or Chicano (nor his felt degrees of alienation from either community): "As a Gay Latino playwright I am most concerned about these two specific communities and the effect they have on each other" (1992a:n.p.). The very title, "Orphan of Aztlán" (echoing Cuadros' "Aztlán" title), and the opening stanza from which it is taken suggest Alfaro's particular interest in unpacking the contradictions of his familial-cum-ethnic nationalist moorings: "I am a Queer Chicano. / A native of no land. / An orphan of Aztlán / The *pocho* son of farmworker parents" (ibid.; original emphasis).

Alfaro renders the contradictions of his familial and ethnic urban landscape in intimate but critically uncompromising terms in various texts of his larger dramatic and poetic corpus. Through the medium of multicharacter dramatic monologues, which Alfaro describes as "memory plays" (1992a), he draws an intimate cognitive map encompassing the downtown milieu of his childhood and young-adult neighborhood in the predominately Latino Pico-Union district. The original full-stage production of his work was developed in residency and later produced in an extended run at the Highways performance space in Santa Monica during 1990–1991, under the title "Downtown." A subsequent version, involving a slightly altered selection of text and characters from the same working manuscript, was called "Pico-Union." A compact-disc recording of Alfaro reading his vignettes as spoken word was also titled *downtown.*

Several titles of his work—such as "Downtown," "Pico-Union," and "On a Street Corner"—and the ambientation of many more, unmistakably call attention to their urban location, and not merely as scenic backdrop: "The majority of my work is about Los Angeles and the pressures/pleasures of urban living. . . . Because I write about my urban reality, I also write about the issues and concerns in my community" (ibid.). Alfaro foregrounds substantial and specific detail about the tangible environment of his central-city milieu. Through this precise representation of urban environments, he performs a localized and critical semiosis of recent urban development impinging upon the physical and cultural habitus of his family and that of his broader community in the predominantly Latino Pico-Union district immediately west of downtown. This richly textured semiosis is evident in the account of his extended family's efforts to live together against the pressures of this exacerbated social space:

> When I was ten, . . . my *Tia Ofelia* lived across the street with my *Tia Tita* who lived with my *Tio Tony* who lived next door to my *Tia Romie*. Back in those days, everybody on the block was either a *Tia* or a *Tio*. They lived in a big beautiful wood-carved two-story house with a balcony overlooking the street below. We were crowded by downtown skyscrapers, packs of roving *cholos*, the newly built Convention Center on Pico and portable *tamale* stands. But our families always managed to live together, Because you see, *blood is thicker than water, family is greater than friends, and the Virgin Mary watches over all of us.* (1992b: 3; original emphasis)

The recollective qualification of "back in those days" intimates the changes wrought upon the built environment and social relations of his youthful neighborhood. Along with the extracommunity encroachments of late-1970s and early-1980s redevelopment ("downtown skyscrapers," "the newly built Convention Center on Pico" [see Fig. 34]), the neighborhood is pressured internally by the competition for space attendant upon the increasing inmigration of Latinos (signaled by the cultural specificity of "portable *tamale* stands") and by the exacerbated intracommunity tensions of gang activity. These multiple social infringements coalesce with destructive force on his aunt's home. Its physical erasure from the neighborhood landscape is both a particular loss for Alfaro's extended family and a representative instance of how the community space of Pico-Union is subject to simultaneous external and internal pressures.

The threat from within the community's social space is demonstrated in a drive-by firebombing of the 18th Street gang members who lived on the first floor of the Tía's house. It consumes the entire structure, and with it the memorially imbued architecture of the aunt's memory, who had recently died

FIGURE 34.   Los Angeles Convention Center, early 1970s, with Pico-Union district in background across Harbor Freeway. Courtesy of Los Angeles Community Redevelopment Agency.

of breast cancer: "My mom cried because the memory of my Tía Ofelia would now be an empty lot where bums would piss and tires would grow" (1992b: 5). To symbolically mark and ritually nurture Tía Ofelia's place in the family's memorial geography, Alfaro's mother tends daily to a flower she planted in the now derelict space of his Tía's home. The mother's ritual consecration of this site enacts a popular Mexican cultural memorial practice: the construction of *descansos*, or shrines, at the sites of violent or accidental death. Typically identified with roadside markers, the concept of the *descanso* has more recently been applied to understanding "urban *lugares de recuerdo* [places of memory]" by cultural critic Amalia Mesa-Bains, who sees them "most apparent in the metropolis of Los Angeles" (1994). Alfaro's mother seeds the memory of her sister's life and home in such a site, which is simultaneously "public and personal."

Sadly, the Tía's *descanso* is relegated to a purely mnemonic geography by the definitive erasure of the site when "the Community Redevelopment Agency built the Pico-Union Projects over the memory of my Tia Ofelia" (1992b:5). The housing project is certainly a less spectacular manifestation of downtown urban development, and one not altogether debilitating to the neighboring residents, ever in need of affordable housing in this most densely populated section of the city. However, the actions of the Community Redevelopment Agency (CRA), often acting as an instrument of powerful private development interests, manifest its public space-making power in ways that are very clear to many residents of this central-city community. The particularly troubled history of the CRA's relations with Chicano residential communities has led many activists to translate the initials of its acronym into "Chicano Removal Agency."

Formed in 1947, the Los Angeles Community Development Agency was enabled by the California Community Redevelopment Act of 1945 (Parson 1982:399). This legislation was designed to help developers bypass public-housing requirements—considered too encumbering and even potentially "socialistic"—attached to federal urban-development subsidies. Through empowerment of local public development corporations, run by political appointees rather than elected representatives, it opened the way for slum clearance and private investment projects to be financed through the sale of public bonds, while granting the CRA necessary police powers of eminent domain. Working closely with the City Planning Department and Bureau of Engineering, the Los Angeles CRA often proved to be the nemesis of local poor and working-class communities—frequently in direct conflict with the city's Housing Authority—through a series of landgrabs and land-use battles continuing up to the present, most infamously in the evisceration of the old Bunker Hill neighborhood in the 1960s.

Although Alfaro does not specifically indict the CRA's historical record, the second-order (or less) of priority that the needs of working-class and poor residents have often occupied in dominant urban plans are clearly an object of his critical scrutiny. In a text entitled "Federal Building," Alfaro describes how those outside the circles of influence are made to understand their place in the landscape of power: "Because a black and white can stop you anytime, anywhere, for whatever reason / Because big beautiful buildings stare down at you with a *chale* stare," and most tellingly, "Because I've lived here all my life and I've never owned anything. Much less this city" (1992b:40). This image of personified buildings directing their potent vision down upon the surrounding communities, who are deprived of cultural ownership of the city, aptly characterizes the authority signaled in the built form of Los Angeles' civic architecture, as well as its newer corporate and cultural landmarks on Bunker Hill (see Fig. 35).

Alfaro's inventive image of the "chale stare" portrays hegemonic power through the twin semiotic registers of confrontational speech (the vernacular

FIGURE 35.   Photograph by Raúl Homero Villa, 1997.

"chale" signifies disdain or defiance, roughly translatable as "no way") and condescending sight (the downward "stare"). By reading these registers in the built form of "big beautiful buildings," Alfaro identifies how urbanistic power involves an important representational or aesthetic dimension in which the architectural "text" of the city signifies authority symbolically in concert with more explicit exercises of force. This conjunction of representation and repression recalls the workings of social power described by Antonio Gramsci in the twin effects of *hegemonio* and *dominio*, or once more, the variants of manifest urban authority identified by Lefebvre as "representations of space" (in the architectural signifier) and "material spatial practices" (in police control of mobility through the city). In either case, within the aesthetic or representational effect, the architecturally expressed contents of the Federal Building's "chale stare" thus function through an expressed "symbiosis of vision and power" (Zukin 1995:261) and, simultaneously, by way of a manifest speech act of the sort described by urban semiotician Raymond Ledut: "If modern monuments speak to the inhabitants of cities, what do they tell them, and who is expressed through them, if not the *powers* that surpass them and that are external to local social life and its character . . . a power transcending the life of the citizens" (1986:132–133; original emphasis).

POETIC *PLAQUEASOS:* GLORIA ALVAREZ' CONTRASTIVE VISION

While Alfaro deconstructs the symbolized gaze and voice of power in the historic Federal Building, the upscale Bunker Hill financial and residential citadel, buttressed to the north by the elite cultural acropolis of the Music Center, is the most spectacular and more recent specular expression of Los Angeles' supercity morphology. From the earliest stages of its development, Bunker Hill was the subject of significant Chicano discursive scrutiny, in letters written to City Councilman Edward Roybal (Parson 1993), as well as in critical reporting by the *Eastside Sun* and in the interventions of activist Rosalío Muñoz, which I treated in the previous chapter.

More recently, poet Gloria Alvarez has contributed to this trajectory. Echoing the sedimented fantasy in Muñoz' essay "Our Moving Barrio: Why?" regarding the demise of Bunker Hill's towers of "phallic Babelism," she depicts a more overt retributive projection in her indignant lyric poem "Contrastes/Contrasts." The title refers to the telling signs of social inequity built into the dichotomous cultural geography of downtown Los Angeles. Bunker Hill's Manhattanized skyline is scrutinized by Alvarez to reveal its devastating impact on those past and present inner-city residents who fall under or are felled

by its omnipotent shadows. The poem opens by describing the looming glacis
of the new corporate citadel:

> Interminables, interminable silver gray cylinders
> reflecting their cool glitter
> against aging brown and brick red porous rectangles
> now dwarfed and anchored on skid row.
> (1989:120)

Like a cinematic establishing shot, this poetic mise-en-scène renders the unspecified contrasts of the title in precise architectonic imagery, indicating to
the reader the importance of the urban landscape as semiotic text. The shiny,
smooth monochrome towers are juxtaposed to the rectilinear, textured poly-
chromatic facades of the old city center, now become skid row. Alvarez extends the filmic imagery and compounds it with olfactory detail to produce a
critically revealing synaesthesia:

> Its slick disinfected shadows slip over
> the wide matte-finish corners of the collapsed tent city,
> as if masking los olores de vida, the smell of life,
> perfumed with pungent mustiness of yesterday.
> (1989:120)

The specific nature and significance of the contrasts reveal themselves as Alvarez implicates the repressive impact of the glittering cylinders over the gritty
landscape around them. Playing on the clinical rhetoric of urban malady with
which growth interests often argue for the necessity of redeveloping socially
"infected" low-income neighborhoods, Alvarez shows Bunker Hill's "dis-
infected shadows" neutralizing the fecund "olores de vida." The conspicuous use of Spanish further implies the intercultural differences of race and
class manifest in the antithetical landscapes of skid row and Bunker Hill. If
growth coalitions strategically appropriate the language of medical or bio-
logical (blight) intervention to justify their transformative actions in the ailing
heart of the city, Alvarez offers a contrasting account of their effects. Far from
curing social ills, the cool sterility of redevelopment has destroyed the very
richness of people's lives and memories figured in the "pungent mustiness of
yesterday."

   This terrible destruction is not left to inference. Instead, through the familiar Chicano figurative language of social death and ghostly presences, Al-

varez portrays the "sex zombies," "living hallucinations," and "pained souls" among the habitués of skid row. Her horrendous characterizations further reveal that these shadowed and shattered lives are not just normal consequences of urban society. In a strong indictment of social cause and effect, these denizens of the urban inferno are shown by the poet to have been specifically "manufactured in the dream factory / of the money gods" and "robbed of their essence" in the process. Here Alvarez exploits the semiotic implications of Bunker Hill topography. Like the mythical pantheon of Mount Olympus, Los Angeles' money gods in their corporate heights transcend the lives of the populations below. The hierarchical city and social structure starkly rendered in the expressionist film classic *Metropolis* is brought to mind by Alvarez' imagery. Like the decadent elites in Fritz Lang's *ouvre*, the Bunker Hill overlords depend on the nether dwellers in skid row, stealing their very life essence and worth.

These poetic intimations of a nefarious and criminal symbiosis between Bunker Hill prosperity and inner-city impoverishment mirror the zero-sum game of downtown redevelopment in the 1970s and 1980s. In this period, the inner-city revitalization that was promised after the urban conflagrations of the 1960s was redirected instead to the monumental reconstruction of Bunker Hill. By this turn of political favor, the downward spiral of life chances for many South Central and East Los Angeles residents was inversely reflected in the skyward spires of trophy-building construction. This spectacular corporate growth helped fuel the equally dramatic expansion of the homeless population in the skid-row badlands. With the social safety net pulled out from under them, poor and working-class inner-city residents had little recourse against the devastating effects of the region's coming deindustrialization. For thousands of Blacks and Chicanos who lost their factory jobs, the struggle to keep a home became a desperate scramble that many would lose.

Recognizing these perverse relationships of inverse benefit, where others praise the aesthetic grandeur of postmodern architecture, Alvarez sees "invading glass giants" aggressively consuming the lives and places of inner-city communities in their path. Los Illegals' narrative of cataclysmic urban restructuring in "Rampage" mirrors the critical thematic vision of "Contrastes/ Contrasts." Both texts bear witness to "wasted rows of innocence" and a "lifestyle—being destroyed" (Herrón and Velo 1983) by aggressively personified constructions (see Figs. 36 and 37). In the final section of her poem, Alvarez depicts this active destruction in a specific historical instance of the dialectic between corporate redevelopment and barrio deterritorialization as the monstrous monoliths confidently "swept aside part of Varrio Diamond" immedi-

FIGURE 36.   Illustration by Lorenzo Flores for *El Popo* (Chicano student newspaper, California State University, Northridge, 1977). Courtesy of *El Popo* and the artist.

ately west of Bunker Hill (see Fig. 38). Speaking for those struck down by the city's thundering destiny, she then evokes a retributive fantasy that retaliates in symbolic measure against the barrio's evisceration. Although the former residents have been displaced from the visible landscape, their hearts remain as phantom spirits who mete out a silent vengeance against their aggressors. Alvarez conjures the spirits of Varrio Diamond's displaced neighborhood, drawing on the community's popular knowledge ("it's said") to recount that the "Diamond Curse—Brillantes Vidriales—freezes the hearts" of Bunker Hill's new inhabitants.

This poetic account of Varrio Diamond's ghostly diurnal presences supports Michel de Certeau's phenomenological argument that an experienced human *place* (as opposed to the abstract and commodified *space* of functionalist urbanism) is "composed by . . . [a] series of displacements and effects among the fragmented strata that form it and that it plays on these moving layers" (1984:108). Alvarez plays precisely on such active layers of Varrio Diamond's place memory and identity, further echoing de Certeau's contention that "[t]here is no place that is not haunted by many different spirits hidden there in silence, spirits one can 'invoke' or not" (ibid.). Alvarez' closing

FIGURE 37. Corporate gravestone of Varrio Diamond. Photograph by Raúl Homero Villa, 1998.

FIGURE 38.   The archeology of downtown renewal: home ruins of Varrio
Diamond; Harbor Freeway in background. Photograph by Raúl Homero Villa, 1998.

FIGURE 39. C/S... ¿y qué?: tagging for the 'hood. Photograph by Raúl Homero
Villa, 1998.

invocation of residential spirits thus serves as a sort of poetic *plaqueaso* (to
borrow from the lexicon of Chicano graffiti) or scripted declaration of territorial integrity and defense for the barrio residents as well as for the captive
inhabitants of skid row on the other side of Bunker Hill's panoptic circumference. More precisely, the retaliatory Diamond Curse functions like the ubiquitous emblem "C/S," or "Con Safos," signed on to Chicano territorial graffiti throughout the city.

Of uncertain origin and without an exact translation, "C/S" is generally
posted as a challenge or warning by the writer-artist to those who would disrespect the neighborhood by disfiguring the public imprint of place identity.
Although such damage has already been done to the social spaces treated by
Alvarez, she nonetheless proffers her poetic *plaqueaso* as an indignant reminder
to her readers of the community that stood in this place. There are compelling instances of how graffiti scripting may act as a material *text*-ile symbolically weaving together torn shreds of barrio social space. One example is offered in Jerry and Sally Romotsky's description of tagging in an Eastside
barrio called Jim Town Hoyo, on the border of Pico Rivera and Whittier,
which was split by the San Gabriel Freeway (Rte. 605) during the 1960s.

Plaqueasos stating "Jim Town Hoyo" bloom all over the general area, both east and west of the freeway. The bridges and streets passing over or under the freeway connect the east neighborhood to the west neighborhood in a strictly geographical fashion. In a symbolic manner, these bridges and streets have attracted a great display of plaqueasos that strive to unify the former neighborhood. The plaqueasos are being used to reunite the once geographically whole neighborhood that the freeway and other forces of progress have ripped asunder. (1976:42)

Cultural activist and musician Rubén Guevara tactically exploits the defiant signification of graffiti plaqueasos in the lyrics to his song "C/S." The text of "C/S" recounts *mexicano* presence and claims to territorial primacy in Nuestra Señora la Reina de Porciúncula de Los Angeles as a direct affront to their erasure by hegemonic ideological apparatuses. In doing so, his revisionary lyrics deploy the ubiquitous graffiti emblem to portend the return of the historically repressed, issuing a warning for all who hear his musical verse to "listen to what the walls have to say LA." Echoing once more the 1877 contestatory proclamation by the Californio editors of *El Joven*, Guevara reminds us—as do the other writers discussed—that contrary to appearances, Chicanos and Chicanas have not gone placidly into the shadows of a dominant urban regime. Clearly, they express their claims to social and discursive space in a manner reminiscent of both their Californio ancestors and those fin-de-siècle avant-garde artists in Europe whom Edward Soja praised for having "perceptively sensed the instrumentality of space and the disciplining effects of the changing geography of capitalism" (1989:34).

Through their textual mediations of the material geographic and existential consequences of life in the shape-shifting center of their world city, Los Angeles Chicana and Chicano writers thus represent compelling local instances of powerful global processes. Quite rightly, the selected texts do not concur in all respects about the determining social forces and cultural characteristics of barrio experience. But precisely *because* of their collective complexity and contradiction, these multiform works underscore and contribute to the production of what de Certeau calls a "local authority" that works like "a crack in the [urbanistic] system that saturates places with signification (1984:106). This interstitial discursive place-making tactic surreptitiously battles dominant strategies of urban space production. This place-space dialectic is at the heart of the struggle for control over the use and significance of the city for differently positioned citizens. As Manuel Castells points out, under the capitalist imperatives of urban growth, "what tends to disappear is the meaning of places for people. Each place . . . will receive its social meaning from its location in the hierarchy of a network whose control and rhythm will escape from each place and, even more, from the people in each place" (1983:314). Against such alienating processes, the local authority mediated by Chicano and Chicana writers discursively recovers some of this expropriated control for the barrio communities of Los Angeles. In this respect, their textual tactics may help make the reified *spaces* of dominant urban planning into habitable *places* of Chicano individual and collective subject formation and cultural reproduction.

Art against Social Death

FOUR   *Symbolic and Material Spaces of Chicano*
         Cultural Re-creation

But our research has concentrated above all on the uses
of space, on the ways of frequenting or dwelling in a
place . . . and on the many ways of establishing a kind
of reliability within the situations imposed on an indi-
vidual, that is, of making it possible to live in them by
reintroducing into them the plural mobility of goals
and desires—an art of manipulating and enjoying.
— MICHEL DE CERTEAU, *The Practice of Everyday Life*

The motif of social death has been shown to be among the most persistent
figures of Chicano structural oppression within an aggressive dominant culture. If many Chicanos in contemporary California, like their *mexicano* and
Californio ancestors, have not yet retired to the land of the dead, it is not for
lack of external pressures to do so. The disparate impacts of hegemonic urban
planning and its attendant social ills continue to pose real material threats
to the cultural well-being—if not the very lives—of poor and working-class
Chicanos. However, the impulse among barrio residents to defend and enrich
their threatened or violated social spaces also continues to flourish in dialectical opposition to the intended or unintended consequences of external domination. In this chapter, I will look at significant expressions—both fictional
and real—of this impulse, manifest in Chicano recreational and residential
spaces in three different urban centers: Elysian Valley (known popularly as
Frog Town) in Los Angeles; the Logan Heights barrio of San Diego; and the

downtown barrios of Sacramento. As an initial gesture toward the broader consideration of California Chicano aesthetic and grassroots barriological activism promised in my introduction, I am moving beyond the parameters of Chicano community places in Greater Los Angeles. The homology of circumstances and effects between the represented and practiced community spatial actions in the various urban sites calls for such a comparative discussion. My intention is to illustrate the multiform creative practices by which Chicanos have attempted to materially reconstitute and expressively represent places of community well-being against the degradations to which those places have been subject.

THE UTOPIAN POETICS OF SOCIAL GEOGRAPHY IN *THE ROAD TO TAMAZUNCHALE*

Mapping the Second City of Los Angeles

Ron Arias' novel *The Road to Tamazunchale* is a deceptively playful and fantastic fiction. As the novel begins, we are introduced to Don Fausto Tejeda, who is apathetically awaiting death in the dystopian confines of his neighborhood on the other side of the tracks from downtown Los Angeles. The actual geographic referent for Fausto's urban milieu is the Elysian Valley barrio immediately northeast of the city center. Known popularly as Frog Town, it is situated at the intersection of the 110 (Pasadena) and Interstate 5 (Golden State) freeways and is an urban residential isthmus produced by a historical succession of infrastructure developments (see Fig. 40). The out-jutting finger of the isthmus is marked by the highway interchange, while its southern and northern barriers are respectively defined by Elysian Park's north-facing escarpment (itself partially carved away by the construction of the parallel Golden State Freeway) and the Los Angeles River and parallel Taylor Yards of the Southern Pacific Railroad. Like Goethe's Faust, who is shaken out of a socially reclusive stupor by the epiphanic tolling of a church bell, Don Fausto suddenly resolves to pursue "the song of life" rather than accept his passive death. Fausto subsequently becomes the Quixotic hero of a fantastic quest, conjured by his imaginative will, embarking on a surreal odyssey across the boundaries of time and space.

Fausto starts his trip on a Los Angeles city bus, meeting up with his fellow traveler, a young street-wise hipster named Mario, whom Fausto identifies as his "apprentice wizard." Mario acts as a *vato loco* (crazy dude) version of Sancho Panza to Fausto's Quixote. Thereupon begins a hallucinatory makeover of the barrio and downtown cityscape, as Fausto and Mario soon come across

FIGURE 40.   Elysian Valley/Frogtown. Courtesy of California Department of
Transportation.

a third wayfarer, Marcelino, an indigenous Andean alpaca herder, who suddenly appears with his herd on a congested freeway on-ramp. In a sometimes
dizzying itinerary, Fausto visits sixteenth-century Peru, leads an "army" of
mojados (undocumented immigrants) from Tijuana to Los Angeles, helps put
on a play for them (also entitled "The Road to Tamazunchale"), initiates a
day of community festivity at the Los Angeles River, and, in the end, heads a
procession of his neighbors and the *mojados* to take over and magically make
over Elysian Park. The certainty of difference between the imagined and the
real is lost, or better, rendered irrelevant for Fausto and those whom he en-
counters on his extraordinary voyage.

Several of Fausto's interventions subvert, or cast in relief, the degradation of his barrio's urban milieu. In this way, Arias obliquely mediates a critical historical-geographical consciousness through the thematic and structural registers of his fantastic narrative. In plotting the alternately incredible and mundane adventures of Fausto, Arias deploys a homologous structure to that of *Don Quixote*, by his "parodied hybridization of the 'alien, miraculous world' chronotope of chivalric [or quest] romances, with the 'high road winding through one's native land' chronotope that is typical of the picaresque novel" (Bakhtin 1981:165). Likewise for Fausto, the hallucinatory "road to Tamazunchale" traverses familiar territory in which "the *sociohistorical heterogeneity* of one's own country" (ibid.:245; original emphasis) corresponds to his barrio's social space. But in the novel's parodic conjuncture of this "native land" with the "miraculous world" of Fausto's invention, the social specificity of the barrio-"country" is critically defamiliarized. In this way, Arias' recurring chronotopic figurations of the Los Angeles freeways, the Elysian Park/Police Academy complex, and the Los Angeles River and freight yards serve as "*prosaic allegorizations*" (ibid.:166) of the larger historical map of Chicano community marginalization within a "Third world and second city" (Davis 1987: 77) in contemporary Los Angeles.

While the novel is structurally fragmented by Fausto's Quixotic interventions, these are set against an actual geography of downtown and Greater East Los Angeles, with reference to specific locations and landmarks. Examples of this specified iconography include the Million Dollar Theater on Broadway, Los Feliz Theater, the Five Points neighborhood of Lincoln Heights, the community of Bell Gardens, Elysian Park, the Market Basket on North Broadway, Las Cuatro Milpas restaurant (now King Taco), Boyle Heights, the Maravilla barrio, as well as the bordering landmarks of Elysian Valley described earlier. Taken together, the variety of place details dispersed throughout the text create a cartographic reality and plot the coordinates for a partial "other" map of a particularly Chicano-resonant Los Angeles.

In various pre-*Tamazunchale* writings about the Chicano Eastside, Arias documented the oppressive social geography of the barrios "existing in the midst of American affluence" (1971:126). Working as a research assistant in the early 1960s for the ground-breaking UCLA Mexican-American Studies Project of Leo Grebler and Joan Moore (Ludwig and Santibáñez 1971:271–272), Arias articulated an explicit social knowledge of barrio social conditions and residents' attitudes about their place in the dominant social map. The conditions that his fieldwork, and the UCLA Project as a whole—which looked comparatively at white, Black, and Chicano communities—brought to light were not surprising: "[For] many Americans home is still the ghetto . . . these pockets of poverty, tin-can alleys and rat nests are today the most serious and explosive fact in urban reality" (Arias 1971:123). Given such environments, the attitudes of the residents largely reflected a sense of despair—as explained in the experience of one interviewee:

> "When I came here I wanted something better for my kids," [Ignacio] Gonzalez said. "But now I don't know what to do. . . ."
> Gonzalez was sitting on the porch of his four-room house in the East Los Angeles ghetto called "Maravilla," or "Paradise." Behind him the windows were broken or cracked, the woodwork unpainted and splitting.
> He explained he had only a sixth-grade education, and was now working part-time. Looking out across the littered street to the distant freeway, *Gonzalez seemed sadly resigned about his future.* "Maybe we'll always live here. Who knows? It costs money to live like a *gabacho* (Anglo-white)."
> For Gonzalez and thousands of others the ghetto is no longer "just a temporary place" before moving into better areas. It has become a permanent home. (Ibid.:123; emphasis added)

This journalistic portrait of Ignacio Gonzalez' resignation, of his dystopian sense of containment in the dilapidated physical, and discouraging psychological, environment of the barrio, reads almost like a draft for the opening description of Fausto in *Tamazunchale:*

> Fausto lay still, listening to the faint groan of freeway traffic. He heard the front door slam shut and relaxed. Slowly he stood, then shuffled to the window and peered through the rusty screen, across the river to the tracks. More smog. For six years he had shuffled to the window, to the bathroom, down to the kitchen, through gloomy rooms, resting, listening to the radio, reading, turning thin, impatient, waiting for the end. (Arias 1987:29)

In both portraits, the barrio is a social and physical "dead-end." The real person of Ignacio Gonzalez may very well have been transposed, ill and older, into the fictional persona of Fausto Tejeda awaiting death. Fausto echoes Gonzalez' despairing sentiments about the barrio when he later confides to his Andean friend: "I won't stay here, Marcelino. This is the worst place in the world to die. Anyplace but here" (ibid.:64).

The omnipresent smog casts a sickly gray pallor over this geography, and the grim scenario is accompanied by the persistent soundtrack of freeway traffic and the "eerie cries of rusty freight car wheels" (ibid.:65). The environmental sights and sounds of the second city in which Fausto awaits death disappear and reappear throughout the text. At the novel's outset, the smoggy pallor and the motorized groan and cries of the traffic and railroad tracks suggest an environment of malaise that exacerbates Fausto's own sense of illness and approaching death: "Now . . . he felt as if his muscles were finally turning to worms, his lungs to leaves and his bones to petrified stone. Suddenly, the monstrous dread of dying seized his mind, his brain itched, and he trembled like a naked child in the snow" (ibid.:29). Fausto's bodily decay is mirrored in the understated decay and malaise of the urban environment. The symbolic correlation between Fausto's body and barrio suggests the synechdochic relationship between Fausto's condition and that of his neighborhood community. In this way, his illness and approaching death symbolize the social "ills" and threatening social death of the community in the dominant spatio-racial formation of Los Angeles.[1]

Fausto's petrifying body allegorizes the oppressive pole of a recurring thematic opposition between mortality and mobility in the novel. Consequently, his will-to-life represents not only a rebellion against death as physical mortality but against death as physical and mental stasis. In light of this thematic opposition, the social symbolism of travel and physical movement in the novel as well as the burlesque histrionics and kinetic play of many scenes acquire specific contextual meaning. Life activity in itself, as the impulse for creative expression or imagination, signals the potential for change and self-determination, qualities that the institutional and policy practices shaping Los Angeles' racial formation regularly attempt to deny inner-city Chicano communities.

Recalling the initial mise-en-scène of Fausto's death-waiting, it becomes apparent that the Los Angeles River, the industrial freight yards, and the various freeways impinge upon Fausto and his barrio in visual, spatial, aural, and psychological ways. To varying degrees, they each serve as explicit border markers between the Chicano Eastside and Greater Los Angeles. As outlined in Chapter 2 of this study, by World War II the Eastside barrios had already been set apart as the space for Chicanos to "stay in their place," thus making the Los Angeles River a limit of containment by the Anglo-American social order upon the Chicano population. Parallel to the river, the railroad yards also mark a border for Eastside Chicanos, as living "across the tracks" becomes a literal and metaphoric designation of working-class and poor Raza residential space. The significance of railroad tracks to these groups is, of course, that they were typically forced to live in the midst of, or in close proximity to, less desirable areas such as the freight yards and industrial or warehouse zones. Part of this was due to the availability of cheaper rents near work sites and part of it to the use of restrictive real estate covenants or discrimination in rental housing. In *Tamazunchale*, the freight yards intimate this social history of racial and labor-specific settlement patterns. Furthermore, the daily activities of the freight yards provide a soundtrack that, like the smog and the "groan of the freeway," symbolically resonates with the illness and social death impinging on Fausto and his community. In fact, the smog, the groan of the freeways, and the shrill freight-car sounds produce a combined visual and aural tone of somber and deathly intimations, as presented in the opening portrait of Fausto at home.

Marcelino's flute intermittently contests the aural dominance of the automobile and railroad traffic. The "song of life" that first inspires Fausto to set forth on his adventures, in fact, "beckoned [him] with the faint, soft sound of a flute" (29). The very textures of the competing sounds and their corresponding "instruments" are figured in symbolic counterpoint. The harsh mechanical sounds of rubber on asphalt or steel on steel are starkly opposed to the soft natural tones of Marcelino's traditional Andean flute. At one point, after Fausto returns from a conjured trip to sixteenth-century Peru, he suffers a seizure as the freight trains intimate the threat of death: "Excitement rose in his throat, and suddenly his fingers had sunk into the carpet. . . . And from outside the house came the shrill, metallic sound of freight car wheels rolling into the yard" (31). Later, Fausto is "listening intently" to the song of life when suddenly the "freeway traffic seemed to have swallowed the flute" (44). And finally, the visual-aural ambience of death battles the life music at Fausto's deathbed when, near the novel's end, Mario asks the others present if they too can hear Marcelino's flute:

"That's his friend," Mario said, "the vato with the flute."
Jess raised the window and searched the scummy haze hanging over the [river] levee and the freightyards. "It's the trains," he said, "them squeaking trains." (117–118)

Like the freight-yard sounds, the freeway sounds are locked in contrapuntal battle with Marcelino's pastoral music. For example, just before Marcelino first appears with his herd on a freeway on-ramp, Fausto was listening to the "high-pitched strains of a flute" (43) and dancing to the music that only he could hear. In the next moment, though, the "freeway traffic seemed to have swallowed the flute" (44). The recurring struggles between buoyant flute songs (Fausto dances to them more than once) and the grim mechanical sounds enact the recurring thematic opposition in the novel between creative life expression and constraining social death.

Of course, the sounds of the freeway and freight-yard traffic could be read with a different symbolism. Produced by activities of transit and transport, the sounds might also signify the possibilities of movement and mobility. Indeed, both the freeways and the railroad tracks could be conduits of escape for members of Fausto's community. The railroads, historically, and the freeways, more recently, have held an aura of positive, democratic freedom of movement in the American popular imagination. However, not all people have equal access to the promises of transportation and travel, and *Tamazunchale* does, I believe, imply the idea that the historical presence of these technologies of mobility have physically and psychologically aggravated the hegemonic constraints on social mobility in the barrio community, a point to which I will turn shortly.

Refiguring the Landscape of Power

Elysian Park, like the freeways, and as another civic monument of Los Angeles' dominant urbanism, embodies a history of particular impact on the Chicano community. In this regard, Mario, Fausto's *vato loco* sidekick, is particularly aware of the park's meanings. His wariness of the police is geographically specified when Fausto asks Mario to drive him to Elysian Park to look for Marcelino and his herd after the initial freeway incident.

> 'I don't know man. Ain't that where the police academy is? I don't wanna push my luck."
> "We won't go near the academy. Just take me to the park."
> "Okay, but then I'm leaving." (50)

Fausto, however, convinces Mario to take him, and to wait in the car while he goes searching. Growing nervous with the long wait, Mario steps out to call for Fausto in the park.

"Vámonos."

"Wait . . . just a few more minutes. Somebody has to help him. You know, he came all the way from Peru."

"I don't care if he came from China. You ain't gonna help nobody if some cop sees us. Them vatos train their dogs around here. Man, them dogs'll rip you up so bad you'll look like chorizo." (52)

Shortly after this exchange, the two cross paths with a "Mr. America" and his Doberman, which "growled and sniffed at the two men" (52). While he is not identified as a police officer, the proximity of the Police Academy in Elysian Park marks Mr. America as a threatening figure of gringo power to Mario's view. The satirical nickname confirms the dominating implications of mainstream authority. Fausto can barely contain Mario's suspicious hostility toward this character. The resulting antagonism between Mario and Mr. America leads to the latter's threat against Mario: "If I ever catch you in this park again, you won't leave in one piece. Now get the hell out!" (53).

This confrontation intimates a long history of conflict over the use of Elysian Park and its environs that has pitted area residents, particularly but not exclusively Chicanos, against the police and land developers. As one example, Mike Davis has described a foundational "conflict of interest between community and law enforcement land use," noting the "extraordinary circumvention of local government [through which] the police department has managed to turn its occupancy of the 1932 Olympic pistol range (under temporary lease to the Police Athletic and Gun Club) into an occupation of the entire park" (1990:254). Aggravating this police expropriation of public lands, the 1943 "taxi cab" invasion of U.S. servicemen on the hunt for "Zoot Suiters" was launched from the Naval and Marine Corps Reserve Training Center in Chávez Ravine. The Chicano community tragedy of the razing of Chávez Ravine's barrios to build Dodger Stadium and the continuing suggestion of plans to build a new football stadium in the Ravine add insult and injury to the thorny historical associations with the Elysian Park area for many Chicanos, as for many other Los Angeles residents.

Against such an implicit trajectory of associations with the park complex, Arias narrates the contestative, utopian impulse to reclaim public space for positive, communitarian use. The targeted spaces for these reclamations are, not surprisingly, the Los Angeles River and Elysian Park. In the case of the river, the appearance of a marvelously animated snow cloud inspires a day of spontaneous, community festivity. Displacing the oppressive haze of smog, the cloud blankets the riverbank in snow, transforming the physical environment and inviting the community to do the same. The introduction of this almost-living cloud demonstrates Arias' strategic use of the fantastic narrative conventions of the romance genre. Fredric Jameson has characterized the particular conventions at work here.

> [T]he strangely active and pulsating vitality of the "world" of romance, much like Stanislaw Lem's sentient ocean in *Solaris*, tends to absorb many of the act- and event-producing functions normally reserved for narrative "characters." . . . [W]e might say that in romance the category of Scene tends to capture and to appropriate the attributes of Agency and Act, making the "hero" over into something like a registering apparatus for transformed states of being, sudden alterations of temperature, mysterious heightenings, . . . in short, the whole semic range of transformation scenes whereby, in romance, higher and lower worlds struggle to overcome each other. (1981:112)

The struggle here is between the "lower" smog world of individual and social death and the "higher" snow-cloud world of life and play. Fausto, the "registering apparatus," knowingly accepts the cloud's invitation to reclaim the river. He dispels his neighbors' suspicious concerns and leads them "past the dead-end barrier" of the street. Symbolically, he opens up their lives to the greater possibility of transcending their socially imposed barriers. Once on the river's edge, Fausto throws caution to the wind and slides down the snow, initiating an outburst of ludic excess, a politics of pleasure: "They played most of the day, sledding on flattened cardboard, throwing snowballs, shaping snowmen, building castles. Whole families came and many people left their jobs" (Arias 1987:60). The form and character of this ludic outburst clearly resonate with two historical traditions of Chicano/*mexicano* cultural practice: the *rasquache* expressive sensibility, and the *días festivos* (holidays) and *ferias* (fairs).

Tomás Ybarra-Frausto has described *rasquachismo* as practical inventiveness motivated by limited material conditions. While it originated and had its most organic manifestations in the expressive practices and ethos of the poor and working classes, Ybarra-Frausto notes that *rasquachismo* has "been appropriated as an aesthetic program of the [Chicano] professional class" (1989:5). As a member of this professional class, Arias incorporates *rasquachismo* into his "aesthetic program" by enacting one of its fundamental premises, identified by Ybarra-Frausto as the way in which "[r]esilience and resourcefulness spring from making do with what's at hand ('hacer rendir las cosas')" (ibid.).

This quality of creative improvisation is clearly manifested in the snow-play scene:

> Someone started a small fire to dry wet socks and pants. Smaldino's eldest boy bought a pair of splintered Salvation Army skis for two dollars and rented them for five cents a ride. And Mrs. Rentería hauled out an old card table and made snow cones with three flavors of syrup.
>
> All this time Cuca had remained at home. The snow had been a blessing for her business, especially fortunes and astrology readings. By early afternoon she had done four of each, plus a half-dozen cures based on some use of snow. (Arias 1987:60)

Relatedly, the traditional market-place celebratory form of *días festivos* and *ferias* is recalled here, as their characteristic paid rides, refreshment stands, spiritualist booths, and whole-family attendance are all transposed onto the spontaneous snow carnival. The crucial detail that "many people left their jobs" is likewise significant. As Arnoldo de León has noted, Chicano workers often took unscheduled days off for saints' days and holidays (1982:66–68, 105). Both real and invented, these Mexican feast days may be seen as incipient, if limited, resistances to the enforced and increasingly routinized conditions of wage labor under capitalism.

Considering the history of repressive intrusions upon urban Chicano public space, the spontaneous reclamation of the border-river topos is a symbolic critique of the dominant urban organization of Los Angeles. Mike Davis describes this counterpractice of Latino and other more recent Third World immigrant peoples in ways that clearly resonate with this example from *Tamazunchale:*

> [T]he immigrant working class . . . is not merely the collective victim of 'urban crisis'; it also strives to transform and create the city, its praxis is a material force, however unrecognized or invisible in most accounts of contemporary Los Angeles. . . . The Spanish-speaking neighborhoods of L.A. are more than melting pots for eventual assimilation to some hyphenated ethnicity. Together with their integral worlds of work and itineraries of movement, these residential environments comprise a virtually parallel urban structure—a second city. (1987:77)

This description accurately notes how the Chicano community actively articulates its own interests and needs within an "other" urban social geography. Furthermore, these constituent elements of a second city are not merely parallel to the elements of the Anglo-dominant first city. In varying degrees of symbolic and practical efficacy, they contest the subordinating spatial-cultural practices into which urban and regional planners would fix the barrios. In this contestative vein, the leisure practices of Chicano Los Angeles manifest the utopian impulse to recover "a horizon of liberation in the world" (Saldívar 1986:212). The neighborhood snow carnival illustrates such a desire. However, the crowning and marvelous example of this impulse is the reappropriation of Elysian Park by Fausto and his friends at the end of the novel.

I have already suggested how, in the novel as in Los Angeles' history, the park is a chronotope for confrontations and conflicts of interest between Chicanos and the law. Recall, for example, how Mario, who dreads the park as the site of the Police Academy, is threatened by "Mr. America" and his Doberman. Elsewhere in the text, Fausto's friend Tiburcio is illegally held by U.S. immigration officials at the Police Academy tennis courts in Elysian Park. He admonishes Fausto to "[r]emember, you could be here too" (50), not because he is "illegal" but because he is racially marked as Mexican and thus vulnerable like Tiburcio. The joint INS-police operation in which Tiburcio is rounded up evokes the actual historical use of the Elysian Park playgrounds as temporary detention centers during the mass roundups of undocumented immigrants begun in 1954 under "Operation Wetback" ("Punishment by Exile" 1972:48). Arias' oblique introduction of U.S. border patrol agents into his critique of urban law effects is tied to a subsequent episode set at the U.S.-Mexico border checkpoint. After Fausto successfully leads a large "army" of undocumented workers past the immigration checkpoint, he is stopped.

> [A]pparently [he] aroused suspicion because of his cape, staff, possibly his dark looks. He was ordered to wait in a small, barren room where his clothes were searched and his body thoroughly examined. "Those are corns," he told the guard, wincing as the metal probe played between his toes. Then in his most exaggerated Oxford English, Fausto recited without a pause the Gettysburg Address, the Pledge of Allegiance and Franklin Roosevelt's death announcement. It was an old trick, but when the guard heard Roosevelt's name, he was convinced. Fausto was given his clothes and told to leave. (Arias 1987:85)

After Fausto fails the visual test of citizenship, he lampoons the contents of discursive citizenship. Specifically, his recitation of "great" American speeches parodies the sorts of canonical, official knowledge that make up E. D. Hirsch's barometer of "cultural literacy," and mocks the superficial performance of national identity that countless people act out daily in crossing the border.

The discursive performance of U.S. nationality is particularly revealed as "*puro* show" ("just an act") in Fausto's exchange with the guards as he passes the checkpoint:

> [Guard] "By the way, where d'you learn that?"
> Fausto stepped into his wrinkled trousers. "I used to sell books of knowledge . . . and that's one of the things you can learn. I sold a lot of sets that way."
> "Well, we're not stupid, you know. You better come up with another number next time." (Ibid.: 85)

The form of Fausto's parodic "number" recalls the verbal gymnastics of the great Mexican comedian Cantinflas (Mario Moreno), who himself was a "master of *cábula*, the subversive (and pleasurable) play with language" (Fregoso 1993: 54). This echo of Cantinflas suggests that, along with the carnivalesque tradition of European narrative, Arias' humorous subversion of authority derives some of its "intertextual logic from its relation to a Mexican tradition of performance," in particular, a "uniquely flavored style of Mexican parody and satire that drew its strength from a critique of power," as Rosa Linda Fregoso argues similarly for Cheech Marin's farcical film *Born in East L.A.* (ibid.: 54). It is interesting to note that the plot point on which Marin's film turns involves the visual conflation of race with nation by INS officers. Like Tiburcio, Marin's protagonist is mistakenly rounded up in an immigration raid, after which he is deported to Tijuana, where most of the film narrative transpires.

Recalling Cantinflas' subversive *palabreo* (wordplay) when threatened by the thinly contained power of authority figures, Fausto resourcefully escapes and ridicules the gate-keeping power of the border guards through a mocking appropriation of authoritative voice and national-cultural discourse. This improvisational maneuvering by Fausto to spontaneously appropriate hegemonic rhetoric and thereby disempower the authority of policing agencies on the international border is subsequently reenacted in the space of Elysian Park, where Fausto directs the army of *mojados* at the end of the novel. Given the implicit historical knowledge and the explicit textual evidence of the park as the misappropriated territory of local and federal police agents, the concluding occupation of Elysian Park by Fausto's entourage is a critically symbolic reappropriation of corrupted public space.

Just prior to this closing episode, the narrative enters the furthest realm of supranaturalism or fantastic realism. In the space between the penultimate and the final chapters, Fausto dies. Arias' concession to mortality would seem to mark the end, if not the failure, of Fausto's hallucinatory quest for the song of life. But this is not the case, for if Fausto set out on his fantastic voyage to combat the death-in-life condition in which we first meet him, the final chapter, taking place after his corporeal death, marks his supreme creative achievement of a life-in-death: "There was no funeral, no burial. Instead, Fausto insisted they take him to the beach so he could look at the sea and the women in bikinis for a while" (Arias 1987:119). From this point on the far west end of the city, Fausto and his band return to their home geography on the northeast edge of downtown in order to reclaim Elysian Park as Fausto's Elysian field and as the community's green urban idyll.

At one level, they go to the park for the seemingly mundane reason that "they could picnic on tables and the children would have someplace to play" (ibid.:122). However, in view of the often overcrowded and dilapidated housing and recreational facilities endemic to the barrios, the mundane and practical desire for open, green recreational areas suggests a significantly charged issue of urban place politics. While the imperative for usable recreational space in many barrios is an effect of social-geographic subordination, the pleasure of using public parks is not merely a reactive necessity. It is also an active expression of another relationship to urban space characteristic of the Chicano second city, "based on gregarious, communitarian uses of markets, boulevards, parks and so on . . . [that] have more in common with the early twentieth-century city . . . than with a deathwish 'postmodernity'" (Davis 1987:78). The Fausto-led return to Elysian Park opposes "deathwish postmodernity" with a life-wish recuperation of recreational public space. Now, the police are conspicuously absent: "Except for the[ir] cars, the park was deserted" (Arias 1987:122). The park is itself re-created as a reinvigorated biotic environment in a fantastic "greening" transformation:

The streets were gone, some trees had shriveled, others had grown. Squirrels poked their heads out of the leaves on the ground, a bank of snow lay gleaming on the ridge below the blue, the richly blue sky. A fantailed pigeon escaped the jaws of a snake by swooping up as a hawk, losing itself among the uppermost pines. And there was silence, then the sounds of other birds, of crickets, of frogs by the eddies of a stream. (Ibid.)

The impinging effects of smog and traffic noises are suppressed. Even the cars of the group, which otherwise contribute to these negative ambiental effects, are freed of pure technological association and contingency as they "shook themselves from bumper to bumper and galloped across the stream and into the trees" (ibid.).

Once in the park, Fausto's group continues the fantastic transformations in themselves, metamorphosing into whatever their imagination dictates. In this way, they literally enact the re-creative power of the park. In the end, Fausto's marvelous and *rasquache* interventions in the lives of his family and friends manifest a carnivalesque, parodic impulse that, in the language of Mikhail Bakhtin, "[o]pposed all that was ready-made and completed, . . . sought a dynamic expression . . . [and] demanded ever-changing playful, un-defined forms" (1984:11). In mock-heroic fashion, Fausto has the last laugh against the physical and social forms of grim death that threatened him at the outset of the novel. He transcends not only his own corporeal demise (he merely "sleeps" in death at the end) but, symbolically, the social death of his community within the racial formation of Los Angeles. This fantastic tran-scendence of an oppressive reality should not be viewed as an escape from the urgencies of the social world, as some critics have argued (Marín 1977), but rather as a utopian critique of precisely those most oppressive conditions that constitute the social world. In this manner, Arias' novel "transcends . . . 'normative assumptions' regarding what shape Chicano/a symbolic creations should take . . . by liberating the 'image' from the constraints of the . . . 'cor-rect' mode for political" representation, as Rosa Linda Fregoso argues else-where for certain commercial Chicano cinema (1993:62). Fausto's imagi-native and marvelous *rasquache* interventions in the lives of barrio residents represent a counterimpulse to the subordination of this community. If in Arias' earlier journalistic reflections on the Chicano condition the barrios "were places few people could point to with pride," their fantastic yet cultur-ally specific re-creation in *Tamazunchale* represents a retelling or countertell-ing of this "second city" of Los Angeles. Arias' novel "injects a liberating imagination back into social and cultural discourses" of Los Angeles' aggra-vated barrios that salvages both pride and a sense of hope in the possibilities of change.

If in Arias' novel Elysian Park was a site of symbolic, magical reclamations by residents in its vicinity, in actual fact, several public parks in East Los Angeles were, like Elysian Park, sites of continued spatial conflict. Among these, Hazard Park and Obregón Park were both threatened by urban-renewal plans throughout the 1960s, becoming issues of concerted and consistent community mobilization in their defense, as well as being topics of regular reporting and commentary in the *Eastside Sun* community weekly. In Elysian Park, along with the various appropriations of public space and residential property discussed in the opening chapters of this book, the park was partially dissected by the construction of the 110 and Interstate 5 freeways, joining nearby Griffith Park as well as Hollenbeck Park in Boyle Heights and Vanowen Park in Van Nuys on the freeway hit list for urban green spaces. More than any of the other parks, however, Elysian Park was a key site of preservationist struggle, although with a broader demographic base of citizen support outside of the barrios. Strong grassroots and electoral-representative pressure during the 1960s prevented even more encroachments on this vulnerable green space when plans were in the works to site a convention center and business complex there (Citizen's Committee to Save Elysian Park).

Even today, Elysian Park continues to be a public card in the private hand of growth interests. Peter O'Malley, son of the original Dodgers owner Walter O'Malley, recently proposed building a state-of-the-art football stadium and entertainment complex adjacent to the existing baseball stadium as an incentive to woo a professional football team back to the city. As one of the principal Latino park-use areas in a city woefully short of public recreational space, the negative impacts of further eroding Elysian Park's green areas would again be disproportionately borne by residents of the adjacent central-city barrios. Knowledge of this fact, along with the aggravated wounds of the remembered violations of Chávez Ravine by the first O'Malley, drew the public ire of many present and former residents, and of many others who created the Citizen's Committee to Save Elysian Park (Moreau 1996; Ramos 1996). Although this latest development initiative had appeared to be headed for defeat—due both to competition from other sites in Los Angeles and Inglewood and to the adamant opposition of Mike Hernández, the City Council representative of the area—the dramatic announcement of the pending sale of the Dodgers franchise to international media mogul Rupert Murdoch has once more raised the specter of future site development in the minds of suspicious citizens.

The continuous struggles for these and other urban green places involved already existing and officially designated public recreational sites. A slightly different, though related, category of community spatial mobilization involves the effort to transform derelict urban land, often produced by clearance for urban development or freeway construction, into symbolically charged spaces of representation for Chicano cultural-identity practices. Perhaps the most significant and richest instance of such grassroots reclamation has been the struggle to establish, maintain, and expand Chicano Park in the Barrio Logan section of San Diego.

LA TIERRA MÍA, LOGAN HEIGHTS, AZTLÁN

Re-greening the Barrio in Chicano Park

Chicano Park exists on the site of what was once the vital core of the second-largest barrio on the West Coast, Logan Heights, but the depredations of urban development in the 1950s and 1960s transformed the area into a waste-land of space underneath the intersecting constructions of the Interstate 5 freeway and the on-ramp for the Coronado Bridge (see Fig. 41). The com-munity's struggles to reclaim this park space span the period from 1967 to the present, constituting a mini-epic of that barrio's attempts to salvage its cul-tural, economic, and social integrity against the cumulative devastations of 1950s rezoning, from residential to industrial, and 1960s physical restructur-ing. After years of progressive degradation, Barrio Logan residents won a concession from the city to build a park in the derelict space created under the interchange of the freeway and the bridge access ramps. However, the city went back on its word by beginning the unannounced construction of a Cali-fornia Highway Patrol substation and parking lot on the designated tract. Pushed beyond their patience, on April 22, 1970, Logan Heights residents and allied supporters from other parts of San Diego literally drew their line in the sand and mobilized to stop the bulldozers. Two days later, community members began to build a park with their own tools and labor (see Fig. 42). Thus began the still-current though much-subdued battle to reclaim several blocks for Chicano Park, which now reaches to the waters of Coronado Bay. An annual Chicano Park Day celebrates the history and progress of this com-munity's exemplary spatio-political struggle.

While this protracted effort clearly expresses a community's desire to re-claim lost land, the fact that it involved a small, poorly situated tract directly beneath the bridge ramps suggests that its importance may lie more in its symbolic than its practical consequences. This is not entirely the case, of course, since the energy mobilized in creating and defending the park has complemented or inspired other practical (and successful) community mob-ilizations to bring health, educational, and social-service programs to the

FIGURE 41. Intersection of Coronado Bridge and Interstate 5 in the heart of Barrio Logan, ca. 1970. Future site of Chicano Park. Courtesy of Salvador Torres and El Museo del Pueblo.

FIGURE 42. Preparing the ground for a people's park. Courtesy of Salvador Torres and El Museo del Pueblo.

barrio. However, in the park site itself, the symbolic resonances are of primary significance to many area residents, as revealed in the comments of several who were interviewed for the documentary film *Chicano Park*. Doña Laura Rodríguez, a particularly active and key participant in the struggles to establish Chicano Park and several social-welfare institutions in Barrio Logan (one of them, a community health center, was named in her honor), comments on this point: "I don't know of any other community that would fight for a park under a bridge where we get the fumes, where we get the pigeon droppings, but it's our park and we love it." In this respect, the use of culturally expressive aesthetic practices in the constitution of Chicano Park is key to its social significance.

While there was a broad range of community participation in the defense, preparation, and maintenance of the tract for a park, a significant element of the leadership in the early mobilizations to secure and constitute the park came from artists. Many of them were affiliated with the recently founded Centro Cultural de la Raza in nearby Balboa Park, in which the neoindigenous nationalism of the Toltecas de Aztlán, a self-designated warrior class of cultural activists, was a significant ideological-aesthetic influence. As a consequence, the founding of the park involved substantial cultural production and ritual activities that were meant to expressively conjure a specific sense of place beyond the construction of a mere physical environment. From the consecration of the ground for the planting of the first greenery, to the design and construction of a central pyramidal *kiosco* (kiosk), to the pictorial embellishments and motifs of the murals painted on the support pillars of the bridge ramps, to the practicing of pre-Columbian *danza* on the site, a spirit of indigenous identification with the land infused the multiform physical embellishments and cultural enactments of the site. By virtue of such practical and symbolic expressions, the constrained physical-spatial scope of the park was greatly expanded in the cultural-spatial resonance of the site as a symbolic recovery of an originary lost land. "La tierra mía Aztlán," the popular motto of park supporters, was emblazoned on the walls, on the Chicano Park flag, and in various printed documents and ephemera produced for subsequent anniversary celebrations of the park's founding (see Fig. 43). With the ensuing community mobilizations to expand the park's acreage "all the way to the Bay," the material impulse to reclaim the actual lost land of the barrio has also continued to imbue Chicano Park with powerful social-geographic significance.

The physical and cultural development of Barrio Logan's Chicano Park

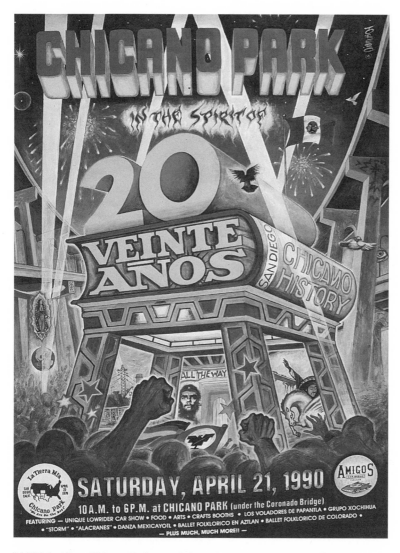

FIGURE 43. Chicano Park twentieth-anniversary poster. Design by Mario Torero, © 1990. Courtesy of the artist.

was a complex collective project involving coordinated and well-planned actions, spontaneous individual accretions, and sometimes conflicting points of view on the form and content of the muralistic embellishments and community uses that would define the park for different groups and individuals. As such, any singular discussion of particular artists and activists will not do full justice to the complex texture of Chicano Park's material and symbolic meaning. Nevertheless, I believe the work and vision of one artist merits particular discussion, for his contributions to, and engagement with, the site have been especially rich and varied.

Salvador "Queso" Torres is a long-time resident of Barrio Logan, living within walking distance of Chicano Park. Though not without some dissenting opinions, Queso is widely acknowledged as being a principal "architect of the dream" of transforming the intruding but monumental columns of the Coronado Bridge into equally monumental "things of beauty reflecting the Mexican-American culture" (Cockcroft 1984:83).[2] What distinguishes his barriological ethos and practice from those of the many other artists involved with Chicano Park are the longevity, complexity, and extent of his expressive engagement with the intruding structures of urban development. On the one hand, he is deeply critical of the social meanings they embody: "They sent this freeway down the heart of our community and nearly killed it. We did not want it. We hated the bridge" (ibid.:84). However, he acknowledges their irreversible presence and accepts the challenge of transforming or subverting their absolute dominion over his community's social space: "But now that we have them, we have to deal with them creatively" (ibid.). These two orientations are identified in conjunctural relation as Torres recalls the tragic yet aesthetically generative context of the bridge's construction:

> I would walk down the streets, passing through, and I'd see this desolate area of our community where the homes had always been. Nothing was there, it was all destroyed. It was such a sad feeling to see this. I thought, what could change this? If only something could change this. So lo and behold, the bridge was built and these great big huge massive columns were built there and the ideas began to evolve in my mind. So I started sketching them and sketching the work that was taking place. (Ibid.; see Figs 44 and 45)

Those initial sketches were the first stirrings of Torres' vision for a monumental aesthetic makeover of the future park site, equally grand but counter-signifying to the designs of hegemonic power that planned and built the

FIGURE 44. Watercolor studies of Coronado Bridge pillars by Salvador Torres, ca. 1976. Courtesy of the artist.

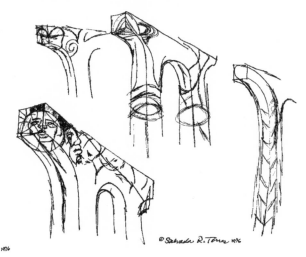

FIGURE 45. Pen-and-ink studies of Coronado Bridge pillars by Salvador Torres, 1976. Courtesy of the artist.

Coronado Bridge. From that moment to the present, Torres has exercised this recuperative vision for the spiritual and social space underneath the bridge in a variety of artistic, documentary, and custodial forms. These include drawing, canvas painting, muralism, video recording, audio recording, ceramics, archiving of press clippings pertaining to the site and its history, tour guiding and lecturing, and maintenance of the grounds and murals.

If Torres has acted as an "architect of the dream" for Chicano Park, he was certainly not alone in sensing its aesthetic possibilities from the outset. Rebecca Castro, a student involved in the original takeover of the site, gave voice to the transformative, aesthetic vision that inspired many of those involved in the site's original reconstitution: "This will make a great park. When the sun is right . . . that [perspective of support pillars] looks like a cathedral" (Cockcroft 1984:84). The exceptional quality of Queso's creative, or re-creative, visionary and material-aesthetic engagement with the park site, therefore, is one of degree rather than of kind. If others saw momentary glimmers of a transcendent architectural form in the monolithic structures dropped into their barrio landscape, Queso has been most possessed by the idea that this fleeting image could be brought into full material-aesthetic being. More than simply making a virtue of necessity, Queso was uniquely inspired to aesthetically transform the site in equal but opposite measure to the epic scale of possibilities manifest in the intruding monolith of the Coronado Bridge.

I hesitate to ascribe Torres' exceptionalism solely to a generational orientation. Nonetheless, his peculiar mix of aversion and awe toward the specific form and monumental scope of the bridge is reminiscent of the similarly complex engagement with the structures of the expressway world by a modernist generation of artists, which Marshall Berman describes as being active at the cusp of the 1950s and 1960s. This period coincides with Torres' own artistic coming-of-age in the San Francisco Bay Area during the early 1960s. Citing a particularly harrowing section of Allen Ginsberg's 1956 epic poem "Howl," in which the built environment of postwar urbanism is figured in nefarious and hallucinatory incantations, Berman points out that along with his emphatic social criticism,

> Ginsberg is urging us to experience modern life not as a hollow wasteland but as an epic and tragic battle of giants. This vision endows the modern environment and its makers with a demonic energy. . . . [but simultaneously] the vision is meant to arouse us . . . to make ourselves

equally great, to enlarge our desire and moral imagination to the point where we will dare to take on the giants. But we cannot do this until we recognize their desires and powers in ourselves—"Moloch who entered my soul early." Hence Ginsberg develops structures and processes of poetic language . . . that recall and rival the skyscrapers, factories and expressways he hates. (1982:311)

In like fashion, Torres' ceaseless figurations for Chicano Park have always manifested a decidedly modernist sensibility. He clearly perceives the simultaneously creative *and* destructive power that the freeway and bridge planners employed in the production of their technostructures. The expressive power suggested to him in this dynamic of creative destruction has inspired him to envision ways of tapping its creative energy in order, as Berman observes of Ginsberg's poetry, "to make ourselves equally great, to enlarge our desire and moral imagination to the point where we will dare to take on the giants."

To hear Torres speak on the history, significance, and unrealized potential of the park site—which he often does in formal and informal tours of the site and slide-show presentations at schools and colleges—is to see this dynamic modernist energy enacted in an oratorical and performative expressive medium. As an occasional tour guide and public lecturer, Torres emphatically performs his engagement with the site and brings his audience actively into the event. In this vein, for example, Torres' vision expanded far beyond the idea of painting the bridge supports or developing social-service agencies out of the momentum of community-based organizing. As part of the Barrio Planning Committee—a community design collective that also included Al "Pelon" Johnson, Abran Quevedo, and Antonia Pérez—Torres imagined a scale of design and redevelopment for the park neighborhood equal to the city's own plans for downtown. The concepts of the Planning Committee were projected onto a master plan, which they commissioned to be drafted by Victor Ochoa, for a full makeover of Barrio Logan based on motifs of pre-Columbian urban form (see Fig. 46). For Torres and others who were moved to realize their various dreams, alternately coincident and conflicting, of a transformed barrio centered around Chicano Park, the limitations of Chicano political and economic power have always thwarted such possibilities. However, like Ginsberg in "Howl," the monolithic expressions of Moloch entered early into Torres' creative soul, compelling him to exercise his own forms of agonistic modernism as he attempted to wrest a space of heaven from the designs of hell imposed on his barrio.

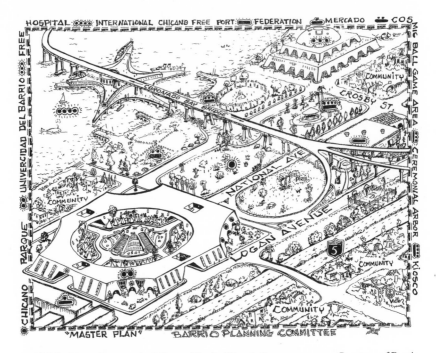

FIGURE 46. Community "Master Plan" of Barrio Logan, ca. 1971. Courtesy of Barrio Planning Committee.

From Space of Representation to Representation of Space: The Textualization of Chicano Park

The meaning of Chicano Park as a symbolic site and expressive figure of spatial reclamation would later be extended well beyond the physical and social parameters of Barrio Logan. This extension would occur in great measure through its mediation as a representative sociospatial "text" in the award-winning documentary film *Chicano Park*, produced in 1988 by Mario Barrera and Marilyn Mulford. This media effect reveals the orientation of many of the film's creative contributors, who clearly meant to represent the park as a synechdochic text-in-action that illustrated a larger utopian impulse toward neoindigenous, Chicano re-territorialization in the mythical and historical homelands of Aztlán and the former Mexican northwest, respectively. The scripted narration of the film, cowritten by Gary Weimberg and the poet Juan Felipe Herrera, is explicit in this figurative rendering of the park.

The narration begins over a breezy montage of generic city views of the sort that might be shown to prospective tourists or investors. This visual track is accompanied by a bubbly catalog of equally generic booster sound bites: "San Diego USA. California's southern gate. Navy town, industry, borderline, factories, Mexicans, Americans, high-rise, businessmen, sun-washed beach sand, tourist-filled vacation land; growing, building, affluences, urban modern development." On cue with the phrase "urban modern development," the film track cuts to a long take of the Interstate 5 freeway, accompanied by a noticeable vocal pause enforced by an ominous synthesizer soundtrack. Thereupon follows an abrupt turn in the vocal tone and narrative content—"That's San Diego today, but it has not always been"—which jointly color the preceding script with a clearly purposeful irony.

The script textually reinscribes a chronology of historical and mythical social spaces displaced from view and erased from public knowledge by the "urban modern development" of "San Diego USA." Now spoken in a sober but proud tone, it offers us a retrospective palimpsest of this region's social geography: "Once this fine land was Mexican, once it was Spanish, once it was Indian, and once in the time of myth and history, San Diego, like all of the American Southwest, was called Aztlán." This revisionist challenge to the hegemonic narrative of contemporary urban progress identifies the film's narrative reclamatory project as ideologically coincident with the material reclamatory project of creating the park itself. Consequently, the twin productions of "Chicano Park" (i.e., as a space of cultural representation and a cultural representation of space) effect a double recovery project (in material and discursive forms) in which the various producers "acquire a measure of imaginary control as a collectivity" (Sánchez 1995 : 303). In fact, the film text identifies this reclamatory project as the theme of its argument: "This is the story of one piece of Aztlán, reborn, and how its people, the Chicanos, rediscovered their culture and history by rediscovering their destiny as a people and as a community. This is the story of Chicano Park." The film's propositional representation of Chicano Park has very specific, determining discursive precedents in the manifest barriological orientations of at least two people centrally involved in crafting this collective film text: coproducer Mario Barrera and co–script writer Juan Felipe Herrera.

Barrera has been a professor of political science and ethnic studies for many years at the University of California, Berkeley, and is the author of the much-cited study of historical Chicano structural subordination *Race and Class in the Southwest: A Theory of Racial Inequality*. Furthermore, prior to publishing this study, Barrera was co-editor of the previously discussed monograph *Action Research: In Defense of the Barrio*. The introductory description of its contents resonates with the statement of documentary purpose in *Chicano*

Park: "The body of the report consists of three interviews that describe projects undertaken in three urban areas to counter these processes [of disruptive urban development] and to give the Chicanos in those areas some small measure of control over their own lives and communities" (Barrera and Vialpando 1974:1). This documentation of the impulse toward community defense and self-determination is also manifest in a precedent barriological text of co-script writer Juan Felipe Herrera, although expressed in a very different medium from Barrera's scholarly investigations.

Herrera lived many of his school-age years in Logan Heights. During this time, he experienced the arrival of the freeway and, while attending UCLA in the late 1960s, saw the further degradation of the barrio by the building of the Coronado Bridge. These lived experiences of urban devastation were strongly etched in his memory and given expressive form in his poem "Logan Heights and the World," published in 1987. The narrative structure of the poem anticipates that of *Chicano Park.* The poem opens, as does the film (after the ironic booster montage), with an assertion of accomplished contestation:

> I come from a neighborhood
> where you can see the Bay from the kitchen.
>
> We kicked the Highway Patrol out
> from our varrio and put a Chicano Park
> in its place. (58)

Having established the prefatory pride in community reclamation of the site, Herrera reconstructs the quotidian, intimate sense of place of his predevastated barrio, echoing the testimonial statements of Logan Heights residents in *Chicano Park* about how the barrio once functioned as a vital social space. The carefully detailed evocation of his childhood milieu is then abruptly interrupted by a statement of how and when that world was shattered: "A couple of years later, / the city administration cut a freeway right through / our barrio. Everything fell apart, vanished" (ibid.: 59).[3] This description is curiously unembellished, given the awful reality that befell the community. However, Herrera's deadpan statement effectively suggests the swiftness of spatial effect and the sense of community numbness in its wake, as if reflecting the incredulity and powerlessness felt by neighborhood residents. The characterizations of the social space that immediately follow this moment are predictably dispirited:

The little houses with the geraniums singing soprano
and the elastic kids
grew transparent over night.

Me & Arnold Luna, Raymond Neri, Johnny
& Eva García would walk out after school,[4] across
the torn structures and sniff glue
in the condemned apartments

Everyone lived in a studio set for a B movie
about the coming of Godzilla;
a kind of urban ghost town. . . . (Ibid.)

Here, the depictions of social death, read in light of similar images that have
recurred intermittently in Raza barriological expression from the earliest period of barrioization, suggest the cyclical nature of devastations tied to successive regimes of urban restructuring that have not ceased to disrupt the
communal living spaces of *mexicanos*.

However, the social death of the barrio, whether intended or not by urban
planners, is not fully realized. Consequently, the survivors of the monstrous
encroachments are seen to reap the bitter but useful harvest of lessons learned
from the past. Thus, when the next show of turf war is initiated by "the Police
Dynasty / . . . and the Mayor / (not to mention the vampire architects)" (ibid.:
60), Herrera coolly and confidently proclaims:

we were ready.
Our little red plastic watch had been ticking
since we were seven years old; playing marbles &
spinning tops in the Sector of the Dead. (Ibid.)

The residents' tactical knowledge of the onslaughts of urban development is
then enacted in "forming a circle in the heart of the wasteland; / a simple
park, *Chicano Park*, / a reminder to the world / that we were on the loose"
(ibid.; original emphasis). As in the film documentary and physical creation of
Chicano Park, there is no illusion in Herrera's poem about the limited, almost
incidental physical scope of the spatial action ("a simple park"). However, the
concluding statement makes it clear that the significance of this microdefense
of turf is meant to be read beyond the parameters of Logan Heights or even
San Diego. It is a statement "to the world" that, as in the narrated conclusion

of *Chicano Park*, is offered for the measure of inspiration and instruction it may provide to those who find themselves in similar circumstances.

REBELS WITH A *CAUSA:* CLAIMING *CULTURA* AND RECLAIMING PLACE IN THE WORK OF THE REBEL CHICANO ART FRONT

The collaborative and collective artistic processes manifest in many aspects of the Chicano Park struggle in San Diego have been mirrored in the work of many Chicano artist groupings—some ephemeral, others of long standing— who employ a variety of media in inventive and hybrid ways to express their claims to cultural space and place-identity. I have in mind, particularly though not exclusively, the aesthetic practices produced during and since the apogee of the Chicano political and cultural movement of the late sixties and early seventies. The reactive exigencies of producing art by all means necessary and with every media available, along with the need for institutionally marginalized and excluded artists in all media to find mutual support, compelled community-based artists to creatively combine their practices in common cultural and political causes. The Chicano mural movement is the most famous of these aesthetic manifestations, but numerous cultural centers, artist collectives, support groups, and grassroots institutional apparatuses, as well as countless spontaneous and ephemeral groupings and projects, contributed to a florescence of alternative expressive practices and institutions.[5] Among the most important and successful of these groups has been the artist collective Rebel Chicano Art Front (RCAF; also known, in a playful twist on their acronym, as the Royal Chicano Air Force). It was founded in Sacramento in 1970 by José Montoya and Esteban Villa, who were teaching in the Art Department of Sacramento State College (now California State University, Sacramento, where they still teach), and a group of their students, including Ricardo Favela, Armando Cid, and Juanishi Orosco.

Both Montoya and Villa, the figureheads and unofficial leaders of the group, have been involved in some of the major Chicano movement struggles for political and cultural integrity. Starting with their participation in the 1965 California farmworker's union march from Delano to Sacramento, the two have been cultural activists for Chicano and Third World social issues as visual artists, poets, musicians, teachers, and cultural organizers. The RCAF, in its multiple political and cultural activities, was the organizational rubric for much of their work. In 1972, with an expanded membership of about twenty, mostly students or former students of Villa and Montoya, the RCAF established the Centro de Artistas Chicanos, a nonprofit public service corporation that became a clearinghouse for Chicano political and cultural activism in Sacramento and, by network and traveling projects of the RCAF, an influential organization throughout the Chicano "nation."

The formation and public activities of the RCAF in the early 1970s coincided with a major period of central-city reconstruction in Sacramento, based on plans that had been laid out in the mid-1960s. The city's and developers' designs for improved commuter transit and middle-class commercial and touristic revitalization of the downtown area were being substantially plotted over the space of many poorer Chicano neighborhoods in the urban core. Consequently, the RCAF was instrumental in the defense of barrio community and spatial integrity as they worked to inform barrio residents of the dangers of selling their homes, knowing full well that the powerful domino effect of gentrification could be set in motion with even a single resident giving up his or her home to speculating entrepreneurs or the local redevelopment agency (Barnett 1984:164). The impulse to counteract the erosion of barrio social space consistently guided the practical, organizational, and cultural-aesthetic agenda of the RCAF. In their successful lobbying for a 2 percent allocation from all public construction projects, they also helped assure that resources would be available for artistic embellishments that could potentially humanize the often inhumane effects of the urban developments that were taking place and those that were yet to come.

For the RCAF, artistic expression was a vital component of their larger social and political agenda. As cultural activists, they worked to develop "a practical body of knowledge which could be used as a relevant point of reference for all Chicanos" (Montoya 1980a:29). In this respect, the RCAF made a practical virtue of producing and disseminating their creative work in ways that would make it as immediately and broadly available as possible to Chicanos in Sacramento and elsewhere. Muralism and poster design were their most recognizable media of popular artistic production, but they were no less committed to presenting their other visual artworks, music, theater, and poetry through Chicano-centered community venues. In Sacramento specifically, the RCAF worked through the Centro de Artistas, in the 1970s and 1980s, to conjoin their artistic work with such community-based social-service and political projects as the low-income Breakfast for Niños program, La Raza Bookstore, the Chicano Culture Committee, the Alkali (public-housing projects) Redevelopment Committee, and the Human Development Unit of Sacramento Concilio. The "practical body of knowledge" the RCAF developed was revealed both in their concrete administration of the Centro and in the praxis of the group's specific cultural and art activities. In conjunction with these community-based groups, the RCAF engaged in strategic battles against the continuing degradation of the barrio's physical, cultural, and social spaces, precisely the conditions that informed the thematic registers, variously manifest, of Arias' fictional narrative and the Chicano Park activists and creative mediators.

Countering Urban Renewal: Implicit Social Knowledge in "Southside Park"

In 1985, Villa and Montoya recorded *Chicano Music All Day* with their group, El Trio Casindio, and the Royal Chicano Air Force. This independent album was produced by the Instituto de Lengua y Cultura of Elmira, California, and its contents copyrighted by the Centro de Artistas Chicanos of Sacramento. The album was produced, promoted, and distributed outside the mainstream channels of the recording industry by a Chicano cultural organization because they were specifically "interested in giving this music to a wider audience in the Chicano community" (Hernández 1985). On this album, the lyrics to the song "Southside Park," written by Esteban Villa, include a pointed critique of the dominant consumer culture and hegemonic urban renewal represented in the figure of downtown Sacramento's consumer mall complex, consisting of the indoor Downtown Plaza shopping center and the connecting, outdoor Merchant Pedestrian Mall, popularly known as K Street Mall. Marking a major urban-renewal project of the Sacramento Downtown Association, the first incarnation of the K Street Mall closed off automobile traffic on eight blocks of a principal downtown thoroughfare to lay down a European-style mall of grass, red brick, and fountains that would entice suburban middle-class consumers back into the ailing downtown corridor adjacent to the State Capitol area. The Downtown Plaza shopping mall was subsequently opened in 1971, the same year that a derelict section of old buildings just across the Interstate 5 freeway from the mall was refurbished as a pseudohistorical tourist and night-life area called Old Sacramento (Sacramento Downtown Association 1993). Villa introduces the mall in his lyrics by immediately distancing himself from it and inviting the listener to do as much:

> Those of you who hate the Mall
> There's el Southside
> Aquí en Sacra [Here in Sacramento]

The green expanse of nearby Southside Park represents an alternative public space to the consumer-centered mall. Located in a downtown barrio, the park is, in its positive manifestation, a place where "Children come and play all day / Mama dreams the hours away" (Villa 1985). Villa's opposition of barrio park and merchant mall encapsulates a broader conflict over the use and meanings of public and pseudopublic urban space, acted out between dominant planners and aggrieved communities of the downtown area, principally Chicano, but including African Americans, the homeless, and other poor area residents.

No reasons are given for hating the mall. Therefore, the source of inspiration for this drastic feeling resides in an implicit understanding of the semiotic resonances of the K Street Mall for the Southside Park users. Mike Davis has described the ideological subtext of similar urban-development practices in downtown Los Angeles. His observations can help us to identify how apparently innocent "pseudopublic spaces," like Sacramento's downtown mall,

> are full of invisible signs warning off the underclass "Other." Although architectural critics are usually oblivious to how the built environment contributes to segregation, pariah groups—whether poor Latino families, young Black men, or elderly homeless white females—read the meaning immediately. (1990:226)

Such invisible signs of exclusion to "undesirables," built into the architectural text of Sacramento's downtown mall, compel the antagonism of Villa's lyrics in "Southside Park." The knowing reader or listener would be quite clear on the hateful resonances of Sacramento's downtown mall, as they might often have had such barring messages directed at them. The fact that the spatial and architectural text of downtown Sacramento's social geography can be "read" semiotically, particularly by those whom it marginalizes, suggests the often forgotten etymology of *semiotic* as a designation of spatial signs. To wit, Edward Soja points out: "The root of semiotic and semiology is the Greek *semeion*, which means sign, mark, spot or *point in space*. You arrange to meet someone at a *semeion*, a particular place. The significance of this connection between semiotics and spatiality is too often forgotten" (1989:246; original emphases).

Of course, the signs of exclusion from pseudopublic spaces are often openly directed and thus made visible to a broad public semiosis. In the case of the downtown malls, José Montoya has identified the hegemonic media effect of demonizing Chicano youth, making them especially vulnerable to police harassment and public disdain. He sarcastically notes Sacramento newspaper reports that "Cholos and Low-riders are gangs of vandals who go around terrorizing downtown merchants and shoppers (Sacra headlines for the past few months), all manipulated by even more vicious Chicano prison gangs" (Montoya 1980b:28). In a later, poetic meditation on the same subject entitled "Cinco de Mayo Poem for '87," Montoya recalls the spate of reports involving disturbances in the downtown area at the time the original pedestrian grass mall was being built over with a light-rail train system and cobblestone streets:

> . . . the recent media-fest of battle grounds
> And concrete pyramids of reinforced steel
> Complete the 'K' street obstacle course of th' seventies
> And the chief and th' merchants and politicos
> Blaming the cholos from downtown barrios
> For most of th' chaos. . . . (1992a:215)

Even though racial and class biases are inscribed in the shape and meanings of the redeveloped downtown, Villa does not figure the park and the mall complex in a moralistic binary (i.e., good/bad) opposition. Rather, he points out that the barrio park, while a space for regenerative leisure, is also where the unemployed go to pass the time with their frustrations:

> Gettin' tired
> Of bein' fired
> Aquí en Sanjo
> En el Southside

While Villa expresses a symbolic critique of American consumer society through the inscribed symptomatic meanings of the mall, he renders the opposed barrio park, complexly, as a space containing elements of both pleasure and despair.

In an effort to wrest the park from increasing dereliction, the RCAF and Centro de Artistas Chicanos had begun to use the park as a designated site for community-wide activities in the early 1970s. José Montoya pointed this out in a report to the Concilio de Arte Popular, an umbrella organization for California Chicano art centers and art collectives:

> May proved to be our busiest month as we took on "5 de Mayo" at
> Southside Park. Traditionally, it involves a collective effort on the part
> of all the Chicano community organizations, college MEChAs [Movi-

miento Estudiantil de Chicanos en Aztlán], and high school MAYAs [Mexican American Youth Association] to organize a big *jamaica* [bazaar] plus *mercado* [market] at Southside Park. Involving such things as entertainment, security, publicity, booths[,] the Centro this year also had the added pressure of finishing a mural there at the park for the occasion. *It was as though the park was finally acknowledged to be a part of our barrio—a Chicano Park.* (1976:7; emphasis added)

The importance of the mural in helping to transform this once-decaying city park into a vital and popularly designated Chicano Park must be emphasized. The RCAF had appropriated the concrete backdrop of an outdoor stage in the park for a sequence of individual artist mural panels. This project was like a collective visual signature and graphic *testimonio* of the group. Alan Barnett describes how in the shadow of Sacramento's downtown gentrification, "the park in the midst of a barrio had been neglected and was the hangout of junkies and winos until the RCAF painted the old concrete structure and then proceeded to turn it into the site of its Mexican and *indio* ceremonies each year. Here was an exemplary instance of a mural that continued to be used after the painting was completed" (1984:276). The mural dedication was thus both a practical action and a symbolic declaration that the park would be used for Chicano holiday celebrations (Cinco de Mayo, 16 de Septiembre), neo-indigenous ceremonies (Fiesta de Maíz, Fiesta de Colores), popular market activities, a series of annual "Barrio Olympics," car shows, and a variety of other formal and informal community cultural events. The use of Southside Park by the RCAF as an effective center for Chicano expressive, ritual, and popular cultural activity was in direct response to the perhaps unintended, but nonetheless dysfunctional, uses to which the park had fallen victim through civic abandonment. This reclamation of recreational "green" space, its embellishment with graphic (typically mural) designs, and the subsequent identification and conversion of the neglected space as an arena for community-specific, popular uses make up the social history within which the understated lyrics of "Southside Park" achieve a fuller meaning (see Figs. 47–49).

The chronology of spatial appropriation, graphic embellishment, and a reinvigorated political-cultural public use of the park space recalls a similar chain of events associated with the founding of Chicano Park in Barrio Logan, as well as other urban Chicano parks during this same period. In fact, the RCAF contributed to the development of San Diego's Chicano Park when they painted a series of murals on the bridge pillars in 1975, and in later years when El Trio Casindio performed in the annual Chicano Park Day festivities.

FIGURE 47. RCAF Southside Park mural in progress. Panels designed by (*left to right*) José Montoya, Juanishi Orosco, and Esteban Villa. Courtesy of José Montoya and the RCAF Collection of the California Ethnic Multicultural Archive, University of California at Santa Barbara.

FIGURE 48. Indigenous celebration at Southside Park. Courtesy of José Montoya and the RCAF Collection of the California Ethnic Multicultural Archive, University of California at Santa Barbara.

FIGURE 49.   Raza jam in Southside Park with Freddy Rodríguez and the RCAF Band.
Courtesy of José Montoya and the RCAF Collection of the California Ethnic Multicultural
Archive, University of California at Santa Barbara.

Furthermore, the sequence of events of this particular park's history are representative of a pattern of similar grassroots spatial actions in the late 1960s
and 1970s, through which many "People's Parks" were founded and defended
by people of color, the urban poor, and other disenfranchised or marginalized
groups, the most recognized of these being in Berkeley. Ron Arias' complex
narrative mediations of Los Angeles' Elysian Park are akin to Villa's meditation upon the social semiotic tension of Sacramento's Southside Park. While
Arias' fiction portrays the wholly utopian transformation of the park as a
reappropriated idyll for Fausto's barrio neighbors, the mediated tension in
"Southside Park" does not strongly favor one or another of its poles. Villa's
urban idyll is both constrained by and contesting of the negative conditions
of the adjacent barrio's social subordination.

    The contradictory significations of the social space in "Southside Park"
suggest, finally but no less importantly, a way of reading its musical form
(composed of meter, rhythm, and instrumentation) as a propositional, meaningful structure supporting the content of the lyrics. Described in the booklet
accompanying the album as a bolero, the musical texture of "Southside Park"
seems, as well, to evoke a blues quality along with the identified Latin Ameri-

can form. The bolero genre denotes a specific metrical pattern and rhythmic feeling of the music. In "Southside Park," this feeling is produced by the lilting tropical backbeat, marked by the conga drum. Relatedly, "Southside Park" subscribes to the traditional narrative contours of the bolero genre, characterized by a personalized, intimate lyricism. The bolero typically expresses longing or nostalgic sentiments for a person (usually a woman) or a place (a town, region, or nation: "mi tierra"), and here these sentiments are transposed by Villa to describe the more idealized aspects of the barrio park:

> Southside Park
> After dark, in the moonlight
> Southside Park
> A summer day, in the sunshine
>
> Children come and play all day
> Mama dreams the hours away

My ascription of a blues feeling to the musico-lyrical text is not based on a metrical analysis, since "Southside Park" clearly does not follow the typical, repeating twelve-bar pattern of the blues. While other songs on the album do use blues chord progressions—"The Derelict Dawg," "Cruzin'," the instrumental "Warm Up," and "Stipend Blues"—the blues quality in "Southside Park" is more obliquely rendered as an impressionistic mood created by the conjunction of the harmonica riffs with the melancholy lyrics of unemployment and despondency. Taken together, the conga and the harmonica respectively represent instrumental and rhythmic correlatives to the tension of utopian and dystopian meanings in "Southside Park." The backbeat of the conga underscores the idyllic associations of the park space, while the harmonica riffs emphasize the tone of despondency in the oppressive social conditions of the contemporary barrio.

The symbolic and practical significance of Sacramento's public parks is central to the organizational and expressive practices of Villa and the RCAF. As a major public site of RCAF- and Centro-organized community activities, Southside Park was a privileged barrio cultural space, but it was not the only one. Six blocks due north of the K Street Mall lies a small barrio park that was recognized by the city as a Chicano park when it was officially designated Zapata Park (after the early-twentieth-century Mexican revolutionary general Emiliano Zapata) in 1975. More than a cosmetic title, the naming of the park was part of a package of hard-won civic concessions—such as a new elementary school with increased community involvement and support for cultural activities—negotiated by the Alkali Redevelopment Committee, an advocacy group for Chicano public-housing projects working through the Centro de Artistas Chicanos (Montoya 1976:6). Armando Cid had earlier put the RCAF artistic signature on the park with a 1973 mosaic mural. In his poetry, José Montoya, like his *compadre* Esteban Villa, also represents the parks of Sacramento as multivalent chronotopes of the city's social-geographic formation; their meanings are assessed principally for their significance to the Chicano community. In the poem "Until They Leave Us a Loan," Montoya recounts a brief period in which barrio residents engage in practical battle with a well-to-do white neighborhood over dominion of an urban park. This text and his 1985 Trio Casindio song lyric "Cruzin'" demonstrate Montoya's understanding of Chicano leisure spatial practices as contestative social texts. I will look first at his poem, before concluding this section by discussing Montoya's song lyric.

Leisure Practices as Intercultural Critique in "Until They Leave Us a Loan" and "Cruzin'"

"Until They Leave Us a Loan" is Montoya's poetic transcription of a friend's ribald tale ("as related to me by / Elias, alias, Eelye") of how the Chicano community claimed the space of a Sacramento park that had previously been the exclusive province of the middle- and upper-middle-class white residents in its area.

> Back then, José, we knew
> McKinley Park as Clunie Pool.
> Fancy, ese [man], with a high-board
> y todo el pedo [and all that shit]—and strictly
> for gavas [Anglos]! (1992b:117)

The barrio community was allowed to look at this segregated urban oasis but not swim in it. Denied access to the "public" pool, Chicanos made *rasquache* leisure use of the Sacramento and American Rivers running through the city. However, when the city rulers decided to restrict even this option, the conditions congealed for the barrio's spontaneous rebellion.

Montoya's recounting of the spatial mobilization is fully carnivalesque. The actions transpire in a bounded period of time and are told in a vernacular language that blends Spanish and English into a rich barrio *caló* (slang). Images of the body's "lower stratum" abound in the activities of urination, copulation, and drinking, as the "colored" (brown and white) bodies themselves become sites of difference and of male-enacted cultural conflict. Finally, the actions are narrated with a mock epic grandeur and a sense of humor that ironically underscore the felt seriousness and pleasure of victory for the participants.

> [W]e invaded Clunie Pool
> and routed the gavas [Anglos]
> and for three beautiful days
> the barrio owned Clunie, ese!
> . . . .
> And we swam and we peed
> in the water for three days
> and three nights—parecía
> una factory de chocolate,
> [—it was like
> a chocolate factory,]
> por dios santito [I swear to God!]!—a bronze
> smelter, ese [man] in the heat
> of July and a glistening,
> blue-silver fish hatchery in
> the moon-light. . . . (Ibid.: 117)

Though told as a mock epic, the barrio mobilization nonetheless produces real and strategic results. The routing of *gavas* was a substantial transgression of the racial map of Sacramento, subject to an equal or greater retaliation, since "back then" not just the pool park but the area surrounding it was clearly a white enclave. These stakes and consequences are evident in the mocking account of the park neighbors' response to this brown "invasion."

> [T]he solid, stolid neighbors
> who were used to the
> solemn, cemetery stillness
> of that beautiful park
> de volada le hablaron a la ley
> [right away they called the cops]
> —but they came too late, ese,
> the park was ours!
> Public park. ¿que no [right]? (Ibid.: 117)

The silent, deathly characterization of the *gava* neighborhood is reproduced in the physical bearing of its residents, whose "solid, stolid" demeanor is the mark of their (f)rigidity. Thus, they embody qualities of ruling social classes that were traditional objects of carnivalesque derision and inversion. In this parodic critique, all fixed and frozen qualities of Being in the ruling culture were eschewed in favor of active, creative principles of Becoming in the popular culture. Consequently, like Fausto in *The Road to Tamazunchale*, the barrio neighbors in Montoya's poem "sought a dynamic expression . . . [and] demanded ever-changing playful, undefined forms" (Bakhtin 1984:11). Antithetical to the cemetery solidity of the *gava* neighbors, the playful dynamism of the barrio "invaders" is shown in multiple forms of creativity and productivity. The power of their re-creational activity is figured, first, in the industrial dynamic of a "factory de chocolate" and a "bronze smelter," which describe their daylight uses of the pool. Subsequently, the evening uses of the pool are rendered in the reproductive sexual metaphor of a "blue-silver fish hatchery in / the moon-light."

The sexual carnivalization of Clunie Pool introduces a masculinist perspective to the poem. In its mock-epic account, the poem enacts a male-centered sexual narrative common to many nationalist resistance struggles.[6] Specifically, in the occupation of the pool, only the active agency of men is identified, if not during the actual "invasion," where the plural pronouns ("we," "our," and "ours") are not gender specific, then certainly in the prized activity given immediate reign by the carnivalesque spatial conquest:

> Y de ahí pa'ca [And before you knew it] it became our
> classroom, ese, a sex education
> forum for young dudes—maniacos [maniacs]!
> and the Rose Garden—right
> there, carnal [brother], in front of
> the Police Academy was the
> place a lot of vatos [dudes]
> lost their maiden-heads and began
> to wonder why white chicks
> fucked and ours went to
> catechism . . . (Montoya 1992b:117–118)

Here, the plural pronouns have clear male referents (dudes, *maniacos*, and *vatos*), so that their possessive grammatical case not only claims proprietary rights to a spontaneously created libidinal zone ("our classroom"), but to fellow Chicanas ("ours went to / catechism"). By extension, the "white chicks" may be not only racially "other" in their physical bodies but, as women *of* white (male) culture, also spoils of war in the narrated sexual-racial conquest. Under the rubric of intercultural conflict, the libidinous activities enacted in McKinley Park recall the body politics noted by Paul Gilroy about Black British popular culture, in which "sex and other types of hedonistic recreation are blurred together in a dense discourse which 'carnivalizes' . . . the residues of work, transposing them into a source of collective pleasure, a funky party" (1987:203). However, as articulated in "Until They Leave Us a Loan," this funky party only celebrates the sexual initiation, freedom, and victory of the young male *maniacos*.

Without minimizing the implications of this male-centered narrative, it must nevertheless be emphasized that the long-term result of the spatial action was to re-create the once exclusively white park as a broad-based Chicano community space. This fact is made clear by Montoya's identification of several festive cultural activities enacted in McKinley Park that would become a trademark of RCAF-led uses of Sacramento's parks. These include neighborhood picnics, community cook-offs ("menudo bowl"), family reunions, athletic tournaments ("Barrio Olympics"), and special fund-raising events. By way of such formal and informal activities the barrio residents used their traditions of gregarious and communitarian recreation to enact a vital public cultural place on the grounds of a beautiful but relatively moribund built environment. From the perspective of the poet-speaker, this reclamation of urban green space expresses a limited wish-fulfillment of the quintessential Chicano nationalist goal, a reconquest of the occupied homeland of Aztlán. Still, the poem does not claim a univalent victory for the Chicano community. Instead, it describes a continuous dialectical conflict over spatial and, by extension, social self-determination. Consequently, the symbolic and practical victory of the barrio residents described in the poem is ever vulnerable to a counterattack by dominant urban interests. Thus Elias, the reported speaker, wonders:

> I heard a new freeway's gonna
> come through here—did you
> hear anything?
>
> Qué quemada, ¿Verdad? [What a burn, right?]
>
> But I've been looking at this
> big park over in Carmichael . . . (Montoya 1992b:119)

Setting his sights on another plot of public space in a comfortable, middle-class zone further east of McKinley, Elias projects the momentum of this localized Chicano territorial reclamation as a sort of reverse Manifest Destiny (i.e., *west*ward imperial expansion): a playful-serious expression of the Chicano nationalist dream.

Thesis begets antithesis and with every synthesis a new struggle will engage the oppressors and the oppressed. The punning title, "Until They Leave Us a Loan," recognizes the tension between the barrio's dependent status ("Loan") and its residents' desire to be independent (left a-lone). In its broad temporal scope, the poem mediates a sequence of precedent ("back then"), present ("And today"), and prescient (what's "gonna come") knowledge of community spatial mobilizations. The latter category of knowledge is a touchstone of the RCAF's community-activist impulse and is voiced in Elias' closing advice to Montoya and the reader:

> I was just thinking, man!
>
> Qué dicen haya en la universidad—
> [What do they say over at the university—]
> Plan your future.
> ¿Tú sabes? [You know?] (Ibid.: 119)

The narrative of intercultural conflict in "Until They Leave Us a Loan" presents an explicit case for reading the practices of public recreation as politically meaningful social acts. Recreation, in this case, mediates cultural conflict in the practical struggle of Chicanos to secure the right to use designated public space for their particular forms of leisure. Similarly, the very forms of leisure activities themselves can be read as meaningful social texts. That is, their form may be interpreted as a signifying content. For example, in the poem, the carnivalized swimming and sexual activities signified cultural differences exacerbated by spatial segregation in which racialized bodies became sites of struggle in a sexualized tension of intercultural contact, conflict, and conquest.

In a related representation of leisure form-as-content, the lyrics to Montoya's Trio Casindio song "Cruzin'" identify a particular Chicano urban pastime as a resonant text of cultural difference and defiance. Like Esteban Villa's "Southside Park," "Cruzin'" contrasts the meanings of specific mainstream leisure pursuits and urban spaces with counterposed Chicano activities and places:

It's not the Boardwalk
In Santa Cruz
It's not a stroll down
In Malibu
. . . .
It's not the Sunset
In Hollywood
We just go cruzin'
In our neighborhood

These unassuming lyrics narrate very little explicit content, employing a minimalism also reminiscent of "Southside Park." However, they implicitly valorize the ethos and expression of Chicano cultural difference that underlies the entire album. In stating that "We [Chicanos] just go cruzin' / In our neighborhood," Montoya is saying little but implying much. The minimizing term "just" is a complex signifier, simultaneously obfuscating cultural meanings to an outsider while flagging those meanings for a knowing insider.

The embedded meanings of "just" are, on the one hand, a knowledge of social containment in the sense that we *can only* "go cruzin' in our neighborhood" with any degree of felt security. On the other hand, it expresses the opposite, contestative appeal of "cruzin' in our neighborhood." This second sense of "just" notes the positive, affective meanings of a circumscribed leisure activity, produced precisely because the mainstream demonization of cruising magnifies its resonant appeal as identity-enhancing expressive performance (Bright 1995:98–99). This demonizing process includes the increasing attempts to suppress the activity, as when police patrol cars "cruise" principal streets to harass or intimidate the participants, or when the designated cruising areas are simply closed down on weekend nights. The unwelcome presence of police is referred to in the background of the recording, where the band members act out a series of representative raps from the street. In one, we hear Montoya warn "ay viene la jura, trucha" (here come the cops, watch out). In spite of such police impositions, one lowrider aficionado interviewed by Brenda Jo Bright clearly expressed the culturally specific and empowering significance of cruising in his community: "Cruising was a tradition . . . it was a Chicano alternative to Disneyland. It brought Raza together from all parts of Southern California. It was unequaled entertainment for a minimal price" (quoted in Bright 1995:99).[7]

Depicted as the product of simultaneous and contrasting social meanings, Chicano cruising serves in Montoya's text as a synecdoche of broader barrio culture. In *The Road to Tamazunchale*, there is an interesting corollary to the cruising effect rendered in "Cruzin'." However, rather than manifesting the dialectical quality of Montoya's text, Arias' novel offers a wholly utopian projection of magically empowered cruising for its protagonists. The very narrative dynamic of *Tamazunchale* is premised, in a sense, on the desire to escape immobility (both physical and social) on the marvelous "road to Tamazunchale." It is not incidental, therefore, that descriptions of intercontinental travels (across history and geography), intercity driving (from the Tijuana border to Los Angeles), and intracity and -barrio excursions figure prominently and repeatedly in the novel. In a manner of speaking, they "drive" the narrative as Fausto et al. cruise toward their utopian self-re-creations. A far more dire vision of automotive mobility was made manifest in my discussion of Helena María Viramontes' story "Neighbors." There, the classic cruiser vehicle, a "candied-apple red Impala," around which a group of neighborhood boys gather to socialize, is significantly immobilized in symbolic resonance with the general social paralysis and death of the neighborhood. Falling somewhere between the respective enabling and disabling cruising of Arias and Viramontes, "Cruzin'" reveals Montoya's rhetorical use of "neighborhood" as a trope for understanding a complex, conjuncturally produced place-identity and cultural consciousness.

This identity and consciousness is not locally circumscribed as a Sacramento phenomenon. In the two stanzas from "Cruzin'" previously cited, the list of mainstream place-names—Santa Cruz Boardwalk, Malibu, Sunset Boulevard, and Hollywood—is set against an unspecified and generalized Chicano geography ("our neighborhood"). Furthermore, in the background of the recording (not transcribed in the printed lyrics), Montoya and his fellow musicians name a series of barrios and some of their principal cruising streets across the country: Barstow (CA); *Calle primera* in Barelas and Broadway in Sanjo (both barrios in Albuquerque, NM); Fresno (CA); and 22nd Street in Chicago's Pilsen barrio. This juxtaposition of identified Chicano and non-Chicano recreational and social spaces produces a similar effect to that section of *Tamazunchale* in which a group of barrio neighbors debate the appropriate setting for the community play about to be produced:

> [Mario:] "You mean, we gotta put the thing on?"
> [Tiburcio?:] "Sure, it's easy, just think of something."
> Cuca suggested a show about Burma.
> "Where's that?" someone asked.
> "Next to India."

"Why not Los Angeles?"
"Hollywood . . ."
"Glendale."
"¡Qué Glendale! ¡Maravilla!"
"Boyle Heights . . ." (Arias 1987 : 100)

In both Montoya's and Arias' texts, the designation of barrio geographies against the perceived mainstream geographies manifests a defiant pride in affirming the inherent value of the Chicano neighborhoods as culturally rich and worthy of expressive mediation in their own right.

Beyond this barriological affirmation of naming Chicano urban places, El Trio Casindio implicitly articulates a more ambitious social-geographic consciousness. The references to Chicano place-names do more than suggest that there are similar communities around the country in which equivalent cultural knowledge and practices exist. This, of course, is one signifying proposition of the background rap. A precursory song text could be identified in Lalo Guerrero's early-1950s classic "Chicas Patas Boogie." As in "Cruzin',," Guerrero's lyrics project the scope of barrio popular-cultural practices—in this case associated with the youth style complex of *pachuquismo* (fashion, language use, dance, music, body marking)—across a range of urban sites in the Southwest Chicano "nation," also identified by their *caló* translations: Tula (Tucson), Sanjo (San Jose), Sacra (Sacramento), El Chuco (El Paso), Alburque (Albuquerque), and Sanfra (San Francisco). The song was one of several by Guerrero adapted for the stage and film versions of the Luis Valdez–directed musical "Zoot Suit." Not coincidentally, José Montoya was consulted by Valdez for authenticity of design in creating the *pachuco* fashions for the original Los Angeles theatrical production.

In Montoya's litany, then, the various barrios are named as if they were points on a projected itinerary: "let's go to Barstow," "vamos a la Broadway, en Sanjo," and so on. They are, moreover, not just compared as related spaces; they are connected as intended destinations for the speakers. The compendium of place-names, therefore, identifies a series of local Chicano geographies connected in a national network. Such an evocation of homologous social spaces has an important precursor in Raúl Salinas' classic poem "A Trip through the Mind Jail." After rendering homage to his recollected childhood barrio of La Loma in Austin, "demolished, erased forever from / the universe" (1972 : 182) by freeway construction, the poem closes with the equation of various barrios as geographies remembered and reclaimed by the poet in an agonistic and existential struggle to retain his spiritual well-being in prison:

> i needed you then . . . identity . . . a sense of belonging.
> i need you now.
> So essential to adult days of imprisonment,
> you keep me away from INSANITY'S hungry jaws;
>   Smiling/Laughing/Crying.
>
>   i respect your having been:
>   My Loma of Austin
>   my Rose Hill of Los Angeles
>   my West Side of San Anto
>   my Quinto of Houston
>   my Jackson of San Jo
>   my Segundo of El Paso
>   my Barelas of Alburque
>   my Westside of Denver
>
> Flats, Los Marcos, Maravilla, Calle Guadalupe, Magnolia,
> Buena Vista, Mateo, La Seis, Chiquis, El Sur and all
>   Chicano neighborhoods that now exist and once
>   existed; somewhere . . . , someone remembers. . . .
> (Ibid.: 186)

Expanding the scope of Chicano "second cities" in individual metropolitan areas, El Trio Casindio—like Salinas' more dire invocation—identifies a Chicano alternative nation in the circuit of barrios connected by the spoken itinerary of "Cruzin'." Ironically, this network is made possible by the very automotive and freeway technologies that have otherwise been major forces of urban Chicano marginalization. El Trio Casindio's subaltern map thus identifies a peculiarly contemporary configuration of the Chicano homeland. In the spoken background, the singular form of "our neighborhood" is multiplied to the plural form of "our neighborhoods." This national nexus of urban Chicano cultural/place-identity expands the constrained localization of any single barrio (as the only place for Chicanos to circulate) even as it multiplies the urban geographic referents of the continuing tension between barrioized containment and barriological expression.

FIGURE 50. Interstate 280 under construction through downtown San Jose. Courtesy of California Department of Transportation.

Between Nationalism and Women's Standpoint

F I V E *Lorna Dee Cervantes' Freeway Poems*

For Chicanos and Mexicans in the Southwest there is a continual tension between the shadow of an earlier central presence and their contemporary marginalization in a homeland. This mapping and remapping adds to the disguised issues of history and identity embedded in the western landscape for Mexicans.

— AMALIA MESA-BAINS,
"Land and Spirituality in the Descansos"

. . . locating ethnic and women's history in urban space can contribute to what might be called a politics of place construction, redefining the mainstream experience, and making visible some of its forgotten parts.

— DOLORES HAYDEN, *The Power of Place*

If the Los Angeles metropolitan region is a paradigmatic site of modern urban restructuring—with all of its attendant problems and promises—it is not the only place in California to have been monumentally refashioned in the contemporary period. While no other city in the state (or the nation) has surpassed the sheer volume of Los Angeles' twentieth-century spatial and demographic expansion, the pace of urban development in the quarter century following World War II was matched by San Jose, its later-blooming doppelganger to the north. The *Los Angeles Times*-led growth interests of the postwar period had their counterparts in San Jose's Progress Committee, formed in 1944. According to the historian John Findlay, the committee's "aggressive growth . . . agenda reached fruition between 1950 and 1970 under the administration of A. P. Hamann, the city manager, who sought to make San Jose 'the Los Angeles of the North'" (1992 : 21). The urban expansion of San Jose and greater Santa Clara County was indeed to be marveled at for the phenomenal pace and scale of its metamorphosis.

The economic engine driving this transformation was, like that of Los Angeles in the same period, primed by the industrial exigencies of wartime defense. If in Los Angeles the boom in defense spending laid the foundation for the region's major aerospace industry, the war years in Santa Clara County planted the seeds of the high-technology electronics industry that would later bloom in the Silicon Valley. As more and more electronics firms developed in or moved to the area, the continuous demand for both highly skilled professionals and low-skilled factory and service employees pushed the region into a leading national position as a center of population gain. As documented by AnnaLee Saxenian (1981 : 63), the figures for Santa Clara County were far ahead of both the California and national averages. From 1950 to 1960 it grew 121 percent compared to 48.5 percent and 18.5 percent for the state and the nation, respectively. Although the average growth rate dropped to 66 percent in the 1960s, this was almost two and one-half times the California rate and five times that for the rest of the country. Within these figures, San Jose easily surpassed all other cities in the county (ibid.) and, for much of the period, in the country as well. The city even achieved mass cultural iconicity as a place to move to by way of the hit song "Do You Know the Way to San Jose," written by Burt Bacharach and Hal David and popularized by Dionne Warwick. With Los Angeles ironically serving as antithesis, the lyrics beckon the listener to leave behind "the great big freeway" for the more open (and breathable) space in San Jose. The California dream, apparently exhausted in the South, moved to (formerly) fertile ground to the north.

With the tremendous influx of new residents, the renowned agricultural fields of the Santa Clara Valley—which were said to rival the prewar orchards of Southern California in production and promotion—were sacrificed to the omnivorous real estate demand for single-family housing units. Thus, while the policies of the Progress Committee "increased the size of the city from 11 square miles in 1940 to 137 square miles in 1970," the same period witnessed a precipitous decline in "the number of acres devoted to orchards in Santa Clara County . . . from 101,666 to 25,511" (Findlay 1992 : 31–32). The specific pattern of spatial restructuring in the county was not enacted willy-nilly. Rather, residential settlement patterns

> replicate[d] the dichotomized occupational and class structure gener-ated by the dominant electronics industry onto the organization of urban space. The affluent [and overwhelmingly white] professional-managerial strata of electronics employees are insulated in the western foothill cities, in Palo Alto, and to a lesser extent in the other north county industrial cities with easy access to the electronics complex clustered around Stanford, while the large low-income minority pro-duction workforce is concentrated in the bedroom city of San Jose and the adjacent cities of Milpitas and Campbell. (Saxenian 1981:81)

This conspicuous segregation of the "Los Angeles of the North" provides the broad spatial context that poet Lorna Dee Cervantes mediates in several of her works. Born in San Francisco's Latino Mission district into a self-described "welfare class," Cervantes moved at the age of five with her mother and brother to her grandmother's home in downtown San Jose, during the peak of its supercity redevelopment. As a child and young woman, she would thus witness, like her generational colleagues in Los Angeles and elsewhere, the tremendous changes in the built environment of the city and its particu-larly harsh impacts upon her centrally situated barrio community. In this case, the signal development was the construction of the region's major arterial freeway, Interstate 280.

In her poem "Declaration on a Day of Little Inspiration," published in 1976, Cervantes identified this technospatial icon in clearly antagonistic lan-guage as "the great piss-stream of freeway / which covers my barrio, / sops my Atlantis." In a concise rendering of its most disruptive geographic and cultural consequences, the freeway simultaneously eviscerates her present community's cultural landscape ("my barrio") and her mythohistorical place-identity ("my Atlantis"). The latter is a syncretic transfiguration of the Chi-cano homeland of Aztlán, by which Cervantes evokes the nationalist motif of a "lost land" via a seemingly more universal Western cultural referent. Her critical spatial perspective in "Declaration" is akin to the broad deconstruc-tive vision of many other barriological writers. However, in a group of poems (from her 1981 collection, *Emplumada*) that employ the freeway as a leit-motif of displacement, Cervantes mediates a wider range of social-geographic consciousness. The specific texts are "Poema para los californios muertos," "Freeway 280," and "Beneath the Shadow of the Freeway."

Within the shadow of this resonant technological icon and a paired food-processing plant in the related poem "Cannery Town in August" (1981:6), Cervantes variously focuses on the historical violations (and the violation of history) done to the greater Californio population through intercultural conquest and the violations done specifically to Chicanas through intracultural gender conflict. Cervantes will thus speak at times from a fundamentally nationalist perspective, defending the present and historical interests of *la raza*, then decry the patriarchal oppressions within that same *raza*. A coordinated analysis of the poems literally reveals a tightening perimeter of geographies. These varying spatial foci figuratively plot the critical ideological coordinates that create Cervantes' "differential consciousness" of place and identity, which moves "between and among . . . separatist modes of oppositional consciousness considered as variables, in order to disclose the distinctions among them" (Sandoval 1991:14).

As a heuristic device, we can therefore identify an emergent graph to be drawn in the intertextual discussion of the three "freeway" poems. This graph illustrates a series of concentric circles in which "Poema para los californios muertos" draws the widest circumference of meaning around the historical process of cultural displacement. "Freeway 280" tightens the circumference of meaning by illustrating the contemporary configurations of an aggrieved San Jose barrio. Finally, "Beneath the Shadow of the Freeway" draws its circle around a domestic, matriarchal home in the barrio community. In its movement between a nationalist ethnic perspective and a Chicana gender standpoint, Cervantes' intertextual map may be read as a figure of the poet's complex location in the postnationalist and emergent-feminist cusp of Chicano cultural history and discourse in the 1970s and early 1980s, the period in which the poems were written and first discussed. The productive tensions that surface in the intertext of the identified poems highlight the shifting status of women's concerns within the dominant masculinist contours of politics and culture in the Chicano movement period.

A BLOOD MEMORY OF PLACE:
"POEMA PARA LOS CALIFORNIAS MUERTOS"

A key objective of "Poema para los californios muertos" (hereafter "Californios") is to deconstruct the Anglo-promoted "fantasy heritage" (McWilliams 1948:35–47) of pre-Anglo California history. As discussed in Chapter 1, this fantasy heritage paints the idyllic picture of benevolent priests "civilizing" the indigenous people, while cultured Spanish dons and lovely señoritas lived a pristine rancho life. The literary origins of this pseudohistory can be traced at least as far back as 1884, with the publication of Helen Hunt Jackson's romantic novel *Ramona*. But the credit for consciously promoting the ideological apparatus of a "Southwest genre" in literary and cultural discourses must go to Charles F. Lummis, around the turn of the century (Calderón 1990: 214–215; Calderón and Saldívar 1991:2–3). These discourses, ostensibly concerned with the celebration and preservation of the distinctive cultures of the U.S. Southwest, were equally deployed to market the first monumental projects of real estate and tourist development of the vast borderlands (Davis 1990:20; McWilliams 1976:70). The idealized histories of "old" California are still celebrated in civic "fiesta days" and "mission days" organized around the state, with regional variations throughout the borderlands states, while its visual imagery is inscribed in the built environment through the ubiquitous "Mission-style" architecture of arcades, interior courtyards, and red-tiled roofs.

Within the context of such fetishized and commodified cultural iconography, the plaque inscription identified in the poem's epigraph (*"Once a refuge for Mexican Californios . . . /*—Plaque outside a restaurant / in Los Altos, California, 1974") documents, to Cervantes' critical view, this ideologically overdetermined Californio heritage. For her, the Southwestern genre masks a history of conflict and conquest beneath a self-serving fiction: that an idyllic "Spanish" era simply ran its course before the inevitable and peaceful expansion of Euro-American influence.

"Californios" exposes this celebratory facade in a cutting rhetorical question: "What refuge did you find here / ancient Californios?" The question is rhetorical (they found none) because it is preceded by an account of the poet's indignation when confronted by the inscribed message.

> I run my fingers
> across this brass plaque.
> Its cold stirs in me a memory
> of silver buckles and spent bullets,
> of embroidered shawls and dark rebozos.
> Yo recuerdo los antepasados muertos.
> Los recuerdo en la sangre,
> la sangre fértil.
> [I remember my dead forebears.
> I remember them in my blood,
> my fertile blood.] [1] (Cervantes 1981:42)

By characterizing her knowledge of a hegemonically erased history as memory rather than institutionally documented fact, the speaker stresses her intimately felt and living link to this other history.

The remembered and embodied quality of the speaker's historical consciousness recalls the visceral and affective impulse that, for Walter Benjamin, motivates a materialist reading of the past: "To articulate the past historically does not mean to recognize it 'the way it really was' (Ranke). It means to seize hold of a memory as it flashes up at a moment of danger" (1968:257). Following Benjamin, I argue that the "moment of danger" that stirs the speaker in "Californios" is not a discrete instant or event in time. Rather, the "danger" is best understood as corresponding to the historical moment of the poem's genesis, in the wake of the nationalist Chicano movement. The movement-as-"moment" exerts a strong residual effect on the social poetics in "Californios," particularly in Cervantes' mediation of the continuous marginalization of Californios-cum-Chicanos in an Anglo-dominant society. "Californios" clearly does not articulate the past "the way it really was." Instead, Cervantes' counterhegemonic articulation of the Californio past is circumscribed by the residual influence of Chicano nationalist ideology. Nevertheless, even within this ideological milieu, Cervantes introduces a woman-centered critique that, in other poems to be discussed, will develop into a more fully realized interrogation of patriarchal culture itself.

This critique is poetically figured in the image of a fertile blood memory that gives a bodily dimension to the poetic deconstruction of the fantasy heritage. Specifically, it materializes the historical practices and consequences of Anglo-American occupation upon Mexican California women (californianas). The violence of intercultural conquest and conflict is figured through the sexual abuse and disfiguring of a woman's body. Los Altos, the predominantly white city with the Spanish-language name, is thus understood as the illegitimate progeny born of a violation of the Californio population, generally, and the californianas, particularly.

> What a bastard child, this city
> lost in the soft
> llorando de las madres [crying of the mothers].
> Californios moan like husbands of the raped,
> husbands de la tierra [of the earth],
> tierra la madre [the mother earth].
> (Cervantes 1981:42)

The metaphoric image of Californio men moaning "like husbands of the raped" expresses a complex ideological position signaling a concern for the specific experiences of women under conquest while it simultaneously reproduces certain ideologies of heterosexual familism. As evidence of the latter point, women are portrayed primarily in their reproductive function as mothers and heterosexual partners. Norma Alarcón has noted the way in which such representations situate *mexicanas* as "the bedrock of the 'ideal family' at the center of the nation-making process, despite discontinuous modes of its construction" (1990:253). Thus, the sounds of women moaning for other women as sisters, friends, or lovers—as an affective register marking a space of social relations among women that is partly or wholly outside the patriarchal purview—are not heard, being subsumed in the tears of the mother-wife figure.

Nevertheless, a woman-centered perspective is intimated through Cervantes' evocation of the physically violated bodies of women. This material emphasis on the body gestures toward a spatial and epistemological orientation fundamental to feminist critiques of women's oppression. Adrienne Rich characterizes this orientation in her prescription to identify the space of women's social being not, in the first instance, "with a continent or a country or a house, but with the geography closest in—the body. Here at least I know I exist, that living human individual whom the young Marx called 'the first premise of all human history'" (1986:212). Her call to situate the politics of women's experience first and foremost in the core geographies of their own bodies—and thus to always be cognizant of "[t]he politics of pregnability and motherhood . . . of orgasm . . . of rape and incest. . . ." (ibid.)—resonates with Cervantes' social poetics in "Californios." Cervantes is similarly "locating the grounds from which to speak with authority *as* [a] wom[a]n. Not to transcend this body but to reclaim it" (ibid.:213; original emphasis) in identification with the violated bodies of her *antepasadas* (forebears).

And yet, the women-centered gestures in "Californios" are not fully divorced from masculinist discourses of nationalism. The most telling residue of masculinism is the metaphorizing of the land, *la tierra*, as the female body of the wife/mother: "husbands de la tierra / tierra la madre." It is a rhetorical convention in nationalist discourse to speak of the national culture and territory in terms of a woman's body. Characteristics such as fertility, nurturance, desire, and penetration are commonly identified with the feminized social geography of the homeland.[2] Particularly in situations of actual or perceived anticolonial struggle, the feminization of land makes the colonizers' occupa-

tion of that land an even more heinous "violation" to the men involved in
resistance. The feminized geography of the motherland becomes a fulcrum of
conflict: as the protected property of resistance and the coveted object of conquest. In the sexualized anticolonial narrative, the colonizers' assault upon the
land-as-woman threatens the purported integrity of the patriarchal culture *(la
patria)* with miscegenation.[3] Intercultural violence done to women thus represents violence against the ethnos through its violation of the very producers
of future bodies for that community. For this reason, masculinist anticolonial
rhetoric often speaks of men defending *their* women, *their* lands, *their* traditions, and other constituent elements of the national *patria*. Whether seen
from the site of resistance or of conquest, the metaphorized body of land-
as-woman is a passive receiving entity, acted upon by men. Cervantes' gendered identification with the historical bodies of violated women is not
entirely separated from such cultural nationalist representations of the land-
as-violated-woman.

The original violence of cultural and socioeconomic dislocation experienced by the Californios under Anglo-American rule is then projected forward to the speaker's own historical moment as the Santa Clara Valley is disfigured by a signal infrastructural development of modern California culture:

> These older towns die
> into stretches of freeway.
> The high scaffolding cuts a clean cesarean
> across belly valleys and fertile dust. (Cervantes 1981:42)

The curving hillside stretch of I-280, which runs behind Los Altos, also runs
along the back side of some of the wealthiest communities on the West Coast,
such as Hillsborough, Burlingame, and Palo Alto, as well as Stanford University (see Fig. 51). A bitter irony registers in the very name of the freeway.
Aside from its numerical designation (I-280), this particular section of the
freeway is named "The Junípero Serra Highway: The Most Beautiful Highway in America." It may very well be, since it was consciously planned with
the highest standards for parkway landscape design. However, this com-
memorative expanse of highway represents another ideologically masked history of conquering violence, although this one is not treated by Cervantes.
In this case, the aggressions were directed by the Spanish missionary priest
Father Junípero Serra, who has been at the center of a continuing debate regarding his possible designation as California's first saint. Native American
groups particularly, but others as well, are vehemently opposing the canoniza-

tion efforts, citing Serra's flagrant abuses and virtual enslavement, in many cases, of indigenous peoples. No homes were razed, families disrupted, or communities disfigured in the construction of this memorial section of the freeway. While the formerly rural lowlands to the south and east were being razed by the Santa Clara Valley's urban-industrial expansion, the towns and cities in the western foothills and Palo Alto were preserved because they were

> an ideal environment for professional and upper-class reproduction.
> As one industry representative noted, "Our firm relocated here
> because it's an ideal place for millionaires to live." . . . The area retains
> the peaceful, orchard-like character which the whole of the Santa
> Clara Valley was so famed for during the first half of the century. . . .
> These communities are designed to remain well insulated from the
> communities to the south and east which house the county's large
> industrial workforce. (Quoted in Saxenian 1981:83–84)

But when the freeway winds down toward San Jose, it leaves the graceful contours of the hillside and "cuts a clean cesarean" line through the valley and the speaker's central urban neighborhood. The effects of this infrastructural traversal of the barrio will be discussed shortly with regard to "Freeway 280."

In Los Altos ("The Heights"), the speaker seeks and speaks to the ghosts of her "antepasados muertos" (dead ancestors) who inhabit "the shadows of these white, high-class homes." In oratorical fashion, she lucidly images the process by which, as Walter Benjamin notes of all histories of conflict and conquest, "the present rulers step over those who are lying prostrate" (1968: 258). Already displaced by historical conquest, her *antepasados* are further obscured as their very ghosts fall under the shadows of "white ghosts."

> Soy la hija pobrecita
> pero puedo maldecir estas fantasmas blancas.
> Las fantasmas tuyas deben aquí quedarse,
> solas las tuyas.
> [I am only your poor daughter
> but I can curse these white ghosts.
> Only your ghosts should remain here,
> only yours.] (Cervantes 1981:42)

The image of obscured Californio ghosts recalls the eclipsing of lived Californio history by the hegemonic operations of a fantasy heritage and Hispani-

FIGURE 51.   Design study (enhanced photograph) of the Junípero Serra Highway.
Hoover Tower of Stanford University visible in upper right. Courtesy of California
Department of Transportation.

cist historiography.[4] It also echoes de Certeau's contention that "[t]here is no
place that is not haunted by many different spirits hidden there in silence,
spirits one can 'invoke' or not. Haunted places are the only ones people can
live in—and this inverts the schema of the *Panopticon*" (1984: 108; original
emphasis). Clearly, the speaker is turning over the hierarchy of power inscribed in the spatial order of things as she casts her gaze up and against the
"white high-class homes" that otherwise look down from their heights to her
location. It is, therefore, against these hegemonic operations that the speaker
angrily invokes the specters of her cultural past: "Las fantasmas tuyas deben
aquí quedarse, / solas las tuyas." Benjamin provides a further perspective for
understanding the impulse that stirs the speaker's materialist reordering of the
phantasmic geography: "Only that historian will have the gift of fanning the

spark of hope in the past who is firmly convinced that *even the dead* will not be safe from the enemy if he wins. And this enemy has not ceased to be victorious" (1968 : 257; original emphasis). The speaker's vehement cursing of "estas fantasmas blancas" is a measure of how she is fanning the spark of hope in her Californio past, returning its ghosts to their proper place in the historical and cultural geography. In reordering the historical geography of the region, Cervantes is also reinscribing herself in its cultural landscape. The poet-speaker's indignation at her *antepasados'* multiple displacements reminds us that "[e]ven when official histories have erased the popular remembrance of belonging, the landscape succeeds in restoring to us the power of our presence" (Mesa-Bains 1994 : n.p.).

Cervantes closes the poem with a meditation upon the artifacts at the restaurant that first stirred the speaker's blood memory. To her deconstructive view, these relics are correlative objects signifying the trivialization or, worse, the erasure of her *antepasados'* experience by the mythologies of California's past that pass for official, and thus hegemonic, history. The stories inscribed in these "yanqui remnants" leave no room for her memory:

> In this place I see nothing but strangers.
> On the shelves there are bitter antiques,
> yanqui remnants
> y estos no de los Californios.
> [and these are not of the Californios.] (Cervantes 1981 : 43)

The poem concludes with what, at first impression, may seem an incongruous use of natural imagery:

> A blue jay shrieks
> above the pungent odor of crushed
> eucalyptus and the pure scent
> of rage. (Ibid.)

While they may appear to lack denotative reference to the preceding narrative, such images harbor a very personal as well as a political significance for the poet:

> I was always very influenced by nature. When I was little, I always
> wanted to go move in the mountains. . . . And [later] . . . when I was
> about sixteen, I really did go through this period where I had this

amazing connection with these birds that talked to me. . . . So the bird
imagery is very real to me. (Binder 1985:48)

The closing allusions to the blue jay and the crushed eucalyptus thus reflect
her childhood fascination for an alternative to her exacerbated urban landscape in central San Jose. A curious consequence of Cervantes' poetic evo-
cations of birds and other such scenic elements is that some readers have
mistaken the setting of her poems: "It's funny, because just recently I am beginning to get feedback on . . . *[Emplumada]* and a lot of the comments, especially from non-Chicanos or from people back East and other places, is that
it is very rural. . . . Well, San Jose could be rural but it is not" (ibid.). More to
the historical point, San Jose *was* a predominantly rural environment for much
of this century. However, when Cervantes was coming of age there, the city's
proportion of open space was a dismal "8 acres . . . per 1000 residents, compared to 35 acres in nearby San Francisco" (Saxenian 1985:90). In this respect, San Jose's postwar leadership further realized its wish of becoming the
Los Angeles of the north.

The curiosity of the topographical misreading of Cervantes' work is that
it reveals the standard dichotomization that identifies natural figurative elements with a "country" setting. By confusing this typical association in some
of her readers, Cervantes unconsciously complicates the traditional rural-
urban binary. The compelling social criticism mediated in much natural literary symbolism, common to both pastoral and romantic narrative, rests in
its critique of the disfigurations of the country by the city. However, Raymond Williams has ably demonstrated that this critical structure of feeling
has become equally manifest in the city, itself a preeminent site of capitalism's deformations of place, labor, and social relations. As in the case of several other texts I have discussed, Cervantes' quasi-romantic critical sensibility
does not so much lament the loss of a geography because it is "natural"—
recall her specification that "San Jose could be rural but it is not"—but rather
because it is "native" to her experience (Williams 1973:138). In "Californios," the chronotopic mediation of the transformations from a Californio
"country" past to a Chicano "city" present shows the disfigurement of a rural
topography and decries the invading technologies responsible. For this reason, nature joins the poet in cursing the "foreign" violators with aggressive
shrieks from the birds and "pungent odors" let loose by the "crushed eucalyptus." The "pure scent of rage," then, is a nonverbal sign of dissent shared
between the poet and the natural-cum-native environment to which she feels
positively bound.

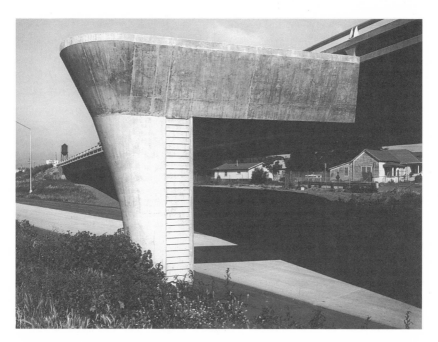

FIGURE 52.   The freeway (I-280) in the barrio. Courtesy of California Department of Transportation.

WOMEN'S WORK: REIFIED LABOR AND SUSTAINING SKILLS IN "FREEWAY 280" AND "CANNERY TOWN IN AUGUST"

"Freeway 280" narrows the spatial-temporal scope represented in "Californios," presenting a close-up view of the freeway's disruptive effects upon the central San Jose barrio it dissects. As it describes the displacement of homes, the poem also evokes a Chicano working-class milieu.

> Las casitas [The little houses] near the gray cannery,
> nestled amid wild abrazos [hugs] of climbing roses
> and man-high red geraniums
> are gone now. The freeway conceals it
> all beneath a raised scar. (Cervantes 1981 : 39)

While little explicit detail is given about the freeway's presence in the life of this San Jose barrio, its ominous impact on the community is implicated in its environmental effect. Not only is the barrio scarred by the freeway, it is enveloped as well by the rancid "smell of tomatoes burning / on swing shift in the greasy summer air."

A fuller rendering of the physical and psychological effects intimated in "Freeway 280" is presented in the companion poem "Cannery Town in August." As if to link the ambience of "Cannery Town" with that of "Freeway 280," Cervantes sets the scene of the former in the same stifling summer season of the latter. Moreover, she opens "Cannery Town" by noting a similarly invasive aspect of the cannery: "All night it humps the air. / Speechless, the steam rises / from the cannery columns." The male-figured cannery assumes itself upon the air of the town, as the cannery work environment does upon the bodies of the women employed there. The monstrous phalluses of the cannery columns call attention to the gendered status and labor conditions affecting Chicana workers. Working men are conspicuously absent from Cervantes' expressionistic scene, suggesting, as well, a critique of the gender politics in the cannery industry's hierarchical production process. In this labor process, women's work has always been secondary to that of men, characterized by a lower piece-rate wage scale and more physically difficult and tedious work (Ruiz 1990; Zavella 1987).

Reading "Freeway 280" and "Cannery Town in August" as a pair evokes the synaesthetic impact of the cannery upon women working in it. In so doing, Cervantes practices a narrative rhetoric that Ann Cvetkovich reads in Karl Marx's account of nineteenth-century factory labor. She points out that in *Capital* "the worker's body is a metaphor or a sensational figure in his account of factory labor. Marx gives the abstract social relations of capitalism a sensational force by representing the physical suffering of the human body" (1992 : 187). Cervantes similarly represents sensational effects upon workers' bodies. The "smell of tomatoes burning" and the tactile feel of "greasy summer air" in "Freeway 280" are repeated and aggravated by the "smell of whiskey and tomatoes," by the taste, touch, and sight of "peach fuzz reddening their lips and eyes" in "Cannery Town." Their very voices are disabled by the industrial process, as the speaker notes that they are "not speaking, dumbed / by the can's clamor" (1982 : 6). The effect of this multisensory assault is summed up in the disturbing image of their "bodyless / uniforms and spinach-specked shoes," in which a devastating reification is represented in the very decorporealization of the women. Cvetkovich's reading of *Capital* is further relevant here as she describes how "[t]he reversal of relations between subjects and objects, or persons and things, that characterizes the relation between capital and labor is represented in microcosm by the image of the machine as a living, and hence monstrous, being and the worker's body as a mechanical, alienated, and inhuman tool" (1992:187). Elsewhere, she observes that the very "flesh, blood, nerves and muscles of the worker give life to the system of production but leave the body itself dead with fatigue and sensory deprivation" (ibid.:183). In like fashion, Cervantes' narrator can only "imagine" the cannery workers as they "drift in monochrome down the dark / moon-possessed streets." Traces of phantom Californios come through in the melancholia of the narrator's speculations: "[the women] walk / like a dream, with no one / waiting in the shadows / to palm them back to living." These women have become disembodied ghosts like their Californio culture and *antepasados*, as their alienated labor is rendered in purgatorial images of death-in-life.

The intimations of social death so strongly rendered in "Cannery Town in August" may be read as an intertext implicit in the image of the gray cannery in "Freeway 280." Consequently, like Ron Arias' Fausto, who resolves to escape the sense of containment and imminent death in his home by the freeway and freight yards, the speaker in "Freeway 280" at one time "wanted out, wanted the rigid lanes / to take me to a place without sun" (Cervantes 1981: 39), far from the stifling cannery environment of her barrio. The irony, of course, is that she looked to one invasive structure to carry her away from the other. And yet, the desire is expressed in the past tense. This temporal detail underscores Cervantes' understanding of "community" in the poem. Although the speaker had wanted to escape the social confinement of her barrio, it is uncertain that she ever left. And if she did leave, she has returned, affirming the knowledge of her community's resilience in revitalizing their scarred social geography. Women's work is key to this sociospatial reclamation.

Following the opening description of the freeway's devastation, the narrative of reclamation is introduced through a disclaiming rejoinder:

> But under the fake windsounds of the open lanes,
> in the abandoned lots below, new grasses sprout,
> wild mustard remembers, old gardens
> come back stronger than they were,
> trees have been left standing in their yards.
> Albaricoqueros, cerezos, nogales . . .
> [Apricot trees, cherry trees, walnut trees}
> Viejitas come here with paper bags to gather greens.
> Espinaca, verdolagas, yerbabuena . . .
> [Spinach, purslane, mint . . .] (Ibid.)

FIGURE 53.   Flora and freeway, downtown San Jose. Photograph by Raúl Homero
Villa, 1995.

At one level, this image of flora versus freeway recalls Cervantes' deep identification with the natural environment. Thus, in a surface reading of the
stanza, the return of plant life suggests a quasi-pastoral opposition to the devastating and subordinating social technologies of the freeway and the cannery.
However, the crucial element here is not simply the resilience of the plant life
and its symbolic associations; rather, it is the knowledge the women exercise
in identifying and making use of these urban gardens. I will say more about
women's horticultural practices shortly. For now, however, it is worth com-
paring Cervantes' poetic narrative of the floral return with the quasi-pastoral
reclamation of Elysian Park in Ron Arias' *The Road to Tamazunchale*. This
comparison is instructive for specifying the woman-centered knowledge that
informs Cervantes' poetics and distinguishes her barriological narrative from
Arias'.

In both Arias' novel and Cervantes' poetry, the dystopian impact of dominant urban spatial practices on Chicano communities is opposed by popular-
cultural counterpractices that combat despair by foregrounding the community's available resources. In *Tamazunchale*, these exist in the *rasquache*
sensibility (Ybarra-Frausto 1989), which is a form of creative adaptation to

the constraints of limited means and oppressive circumstances. The community reappropriations of the Los Angeles River "dead-end" zone for the snow carnival and the abandoned theater for the play are examples of this sensibility in practice. The reappropriation of Elysian Park that concludes *Tamazunchale* is, in a more magical manifestation, the third major example of *rasquache* counterhegemonic practice. In this closing scene, in all the magical transformations, one female character's metamorphosis suggests Arias' intuition about the sphere of women's productive domestic culture, a domain foregrounded by Cervantes: "In the distance Cuca trotted around like a fox, sniffing, poking, tasting every usable herb and plant, from pole to pole, from arctic ferns and alpine reeds to the mosses of Tierra del Fuego" (Arias 1987:123).

The very same activity is described in "Freeway 280": "Viejitas come here with paper bags to gather greens. / Espinaca, verdolagas, yerbabuena. . . ." This detail, like so many others in Arias' and Cervantes' works, yields social meanings when mined for its embedded historical contents. As in "Californios," however, Cervantes does not pretend to represent an objective social history "the way it really was" (recalling Benjamin). Rather, she draws liberally upon a broad historical analysis of the gendered division of labor, using it as an ur-myth for a valorization of women's productive skills in her community. The broad feminist and historical-material analysis that resonates in Cervantes' poem is summarized by Maria Mies, who argues persuasively that women's productivity is historically

> the precondition of all other human productivity, not only in the sense that they are *always* the producers of new men and women, but also in the sense that the first social division of labour, that between female gatherers (later also cultivators) and predominantly male hunters, could take place only on the basis of a developed female productivity.
>
> Female productivity consisted, above all, in the ability to provide the daily subsistence, the guarantee of survival, for the members of the clan or band. . . . It has been proved conclusively, particularly by the critical research of feminist scholars, that the survival of mankind has been due much more to "woman-the-gatherer" than to "man-the-hunter." (1986:58)

In "Freeway 280," Cervantes relates a more immediate and specific manifestation of this larger history, evoking the mestiza culture of her own ethnic community. Within a wasteland of urban development, the *viejitas* exercise their traditional agricultural knowledge and skills for the subsistence and survival of themselves, their families, and their community. *They* know where the wild mustard grows and the old gardens stood.

A brief catalog of fruit and nut trees ("Albaricoqueros, cerezos, nogales") as well as edible and medicinal greens and herbs ("Espinaca, verdolagas, yer-babuena") in "Freeway 280" symbolizes the central role of woman in guaranteeing the survival of the community. The *viejitas* unwaveringly exercise this productive role. In spite of the devastations of the freeway, they return to the old gardens that, we might infer, they had previously tended, if not planted in the first place. The *viejitas*, like the old gardens, "come back stronger than they were," never capitulating in despair to the dystopian effects of hegemonic urban planning. Their "garden" activities, however, also contain less-empowering associations. If, in "Freeway 280," women's domestic horticultural labor is a symbol and practice against their domination, in "Cannery Town," women's industrial agricultural labor is the sign and exercise of their abject subordination. The tension of these two agricultural images, which simultaneously represent women's productive resilience and women's productive reification, points out a key difference between Ron Arias' decidedly utopian *rasquachismo* and the distinctively female and more tenuous expressions of this cultural sensibility in Cervantes' two poems.

Within "Freeway 280" alone, the range of meanings attached to the *viejitas'* horticultural labor is not solely enabling. The narrative privileging of woman's skills in guaranteeing the life needs (nutritional, medicinal) of the community does not consider that they may be socially bound to such labors by a patriarchal division of labor. The latter has been a major point of contention in radical feminist interrogations of the linked concepts of "home" and "community." For example, in her powerful criticism of humanistic geography for its claims that home and community provide the "ultimate sense of place" underlying one's subject-formation, Gillian Rose draws on several feminist scholars who, "[f]ar from celebrating women's involvement in community and place, . . . saw such involvement as a symptom of women's oppression . . . associat[ing] 'the power of women' with the 'subversion of community,'" and further characterized "community as the social locale through which the state maintained the traditional [exploitative] family form . . ." (1993:54). Seen through such critical lenses, the *viejitas'* likely unpaid work would be more properly re-productive than productive, securing the "private," domestic conditions necessary to support "public" (and historically male) paid labor.

The tension between considering women's reproductive labors as instances of female resilience or as evidence of patriarchal repression calls attention to the *"domesticana"* standpoint in Cervantes' work. I introduced this concept, drawn from the Chicana *altarista* (altar maker) and cultural critic Amalia Mesa-Bains, in the discussion of Helena María Viramontes' story "Neighbors" in Chapter 3. This complex Chicana critical epistemology is also relevant to the conflicting associations of women's reproductive domestic labor represented in Cervantes' poetry. In an essay theorizing the ways in which certain contemporary Chicana visual artists evoke, interpret, and reconfigure the gendered constraints and roles of their *antepasadas*, Mesa-Bains characterizes this Chicana survivalist ethos and practice as being "like its male counterpart *[rasquachismo]*, the product of resistance to the majority culture and the affirmation of other cultural values. It also grows out of women's restrictions within the [Chicano] culture" (1991:132).

In "Freeway 280," the *domesticana* resourcefulness of the speaker's female elders in the face of devastating urban modernization provides her with a model of active resilience and cultural survival. It is, as Caren Kaplan has noted of recent feminist discourse, "a view of cultural marginality [that] necessitates the recognition of specific skills" (1987:187). While Kaplan's observations refer to the oppositional consciousness manifested in women's reading and writing practices (as such, they are more directly applicable to the textual practice of Cervantes' own "specific skills" as a poet), Cervantes takes this "view of cultural marginality" in representing the specific practical knowledge of the female elders. Observing and reflecting upon the labors of the *viejitas*, the speaker reconsiders her wish to leave the barrio ("Once I wanted out"). Drawn back to this aggrieved social geography, she searches for a cultural identity and consciousness severed from her by the pressures and demands of a contradictory cultural citizenship:

> Maybe it's here
> en los campos extraños de esta ciudad
> [in the strange fields of this city]
> where I'll find it, that part of me
> mown under
> like a corpse
> or a loose seed. (Cervantes 1981:39)

Here, Cervantes portrays a struggle between dystopian and utopian possibilities in the opposition between the corpse's death and the loose seed's potential rebirth, without indicating a necessary resolution.

But in closing with the image of the loose seed, Cervantes hints at the

FIGURE 54. "...los campos extraños de esta ciudad...." Photographs by Raúl
Homero Villa, 1995.

speaker's recovered desire for connection with the community she had wished to leave. Recalling the poem's narrative of floral resilience and return, the potential is strong that the loose seed can find root in the strange fields of the city. Yet even within this optimistic prognosis, there is an uncertainty: if the speaker had left her barrio, how might she be received upon her return? The strong element of moral and cultural conservatism in the *mexicano* population, particularly with regard to women's activities and roles, could impede the easy reintegration of the returning speaker, particularly if she is considered "loose," in the moral sense, by the community. In "Oaxaca, 1974," Cervantes shows precisely how greater Mexican society did reject her on the grounds of moral and cultural impurity. On a larger voyage of "return" to a homeland, she is met with derision: "México gags, / ¡Esputa! / on this bland pochaseed." The conjunctive term "Esputa" plays on the aural similarities and signified meanings of *escupar* (to spit) and *es puta* (she is a whore). Like the "loose seed" of "Freeway 280," the "Pocha" (assimilated Mexican) is a seed that has not and may not find soil to root in.

By underscoring the ideological tensions intimated in "Freeway 280," I mean to caution against too easily glorifying the traditional cultural practices of the *viejitas*. Cordelia Candelaria, for example, argues that the "poem's most important revelation . . . is that the physical impediment of the highway cannot hide or destroy the irrepressible life of the people uprooted by the 'gray cannery.'" Citing the same images, discussed above, of floral return and of the *viejitas'* reharvesting the old gardens, she concludes that these "descriptions celebrate the traditional life of *el pueblo* and how that life asserts itself in spite of the most imposing obstacles set against it from without" (1986:158–159). I certainly echo Candelaria's emphasis on the figures of resilience, but I differ with her assertion that they embody the principal revelation of the poem. Unmediated by a theoretical perspective, this interpretation of "the traditional life of *el pueblo*" rings truer as an account of the more wholly utopian *rasquachismo* of *Tamazunchale*. Such a reading runs the danger of fixing the "traditional life" as an anti-urban, premodern idyll. I would, instead, characterize the resilient agriculture as a symbolic figure, and women's horticultural practices as a cultural model, of adaptation and survival in the present, not just remembered in another place and time of *el pueblo*.

Within the paired reading of "Freeway 280" and "Cannery Town in August," it is clear that Cervantes acknowledges *both* the resilient practices and real constraints of women's "public" and "private" work. Consequently, the most positive revelation for her lies in identifying residual aspects of traditional mestiza culture in her present life. Cervantes identifies these characteristics in "Freeway 280," not in elegiac or nostalgic celebration, but in the active discovery of potential skills or models of action she may draw upon for her own cultural survival. However, these potential energies of traditional mestiza culture remain problematic within "the idiom of feminist Chicanas," as Mesa-Bains observes:

> The idiom of feminist Chicanas inhibit[s] the traditional roles and images [of women], a change that called for negotiation within the cultural group. This reorchestration . . . [is] problematic. The balancing of enduring, sustaining aspects of cherished cultural roles and practices, and the strengthening of emancipatory devices is never accomplished easily. Tradition and innovation are intertwined and reflected in the degree to which Chicana[s] . . . [draw] images, themes, and contents from the apparently constricting and contradictory roles. (1991:140)

This tension between innovation and tradition, between the *domesticana* standpoints and practices exercised by Chicanas of different generations in the same family and within a patriarchal cultural context, is cast in sharp relief in Cervantes' poem "Beneath the Shadow of the Freeway."

"BENEATH THE SHADOW OF THE FREEWAY": AGAINST THE FAMILY OF THE PATRIARCH

As I argued with regard to "Poema para los californios muertos," the critical meditation on Californio historical geography leaves relatively intact certain masculinist and heterosexist ideologies regarding "land," "culture," and "family." Most tellingly, it employs the conventional trope of conquest as rape—in which culture and land are figured symbolically as female—and the related ideological representation of women in their reproductive functions as mothers and wives. In "Freeway 280," similarly, the account of the *viejitas'* resilience in exercising their traditional productive knowledge and roles as material providers does not address the extent to which they may be fixed in those roles within their own ethnic community. And while the reification of women's productive labor in "Cannery Town in August" is a strong indictment of industrial proletarianization, it marks only the public sphere of women's labor subordination. The possibility of private domestic labor subordination remains outside the poem's critical purview.

The intracultural interrogations and critiques absent from or subordinated in the two previous poems are forcefully addressed in "Beneath the Shadow of the Freeway" (Cervantes 1981:11–14), as Cervantes explicitly contests the authority of patriarchal models of Chicano culture. Although I treat this poem last in order, it might be argued that its Chicana gender standpoint is foundational, or at least primary, within the range of ideological frameworks I discuss in the three poems. It preceded the others in conception and execution, as it was written and revised between 1971 and 1976, during the waning period of the Chicano movement. "Beneath the Shadow of the Freeway" (hereafter "Shadow") questioned the masculinist discourses and practices of the movement from a critical Chicana standpoint that was increasingly unwilling to see its concerns trivialized or dismissed as peripheral to *la causa*. Cervantes has explicitly stated this intention in her work.

> The poem "Beneath the Shadow of the Freeway" was written specifically to address the whole notion of *machismo*. I started the poem when I was very young, I was 17 [1971]. . . . There are parts in that poem that were written in that time, and I worked on that poem until I felt that I really had it finished. That was like in '76. But the reason why I wanted to write that poem [was] that at that time I was going to college and was taking a lot of Chicano culture and sociology courses, and the whole notion of the family of the patriarch . . . I could not buy at all. It was not the situation of a lot of my friends I was growing up with. (Quoted in Binder 1985:44)

Although the Chicano studies courses to which she alludes were most likely an improvement over the minimal-to-absent Chicano studies curricula offered in most universities at the time, Cervantes' life experience as a woman was inadequately represented by the models of culture then dominant in the field of Chicano studies.

The reigning patriarchal and familial models of Chicano culture had at their core a vision of ethnic-group unanimity integrated with an essential racial-cultural identity of "Chicanismo." In a strategic ideological vein, the professed Chicano "family" was meant to serve as an organizational model of community cohesion that would both spiritually and materially oppose the subordination of Chicanos. The strategic familism was clearly evinced in "El Plan Espiritual de Aztlán," a founding nationalist manifesto of the Chicano movement: "Cultural values of our peoples strengthen our identity and give moral backbone to the movement. Our culture unites and educates the family of La Raza toward liberation with one heart and one mind" ("El Plan Espiritual de Aztlán" 1972:404). The desired unity of cultural nationalist rhetoric commonly disavowed women's oppression within the culture as an issue of political importance. Only homosexual difference was more insidiously and forcefully repressed as a concern within the reigning bounds of Chicano nationalist ideological discourse. Witness, for example, how gender and sexual preference were rendered invisible as categories of social analysis in the homogenizing construct of the same manifesto: "Punto Primero: Nationalism as the key to organization transcends all religious, political, class and economic factions or boundaries. Nationalism is the common denominator upon which all members of La Raza can agree" (ibid.).

Chicana feminist, gay, and lesbian scholars have consistently targeted this patriarchal, heterosexual familism as a central ideological nexus for the subordination of "irrelevant" or "divisive" differences within the Chicano community. Attention to these differences was considered at best superfluous, and at worst traitorous to the political cause. Those who deigned to insist on the centrality of such "personal" and "private" concerns were commonly dismissed with the deprecatory title of *malinchistas.* The effect of this designation was to associate them with the much-maligned historical figure of Malintzín Tenepal, the Tlaxcalan translator and courtesan to Hernán Cortés, conquering leader of the Spaniards against the Aztecs. While stopping short of embracing or resemanticizing the figure of Malinche,[5] Cervantes entered this field of ideological contention by crafting "Beneath the Shadow of the Freeway," probably her most well-known poem, as a strategic intervention against hegemonic discourses of Chicano masculinist nationalism. This text differed from other work by narrating a specifically Chicana-centered experience of simultaneous extracultural racial-class subordination and intracultural gender conflict, while showing the resistive knowledge and various modes of survival enacted in the speaker's house of women.

The poem opens with a semiotically resonant condensation of the histories of oppression and cultural resilience associated with the freeway in the other poems I have discussed.

> Across the street—the freeway,
> blind worm, wrapping the valley up
> from Los Altos to Sal Si Puedes.
> I watched it from my porch
> unwinding. Every day at dusk
> as Grandma watered geraniums
> the shadow of the freeway lengthened. (Cervantes 1981:11)

The history of Anglo-American land appropriations and the unequal organization of social space are collapsed in the image of the freeway as a "blind worm" that consumes the earth in its path. In an ironic coincidence of objective reality and poetic metaphor, the racial division of Santa Clara County's residential space is described in two aptly named geographies. The mostly white suburban idyll of Los Altos (The Heights) is opposed to the urban milieu of Sal Si Puedes (Get Out If You Can), the Chicano neighborhood the freeway traverses.

The very title of the poem suggests the freeway's monumental disruptions. On a daily basis—animated by the daily rotation of the earth—the shadow of the freeway casts its pall across a broad swath of the central city, as if reminding its residents of their place in the spatial designs of the city. And yet, with the same persevering spirit of the *viejitas* in "Freeway 280," the grandmother still cultivates her plants. Cervantes, however, quickly moves away from these broad social-geographic innuendoes to focus her attention on an intimate account of a "woman family" in the barrio, composed of the speaker, her mother, and her grandmother. The subsequent narrative transpires in a clearly female social space defined by matriarchal lineage and the domestic milieu of the grandmother's house. Within this intimate circumference, the three women carry out their lives and labors against the ever present intrusions of extracultural social regulation and intracultural threats of male violence. The former is obliquely manifest in the labors of the young speaker, who must act as "translator of Foreign Mail," those documents from the bureaucratic and regulatory apparatuses of the state, including "letters from the government, notices / of dissolved marriages and Welfare stipulations" (ibid.). More central to the intimate focus of the poem, however, are the conflicting orientations to intracultural gender violence represented to the speaker through the respective experiences and perspectives of her grandmother and mother. Home, in the shelter literally constructed by the grandmother, is alternately safe from and threatened by male violation. Here, grandmother, mother, and daughter cultivate their own relationships, and the youngest daughter is ultimately empowered to escape the cycle of domestic male violence in her family.

The grandmother was clearly the victim of an abusive relationship, "living twenty-five years with a man who tried to kill her" (ibid.: 12). The speaker's mother ("Mama") likewise appears to be in a dysfunctional and threatening relationship. This is suggested in a horrific description of a drunken man, characterized as an animalistic "it," who visits their house:

> in the night I would hear it
> glass bottles shattering the street
> words cracked into shrill screams
> inside my throat a cold fear
> as it entered the house (ibid.: 13)

The daughter's response to his repeated invasions of the home-space is to offer to call the police on him. Her potential recourse to extracommunity intervention is a telling sign of the poem's intracultural critique. Like the intruding government documents the daughter must translate, and whose dictates she must negotiate for the family, the police are a function of state power largely antagonistic to her greater barrio community. This point recalls the broader historical context of barrio-police relations (Mirandé 1987; Trujillo 1983), which has been mediated in so many ways by the lived practices and textual expressions discussed in preceding chapters. The "Shadow" speaker's readiness to transgress this implicit social knowledge underscores a patriarchal dysfunction within her community. Cervantes, like the daughter in the poem, does not hesitate to bring "public" scrutiny to bear on such "private" conflict by mediating this dysfunction through her writing. In the process, the traditional binary distinction and hierarchical opposition between public and private spheres, which has so long been exploited by patriarchy to structure its subordination of women (Rose 1993: 34–38), is implicitly disempowered by Cervantes.

Since the police are not actually brought into the home, the women negotiate their own, divergent responses to male aggression. Having witnessed twenty-five years of the grandmother's victimization, the mother can only conclude that it was the grandmother's "own fault, / getting screwed by a man for that long" (Cervantes 1981: 12). Convinced of the male propensity for violence, the speaker's Mama imparts her variety of maternal wisdom to the young narrator. Fearing that the daughter's inexperience may lead her to suffer like the grandmother, her Mama warns: "You're too soft . . . always were, / You'll get nothing but shit. / Baby don't count on nobody" (ibid.: 13). The young daughter, however, sees another dimension to her grandmother's prolonged abuse that ultimately gives her the healing strength to mend at least her own relationship with a man. Immediately following the stanza describing the drunken intrusion, an omniscient narration suggests the young girl's sense of refuge against the threatening male violence lurking outside her bedroom door:

> inside
> a gray kitten a touchstone
> purring beneath the quilts
> grandma stitched
> from his suits
> the patchwork singing
> of mockingbirds. (ibid.)

The safety, however tenuous, that the young girl feels underneath the quilts intimates how the grandmother's *domesticana* skills are a source of strength. Cordelia Candelaria identifies this evocation of resilient strength and "power derived from . . . [the grandmother's] skill in transforming 'his suits' into a 'patchwork singing of mockingbirds.' These interwoven images create a symbol of the artist transmuting objective reality, however unpleasant, into art, and they remind us that the same transmutation is at work in 'Beneath the Shadow of the Freeway'" (1986:231). What the daughter identifies in the experience of her grandmother is represented in the very texture of the quilts stitched from the suits of an abusive man: her ability to survive with her imaginative, creative, and productive skills intact. More precisely, she survived her domestic oppression in part *because* she maintained and exercised those skills.

> She trusts only what she builds
> with her own hands.
> She built her house,
> cocky, disheveled carpentry
> after living twenty-five years
> with a man who tried to kill her. (Cervantes 1981:12)

The very softness of the grandmother engendered the hardness of her daughter's (Mama's) negative wisdom, "Baby, don't count on nobody." To the young speaker's view, however, her Grandma's "soft" capacities mirror or even give rise to her own. Thus, she characterizes herself similarly: "Soft. I haven't changed" (ibid.:14). Given the daughter's affinity for her Grandma, the latter's unspoken lessons become a model of survival that shows the daughter how to draw on her own creative capacities as a buffer to oppression.

The daughter's faith in her grandmother's lessons is first expressed when, apparently still a young girl, she offers her own redemptive and poetic strength as a salve for her own and her mother's shells of cynicism and distrust: "O Mama, with what's inside of me / I could wash that all away. I could" (ibid.). By the end of the poem, the adult daughter has exercised to great effect the models of survival she learned from her Grandma. The freeway, chronotope of historical displacement in the urban barrio, remains "across the street" from where the grown daughter now lives, perhaps in the same house her grandmother built. However, at least for the moment, the dystopian cycle of domestic violence is being kept in check, as she now "sleep[s] with a gentle man / to the hymn of mockingbirds" (ibid.). With the consciousness accrued from the cumulative generational experiences in her woman family, the granddaughter embodies and enacts the lessons of a female, *domesticana* barriology. Male oppression within the community threatens to crush any redemptive forms of social knowledge. This dystopian tendency is clearly suggested in the Mama's justifiably cynical wisdom. Her daughter, however, looks to the wisdom inscribed in the grandmother's life experience. To the extent that Cervantes, through the speaker, identifies the exemplary character of the grandmother's *domesticana* skills (or, similarly, those of the *viejitas* in "Freeway 280"), she is performing a theoretical function in a qualitatively different register from that of academic discourse. The emphasis on *domesticana* practices and knowledge in "Shadow" validates the expressive cultural modes of the grandmother as forms of critical reflexivity invisible to an outside viewpoint (male, academic, elite) but clear to Cervantes.

> In California in the summer,
> mockingbirds sing all night.
> Grandma says they are singing for their nesting wives.
> "They don't leave their families
> borrachando."
> . . . .
> She believes in myths and birds.
> she trusts only what she builds
> with her own hands. (Ibid.: 12)

The popular sensibilities of the grandmother are clearly meditative and critical, though not expressed in the discourses of literate reflection. As Marta Esther Sánchez points out, the grandmother "lives by standards connected more with an oral way of life than with a culture dependent on writing" (1985:124). In a description that echoes the particular, traditional strengths of Grandma's wisdom, Cervantes refers, in "Visions of Mexico While at a

Writing Symposium at Port Townsend, Washington," to her own ascendancy from "a long line of eloquent illiterates / whose history reveals what words don't say" (1981:45).

Cervantes, like the daughter-scribe in "Shadow," has also had to negotiate a place and language—what Emma Pérez describes as Chicana/mestiza "women-tempered *sitios y lenguas*" (1993:62)—in the culture of "books, those staunch, upright men" (Cervantes 1981:11). From this different discursive location on the oral-print continuum, the granddaughter builds a bridge of identity to the "myths and birds" epistemology of her grandmother:

> . . . in time, I plant geraniums.
> I tie up my hair into loose braids,
> and trust only what I have built
> with my own hands. (Ibid.:14)

The circle of identity is completed between grandmother and granddaughter, down to the visual mirroring of the grandmother's braids, as the granddaughter reenacts the *domesticana* skills learned from her grandmother.

Cervantes does not merely celebrate the grandmother's strength in surviving impossible circumstances. She also implicitly contests the elite cultural dismissal of "illiterate" and oppressed working-women's forms and practices of knowledge. Elsewhere, Adrienne Rich has made this same point explicitly.

> In my white North American world they have tried to tell me that this woman—politicized by intersecting forces—doesn't think and reflect on her life. That her ideas are not real ideas like those of Karl Marx and Simone de Beauvoir. That her calculations, her spiritual philosophy, her gift for law and ethics, her daily emergency political decisions are merely instinctual or conditioned reactions. (1986:230)

This is a stinging critique of elitist attitudes. It suggests that in their worst form, they render the modes of thought among poor and working women as quasi-animalistic "instinctual or conditioned reactions." Furthermore, Rich identifies a particular social space, her "white North American world," as the locus for such dismissive attitudes toward the quotidian epistemological exercises of working-class women of color. But, unlike many of her cohabitants in that world—including many white feminists—Rich is cognizant of the strong reflective consciousness exercised in the seemingly mundane practices of these "other" women. In this respect, she concurs with Third World and women-of-color feminists like Cherrie Moraga, who have foregrounded the multiform strategies by which women of color daily "measure and weigh what is to be said and when, what is to be done and how" (1983:xviii). In an ideological sisterhood with Rich, Moraga, and others, Cervantes underscores the reflective-critical insights embodied in the grandmother's expressive and productive skills. She does this specifically in the social space of her *Chicana* North American world, from a woman's barriological point of view and filtered through the literate media of her own academic and poetic education.

In spite of the proviso I offered when first describing my heuristic graph of Cervantes' poems, the sequential structure of my argument might be taken to imply a teleological progression or refinement of Cervantes' consciousness: moving from a nationalist *inter*cultural critique to a contrasting feminist *intra*cultural interrogation. I want, therefore, to repeat and make clear my distance from such an evolutionary configuration of the three poems. Instead, I would hope that my discussion of ideological diversity and figural (spatial) variation among the selected texts suggests the complexity of Cervantes' sociopoetic consciousness, which is not sequential but strategic, not fixed but mobile, and not exclusive but inclusive of contradiction. The motif of mobility is particularly useful for understanding Cervantes' differential consciousness and subsequent poetic images of multiple social spaces and ideological points of view. My use of "differential consciousness" in regard to Cervantes' work is derived from Chela Sandoval's definition of it as

> the strategy of another form of oppositional ideology that functions
> on an altogether different register [from hegemonic norms and forms
> of critical epistemology]. *Its power can be thought of as mobile—not
> nomadic but rather cinematographic:* a kinetic motion that maneuvers,
> poetically transfigures, and orchestrates while demanding alienation,
> perversion, and reformation in both spectators and practitioners.
> (1991:3; emphasis added)

Sandoval's specification of "mobility" is pertinent to Cervantes' poetry. It does not identify a nomadic movement through space, but a shifting configuration of perspectives in place, as in the cinematographic mobility between long-, medium-, and close-range frames of view. The specific *sequence of movement* among the varying frames of view (as, for example, in my own organization of this essay) is less crucial than the *ability to move* among them (which corresponds to Cervantes' sociopoetic activity). In the "kinetic motion" among varying spatial fields and ideological perspectives, Cervantes' cumulative sociopoesis (as opposed to any single poem) reveals her differential consciousness to be the "variant emerging out of correlations, intensities, junctures, crises" (Sandoval 1991:14). Her poetry, therefore, participates in the trajectory of much U.S.–Third World feminist critical-cultural praxis, as it "demands . . . a new subjectivity, a political revision that denies any one ideology as the final answer, . . . instead positing a *tactical subjectivity* with the capacity to recenter [and to remap, I would add] depending upon the kinds of oppression to be confronted" (ibid.; original emphasis). Given the multiple constitutive elements of her own subjectivity—ranging between and across social categories of race, class, gender, and sexuality—it appears both proper and necessary that Lorna Dee Cervantes should have developed a complex and contradictory poetic vision. As a practice against ideological schizophrenia, her mobile trajectory of sociospatial representations serves her well and offers her readers an instructive map of a variegated cultural landscape.

Epilogue

Return to the Source

From an initial dissertation inquiry into the literary representations of urban Chicano experience, this study has grown and deepened in proportion to my expanding relationship with the city where I am making my place. Being in Los Angeles regularly compels me to reflect upon the intersections of urbanism, identity, and expressive practice in Chicano culture. In *Paris Spleen*, Charles Baudelaire noted that "it was, above all, out of my exploration of huge cities, out of the medley of their innumerable relationships," that the inspiration for his poetic urban discourse "was born" (1970:x). Without pretending any poetic quality for my own writing, I can nonetheless modify his observation to my own circumstances: It was, above all, in the exploration of Los Angeles that a "haunting ideal" (ibid.) possessed me to expand the expressive range of my inquiry and produce this academic urban discourse. In various modes of passage through Los Angeles' material and expressive landscapes—reading newspapers, attending cultural events, walking through neighborhoods, riding buses and trains through the central city, and driving the freeways everywhere and nowhere in particular—I have encountered a multiplying range of Chicano spatial practices, as well as those of other more recent Latino immigrants. If not always with the producers' awareness of their collective effect, these practices cumulatively produce and reproduce a mexopolis within the metropolis, a near order within the far order (Lefebvre 1996:101). This Raza second city—contrary to the rigid laws of physics but consonant with the fluid arts of urbanity—exists in the same *space* of the putative Anglo-American first city (signs of its diminution are everywhere to be seen), yet in a significantly other *place* from its dominant cultural milieu.

And so I move through this city that is not one, but many. Like a neophyte of some new faith, I find signs at every turn of the truth in Sharon Zukin's observation that

> space . . . structures people's perceptions, interactions, and sense of well-being or despair, belonging or alienation. . . . [It] stimulates both memory and desire; it indicates categories and relations between them. . . . The key structural shifts in the twentieth-century political economy are located in a symbolic geography of space . . . , and localized in spatial metaphors that explore the relation between economic power and cultural representation. (1991:268)

Clearly Los Angeles is only one of many cities where the material and metaphorical structuring of lived experience finds form. However, as I hope has become evident in this study, the many-layered metropolitan palimpsest laid over the original landscape of El Pueblo de Nuestra Señora la Reina de Los Angeles de Porciúncula makes *this* city a prototypical site for mapping the unending struggles of working-class Raza to make and to mark their place in the larger space of urban capitalist society.

In these struggles, the persistence and power of memory is crucial, being simultaneously effective—as practically informing *history* in the politics of community defense—and affective—as emotionally orienting *story* in the politics of textual representation. Memory, therefore, acts as a common denominator bridging narratives of place in the "real" and represented cities of Chicano barrio dwellers or, as Willa Cather describes them, the inseparable "city of fact" and "city of feeling" (1976:24).[1] Thus, as I reflect upon the metamorphoses of twentieth-century Los Angeles and their repercussions in Chicano expressive culture, I have been struck in a way similar to Baudelaire's poetic persona, who, observing Haussman's reconstruction of nineteenth-century Paris, noted that "tout pour moi devient allégorie" (everything for me becomes an allegory; 1993:174).

As in the formal structure of literary allegory, the primary or "literal" narrative of Los Angeles' development is one of ceaseless modernization, of manifest improvements in the form and function of the city as an economic growth machine. At the secondary or allegorical level of conceptual significance, this master narrative of modernization has had radically contrary interpretations, depending on one's location in the metropolitan landscape of power. Los Angeles' dominant history, as narrated by and for the victors in the city's protracted turf wars, heralds the continuous achievements of "progress," "civilization," and "the good life." For those who find themselves in the path of Los Angeles' development, this dominant narrative of urban growth inspires contrary interpretation, as we have seen throughout the range of barriological texts treated in this study. This critical interpretive legacy, fueled by the history of "our moving barrios" (Muñoz 1973:5), continues to inform the attitudes and actions of barrio residents as they question the multilayered significance of urban development.

An example that reveals the continuing ideological tension around urban renewal in the barrios is the protracted and embattled public debate concerning the major redevelopment plan of the 1990s for the Eastside neighborhoods of El Sereno and Boyle Heights. In 1993 the Community Redevelopment Agency (CRA) of Los Angeles completed an initial physical and fiscal evaluation in a composite area of three square miles, assessing its current conditions and future prospects. The CRA report made specific recommendations for reinvigorating the area's declining commercial and industrial corridors through a combination of physical renovation and economic incentives to attract new businesses and create new jobs. Public redevelopment funds of approximately $93 million were asked for to support the project, known as Adelante Eastside.

From the outset, area residents have been "wrestling with the legacy of distrust, even as they hope the project will launch a new era on the Eastside" (Gold 1997:B-3). At the first public presentation of the CRA plan, community members cast doubt on its stated goals, fearing they might lose their homes, as in previous projects of central-city renovation (Pérez 1994:6). Many residents angrily recalled the community displacements in Bunker Hill, Chávez Ravine, and the Eastside freeway construction. Since 1994, then, the project proposal has been traveling a fractious route of local committee review and revision, bringing together CRA officials, political appointees, and local community representatives. All sides in this delicate collective process appear to want to bring needed resources to the targeted Eastside areas. However, historically informed misgivings about how the power of land-use determinations will be coordinated among local residents, business owners, private developers, and public agencies (with particular attention to how residential areas will be safeguarded) have drawn out the deliberations through successive stages of initial antagonism, later stalemate, and now imminent resolution. As I am revising this epilogue, the final draft of a consensus redevelopment plan is being prepared for presentation to the City Council. Two linchpins of the collectively approved plan are (1) the waiver of governmental eminent-domain powers on any 100-percent residential property and (2) the guarantee of continuing community voice in the administration of the redevelopment plan throughout its thirty-year life span (Santillanes 1999). The project proposal is likely to be approved by the City Council. Its practical results will fall to a future generation to evaluate and perhaps to imaginatively represent.

While the effects of the Adelante Eastside plan remain to be seen, the troubled history of infrastructural impacts upon Chicano social spaces in Los Angeles continues to be represented in a variety of textual forms. Three brief examples suggest the expressive range of the continuing barriological impulse in Los Angeles. At one end of the spectrum, Lalo Alcaraz has used the editorial cartoon format to project a historical-geographic consciousness to a broad audience in the city's public sphere. Two panels from his *L.A. Cucaracha* series, appearing locally in the *L.A. Weekly*, satirize the dispositions of planners and the projects they impose upon (or withhold from) the barrios (see Figs. 55 and 56).

At an opposite extreme, Julio Elguezabal works in a private sphere of expression to construct a personal memorial to barrios "developed" out of existence. Salvaging materials from the detritus of homes razed in Chávez Ravine, Lincoln Heights, Chinatown, and in his own Elysian Valley neighborhood (which is the real referent for the fictional barrio in Ron Arias' *The Road to Tamazunchale*), Elguezabal has, in his daughter's words, turned his backyard "into a living museum over the past thirty years" (quoted in Pool 1997:B-2). Beginning with a miniature Victorian playhouse for his daughters (see Fig. 57), Elguezabal continued to recycle found materials into a western facade, a miniature chapel, and a garden landscape. These intimate creations are not merely playful or decorative. Elguezabal clearly values the memorial substance embedded in the materials. Recalling a time when a coworker asked him why he was drawn to "junk," Elguezabal noted: "I told him it's not junk to me. I told him there was always a story attached to something like this" (quoted in Pool, 1997:B-2).

Finally, in a milieu altogether different from either the public satire of López or the private architecture of Elguezabal, there are those texts that exist in a phantom sphere of pure remembrance. In my research for this project, I came upon the mnemonic traces of such a text by Félix Montoya, a longtime resident of East Los Angeles, now deceased. In the early 1970s, Raúl Escobedo (a Chicano urban planner whom I quoted in Chapter 2) met Mr. Mon-

FIGURE 55.   *Cuando les conviene . . .* : antinomies in the routes and detours of "superhighways." Editorial cartoon by Lalo Alcaraz, courtesy of the artist. First appeared in *L.A. Weekly.*

toya while conducting research on the visual environment of East Los Angeles. Montoya became one of his primary informants. The phantom text in question, which contained Montoya's literal and allegorical narratives of his neighborhood's history, was an extended personal chronicle, begun after he retired in the 1960s. The voluminous meditations were handwritten, chronologically organized, and titled by Montoya "The Destruction of East Los Angeles." Because the collection was lost after Montoya's death, the objective details of urban change and the subjective representations of his community's transformation contained in this protomanuscript can only be guessed at,

LA'S ANGEL MONUMENT — PROPOSAL BY LA CUCARACHA

LALO ALCARAZ ©994

THE ETERNAL LEAF BLOWER (DOUBLES AS WATERHOSE DURING RIOT SEASON)

MECHANICAL WINGS FLAP AWAY SMOG FOR CLEAR VIEW OF TOWER.

HIGH SPEED CHASE CAMERAS

KEY TO THE CITY? MORE LIKELY THE KEY TO YOUR... VALET PARKED S.U.V

YOUR CORPORATE SPONSOR NAME HERE

INSIDE: • A LIQUOR STORE ON EVERY FLOOR
• LOW-COST SWEATSHOP RENTALS HELP KEEP JOBS IN L.A.!
• GUNSHOT FIRST AID KIT EVERY 2 FLOORS

FRANK O. GEHRY DESIGNED KARAOKE BAR

PROPOSED UNFINISHED MTA SUBWAY TUBE

GATED COMMUNITY, AKA ENTERTAINMENT INDUSTRY OFFICE SPACE
...PLENTY OF BILLBOARD SPACE

HIGH SPEED CHASE NEWSCHOPPER LANDING PAD

FREEWAY INTERCHANGE

MOVABLE, DETACHABLE SECTION APPEASE VALLEY SECESSIONISTS

TEMPORARY FOOTBALL STADIUM WITH RETRACTABLE FIELD

MALL OF L.A.: 15 STARBUCKS, 22 DONUTS AND CHINESE FOOD JOINTS

QUAKE FRIENDLY SPRING LOADED BASE

LOCATION: RIGHT OVER BARRIO!

FIGURE 56. A monumental parody. Responding to a strange proposal by a downtown development group for a new monument to the City of the Angels, López recasts the design with an entirely different set of signifiers. Of the many farcical elements, note particularly the inclusion of a freeway interchange at the base and the indication (bottom right corner) of where the monument will be located: "Right over the barrio!" Editorial cartoon by Lalo Alcaraz, courtesy of the artist. First appeared in *L.A. Weekly*.

FIGURE 57.   *Rasquache* architecture as memorial design. Playhouse in Julio
Elguezabal's backyard. Photograph by Raúl Homero Villa, 1998.

although the title points to the author's critical perspective. But in the recollection of Raúl Escobedo, passed along to me and recorded as a closing allusion in this book, perhaps "The Destruction of East Los Angeles" can haunt readers today. While it was, in Escobedo's (1998) description, a clear elegy for the Eastside written in the wake of its most violent "renewals" during the 1950s and 1960s, it was also an impassioned critique of the aggressive deterritorialization effected upon the central-city barrios.

Edward Soja, among other postmodern geographers, has eloquently articulated the reemergent concern in critical and theoretical social studies with "how human geographies become filled with politics and ideology" (1989: 6). Describing the exemplary spatial consciousness in the writings of Henri Lefebvre, Michel Foucault, Fredric Jameson, Marshall Berman, and John Berger, Soja makes a powerful theoretical argument that geography, like history, is a foundational category in the constitution of the social world. However, *why* geography matters is not exclusively (nor perhaps even primarily) a theoretical issue but a function of its felt consequences in people's lives. In this regard, I hope it has become clear, if not imperative, that we must supplement Soja's intellectual history of the "insistent voices of . . . critical human geography" (12) to include the chorus of urban Chicanos and Chicanas whose historical experiences, creative expressions, and everyday cultural activities speak to the politics and power of place for working-class people.

The collective energies applied by Chicanos and Chicanas in Los Angeles to create, enrich, and represent their urban milieu is representative of similar barriological impulses enacted throughout California and across the "nation" of cities in Aztlán. Their evolving urban culture, as both a practical and symbolic enterprise, is ever engaged in a tactical war of positions with top-down urban plans and ideologies. My point, therefore, is to draw attention to a fundamental fact of metropolitan life and civic culture: that the city is a meeting ground of contending social forces and contentious wills to being-in-place. To foreground this urban dialectic is not to underestimate the predominant capacity of ruling groups or classes to shape the broad contours of social space in Los Angeles or elsewhere. Rather, I mean to stress that the forms, functions, and cultural meanings of urbanity are produced simultaneously, and differently, by Chicanos and Chicanas who, like other predominately working-class citizens, contribute significantly, if not always in acknowledged ways, to the development of the cities in which they live.

INTRODUCTION

1. Among the many fine studies on this point are the following: Rodolfo Acuña's *Occupied America*; Patricia Nelson Limerick's *The Legacy of Conquest*; Mario Barrera's *Race and Class in the Southwest*; and Carey McWilliams' *Southern California: An Island on the Land*.

2. While I believe that *law* and *media* evoke a certain self-evident or commonsense understanding as active hegemonic effects, the same may not be true of *landscape*. At first glance, this term may appear to designate a static object rather than an active operation or social apparatus. While *law* and *media* readily suggest agents and agency, *landscape* might be seen as the inert stage upon which social processes take place. Quite the contrary. For clarification, I offer Sharon Zukin's lucid characterization of landscape as an active mechanism of power, from which I derive my usage:

> *Landscape*, as I use the term here, stretches the imagination. Not only does it denote the usual geographical meaning of "physical surroundings," but it also refers to an ensemble of material and social practices and their symbolic representation. . . .
>
> . . . A landscape mediates, both symbolically and materially, between the socio-spatial differentiation of capital implied by *market* and the socio-spatial homogeneity of labor suggested by *place*.
>
> The concept *landscape* has recently emerged from a long period of reification to become a potent tool of cultural analysis. It connotes a contentious, compromised product of society. It also embodies a point of view . . . powerful institutions have a preeminent capacity to impose their view on the landscape—weakening, reshaping, and displacing the view from the vernacular. (1991, 16; original emphasis)

ONE

1. My account of this signal historical episode is informed by various sources, but most substantially by Richard Griswold del Castillo (1979:105–115) and Edward Escobar 1983 (80–95).

2. This implicit social knowledge was by no means limited to the urbanizing zones of Southern California. Américo Paredes' well-known study of the border balladry, *With His Pistol in His Hand*, offers evidence of such popularly manifest and transmitted knowledge in the rural milieu of South Texas during the same period as the early constitution of urban Los Angeles. Carl Gutiérrez-Jones' 1995 work on the hegemonic discourses of criminality and their impact on the critical expressive consciousness of Chicano writers, *Rethinking the Borderlands: Between Chicano Culture and Legal Discourse*, treats this issue in great descriptive and theoretical detail, although the emphasis is almost entirely on Chicano literary and legal critiques of the United States' juridico-legal ideological state apparatuses rather than on the direct repressive activities of police agents.

3. Although it refers to a very different social and temporal milieu, Avery Gordon's treatment of ghosts and haunting in the work of Argentinean novelist Luisa Valenzuela suggests similar uses of these spectral tropes within her critical ideological discourse. I will have much more to say about this phantom element in past and present Chicano spatial discourse throughout this study.

4. I am not suggesting that apart from these print-textual manifestations of critique there were no oral expressive practices critical of *mexicano* subordination within an emerging American social order. The "critical common sense" I refer to was no doubt manifest in various popular "texts" such as gossip, jokes, stories, *corridos*, derogatory appellations ("name-calling"), and the like. However, the systematic documentation and study of these practices in late-1800s California has not been undertaken in the manner or degree that would allow me to comment substantially on these popular expressions of critical consciousness. For a summary discussion of such folkloric expressions in South Texas, see Américo Paredes' 1978 essay "The Problem of Identity in a Changing Culture: Popular Expressions of Culture Conflict along the Lower Rio Grande Border." The *corrido*, or ballad, of the greater Mexican borderlands has been the most well researched of these popular expressive practices, generating a plethora of studies beginning with Paredes' foundational classic *"With His Pistol in His Hand": A Border Ballad and Its Hero*.

5. Original Spanish: "Que un pueblo civilizado . . . se converta [*sic*] en asesino voluntario y despreciando las autoridades . . . es realmente repugnante y escandoloso [*sic*]. . . . Nuestra raza en general debe abrir los ojos a la luz de la verdad y ver lo que pueden esperar de la justicia de nuestros amables primos" (*Las Dos Repúblicas*, April 9, 1893).

6. William Estrada, curator at El Pueblo [La Placita] State Historical Monument, has been documenting, interpreting, and speaking on the significance of the Plaza area as a site of political and semiotic conflict between community use-value and commodity exchange-value orientations. He is currently completing a doctoral dissertation on this subject entitled "The Los Angeles Plaza: Myth, Memory, Symbol, and the

Struggle for Place in a Changing Metropolis." It promises to be a definitive historical and cultural study of this contentious urban landmark.

Similar struggles over the significance of historical *mexicano* urban places and cultural practices have been played out throughout the Southwest since Charles Fletcher Lummis first conceived of and promoted the ideological apparatus of a "Southwest genre" in literary and cultural discourses (Calderón 1990:214–215; Calderón and Saldívar 1991:2–3). This process has perhaps been most strikingly enacted in New Mexico. In cities like Taos and Santa Fe, the commercial promotion of *mexicano* culture has created such an explosion of real estate values that the native *manito* and *manita* residents of those cities will be forced to live elsewhere to make room for the Hispanophilic artisans, entrepreneurs, and retirees settling there from far off lands. For a study of this phenomenon, see Chris Wilson, *The Myth of Santa Fe.*

TWO

1. This episode has received other significant literary and artistic treatments, beginning soon after it occurred. In 1948, for example, Beatrice Griffith published *American Me,* which was structured as sociological interpretations and fictionalized narrations of barrio youth experience in the war years. More recently, Luis Valdez' theatrical-cum-film treatment in *Zoot Suit* (which conflates elements of the Sleepy Lagoon trial with the hysteria of the "riots") is perhaps the most widely known representation of this seamy moment in Los Angeles history. However, the single most disturbing representation is probably the opening sequence from the 1991 film *American Me,* which was inspired by Griffith's work. The scene painfully re-creates the beating and stripping of young Chicanos and graphically shows the rape of a young Chicana by Anglo servicemen. Less recognized, being an independent production principally screened in film festivals or Chicano studies courses, is Carlos Avila's poignant short film *Distant Water.* Avila simultaneously narrates the intercultural conflict of the "riots" in its spectacular public manifestation of sailors versus Chicanos and in its reproduction as a playground battle between young Chicano and Anglo schoolboys battling over rights to use the segregated public pools of Los Angeles.

2. The quoted phrase is from Lee Shippey's 1950 *The Los Angeles Book,* where it served as the title for Chapter 12. The explanatory text that opened that chapter is a wonderful exemplar of postwar technoeuphoric historical discourse: "Ever since its founding, Los Angeles has been changing so rapidly that tomorrow has never been just another day. Tomorrow has always been another town" (103).

3. Banham's unfettered *jouissance* of the Los Angeles freeways recalls the epiphanic moment of motorized mobility that seduced Le Corbusier to "go with the flow" of an unprecedented urbanism in the nascent automobile age, and to likewise preach its virtues as the coming metropolitan technotopia: "On that 1st of October, 1924, I was assisting in the titanic rebirth *[renaissance]* of a new phenomenon . . . traffic. Cars, cars, fast, fast! One is seized, filled with enthusiasm, with joy . . . the joy of power. The simple and naive pleasure of being in the midst of power, of strength. One participates in it. One takes part in this society that is just dawning. One has confidence in this new

society: it will find a magnificent expression of its power. One believes in it" (quoted in Berman 1982 : 166).

In less transcendental language that more closely anticipates Banham's experiential analysis of the freeway *gestalt*, Siegfried Giedion described his own canonizing view of the expressway time-space phenomenon emergent in the late 1930s: "As with many of the creations born out of the spirit of this age, the meaning and beauty of the parkway cannot be grasped from a single point of observation, as was possible from a window of the chateau at Versailles. It can be revealed only by movement, by going along in a steady flow, as the rules of traffic prescribe. The space-time feeling of our period can seldom be felt so keenly as when driving" (quoted in Berman 1982 : 302).

4. Chicano journalistic and literary responses to the displacement of Bunker Hill will be discussed later in this chapter and in Chapter 3. For a concise account of the historical morphology of Bunker Hill, from its early modern status as an exclusive residential enclave through its transformation into the densest working-class neighborhood in the city, and up to its wholesale erasure and postmodern refashioning after the 1960s, see Loukaitou-Sideris and Sansbury's 1995–1996 "Lost Streets of Bunker Hill."

5. The "Prayer for America's Road Builders," an official text of the American Road Builders' Association, is among the more audacious examples of this self-worth rendered as hyperbolic rhetoric:

O Almighty God, who has given us this earth and has appointed men to have domination over it; who had commanded us to make straight the highways, to lift up the valleys and to make the mountains low, we ask thy blessing upon these men who do just that. Fill them with a sense of accomplishment, not just for the roads built, but for the ways opened for the lengthening of visions, the broader hopes and the greater joys which make these highways a possibility for mankind.

Bless these, our Nation's road builders, and their friends. For the benefits we reap from their labors, we praise thee; may thy glory be revealed in us. Amen. (Quoted in Goodman 1971 : 78–79)

6. Mike Davis has classified such hegemonic representations in a specific genre of "hagiographic 'brag books'—so common in the early twentieth century—that depicted local history as the heroic activity of the leading men of business and industry" (1990 : 83). Although he does not offer any titles, I might suggest the following as representative: Boyle Workman's *The City That Grew;* William Andrew Spalding's *History and Reminiscences: Los Angeles City and County, California;* and Charles P. Grossman's *Los Angeles, the Wonder City: A Pictorial Representation of Life in This Great and Growing Metropolis on the West Coast.* If such works were more common in the early twentieth century, the genre has not ceased to produce texts up to the present. Davis cites Kevin Starr's *Material Dreams* as the most important inheritor of this rhetorical legacy.

7. The relationship between the city's business elites and the repressive exercise of police power is not a fanciful connotation of Valle's text. The notorious "Red Squad" of the Los Angeles Police Department, led by Captain William "Red" Hynes, was organized by local capitalists as the public servants of their private union-busting in-

terests, a counterinsurgent task at which they were brutally effective. Among the young officers trained in this unit was Eugene Biscailuz, who would go on to become Sheriff of Los Angeles County, in which capacity he came under regular fire from the Civil Rights Commission of the Eastside Community Service Organization because of his department's abuse of Chicanos during the repressive 1950s.

8. The original publication does not identify the specific author of the introduction. However, in conversations I had with Victor Valle while researching this material, I learned that he drafted the actual text, with input from other members of the editorial group.

THREE

1. Consider as evidence the representative rhetoric of the Automobile Club of Southern California, whose *Guide to Los Angeles Area Freeway System* proclaims that "The Los Angeles area's vital freeway system has grown along with Southern California's unprecedented population expansion and has contributed significantly to the region's economic development. Southern California's much-publicized way of life has been made possible largely because of the automobile and its remarkable ease of movement along the freeways and highways—especially remarkable considering the vast area and population involved" (1980).

2. For a full discussion of Gamboa's personal history, creative influences, and multimedia art projects during his early years as a founding member of the avant-garde Chicano artists' collective Asco (Spanish for "nausea"), see the 1988 dissertation of Zaneta Kosiba-Vargas, or Gamboa's own recollective essay "In the City of Angels, Chameleons, and Phantoms: Asco, a Case Study of Chicano Art in Urban Tones (or Asco Was a Four-Member Word)." For specific reflections on the freeway as a foundational image in Gamboa's cognitive map of Los Angeles, see Ondine Chavoya's 1999 "Social Unwest: An Interview with Harry Gamboa, Jr."

3. By way of comparison, it is worth anticipating my discussions of intergenerational communitarian relations in Ron Arias' novel *The Road to Tamazunchale* (Chapter 4) and in my analysis of Lorna Dee Cervantes' poetry (Chapter 5). I have in mind the high regard given to the traditional skills and knowledge of *ancianos* like Fausto and Cuca in *Tamazunchale* or the *viejitas* (female elders) in Cervantes' work. For the latter, the evocation and valuation of women's knowledge and practical, expressive cultural practices mark respect for their foremothers. This valuation goes beyond well-mannered deference. It is a critical recognition of practical and critical contents, or the "social and cultural capital" (Fernández-Kelly 1995), in the *ancianas'* accumulated life experience.

4. That this issue is of significant concern to Viramontes is manifest in its repeated, though contrary, representation elsewhere in her story collection. Specifically in "The Moths," Viramontes describes an effective and emotionally bonding intergenerational transmission of knowledge and practice. We see there that the healing and care-giving attentions of a grandmother *(abuela)* toward her granddaughter are reciprocated in the granddaughter's regular visits to her *abuela* and in her final attendance to the *abuela's* needs on her deathbed and after her death.

5. "Jack the Ripper" might ring truer as a moniker for Robert Moses, particularly

considering the megalomaniacal challenge he directed to those who opposed the construction of his socially devastating Cross-Bronx Expressway: "When you operate in an overbuilt metropolis, you have to hack your way with a meat ax. I'm going to keep right on building. You do the best you can to stop it" (quoted in Berman 1982 : 290).

6. The conspiratorial perception of urban infrastructural development is a regular motif in Chicano urban narrative and popular culture. For example, in *Always Running, La Vida Loca: Gang Days in L.A.*, the poet and journalist Luis Rodríguez describes scripting an *acto*, or brief didactic theatrical sketch, in which he represents the willful actions of urban planners. The sketch portrays territorial gang conflict between two rival gangs, but "[t]he upshot is as the two barrios fight, local government officials are on the side determining the site of a new mall or where the next freeway will go while making plans to uproot the very land the dudes were killing each other for" (1993 : 177). Rodríguez' expository sketch echoes a popular Eastside opinion that perceives the routing of freeways as a strategic assault by the city on the territorial integrity of the gangs (Moore 1978 : 16).

7. Many Chicana writers and critics have called to task the patriarchal power endemic to the familial community sphere of the barrio, even as they still "throw punches for their race" (Chabram-Dernersesian 1992) against external social threats. While numerous texts engage in simultaneous intra- and intercultural critiques, several key works do so with specific reference to the material-spatial organization of patriarchy: Helena María Viramontes' story "The Moths," in which the authoritarian and alienating sites of a father's home and the patriarchal church are indicted by contrast with the security and nurturing milieu of the Chicana protagonist's *abuela*'s home; several poems in Lorna Dee Cervantes' collection *Emplumada* that are related by key figurations of freeways and women's domestic spaces (gardens and houses); and the widely recognized vignettes of intimate Chicana social spaces in Sandra Cisneros' *The House on Mango Street*. I should note that only Viramontes' fiction refers to Los Angeles. Cervantes' and Cisneros' texts are set in San Jose and Chicago, respectively. The concluding chapter on Cervantes' poetry will elaborate on this thematic trajectory.

FOUR

1. Elaborating on Omi and Winant's concept of "racial formation," I use "spatioracial formation" to identify both the structural primacy of racial categories as subject-placing criteria in urban geographic organization, and the attendant objective and subjective effects upon residents of various racially circumscribed social spaces. This particular mapping of social difference onto the very fabric of the city does not mean that other variables of subject formation (such as class, gender, age, sexual orientation, etc.) are less significant than race. In fact, they are regularly interwoven with race to further structure and place individuals and groups within a given social and spatial order.

2. According to Torres, the quotations from him used in the Cockcroft article were originally part of an article about Chicano Park by Barbara Herrera in the *San Diego Evening Tribune* in August of 1994.

3. Although Raúl Salinas is not a California-based or California-referent artist, his justly famous poem "Un Trip through the Mind Jail" bears mentioning in the context of Herrera's work. "Un Trip" is considered exemplary of a socioaesthetic that deploys

the revisionary power of memory in the textual reconstruction of barrio social space, anticipating (and possibly informing) the related poetics of Herrera.

First published in 1969, while Salinas was incarcerated in Leavenworth Federal Penitentiary, this lyrical eulogy to La Loma, in East Austin, Texas ("Neighborhood of my youth / demolished forever from / the universe" [Castañeda-Shular et al. 1972: 182]), undertakes the agonistic task of memorially reconstituting the material and experientially felt sense of place of his childhood barrio paved over by the routing of the Interstate 35 highway. Contrary to Herrera, however, Salinas never explicitly mentions the freeway, which belies Salinas' critical-aesthetic intention to mnemonically re-site (by textually re-citing) the predevastated physical and cultural integrity of his native social space and, by extension, that of "all / Chicano neighborhoods that now exist and once / existed" (ibid.:186). In effect, then, he is re-membering the dis-membered place of his individual and collective identity formation by a willful return to a time when the freeway was not present. Consequently, his conspicuous nonnaming of the freeway signals his determination to not grant the freeway the violating presence in his memorial landscape that it has in the physical landscape of power in Austin. Although it refers to Austin, Texas, "Un Trip" does have a direct textual-material link to, and an expressive affinity with, Southern California barriological discourse. After its initial publication in a Chicano inmate's journal from Leavenworth, Salinas' poem was next published in the East Los Angeles cultural arts journal *Con Safos*, in which the term *barriology* was first coined.

4. The published version of the poem erroneously printed these lines as "Me and Arnold Leyva, Raymond Nieto, Johnny / & Eva Estrada." The version that I quote in this study is corrected according to the poet's specifications.

5. For the history of some of the more characteristic, outstanding, and long-lived cultural formations and practices, see "The Chicano Movement and the Emergence of Chicano Poetic Consciousness," by Tomás Ybarra-Frausto; *Chicano Art: Resistance and Affirmation*, edited by Richard Griswold del Castillo et al.; *Signs from the Heart: California Chicano Murals*, edited by Eva Sperling Cockcroft and Holly Barnet-Sánchez; *Community Murals*, by Alan Barnett; and *Made in Aztlán*, edited by Philip Brookman and Guillermo Gómez-Peña.

6. For a fuller discussion of this nationalist masculinist ethos, refer to Chapter 5, where I discuss these issues with reference to the poetry of Lorna Dee Cervantes, particularly in "Poema para los californios muertos."

7. For a striking visual rendering of police actions against cruising, see Frank Romero's 1984 painting "The Closing of Whittier Boulevard," which memorializes the infamous police shutdown of the principal cruising strip of East Los Angeles during the weekend of March 23–25, 1979. Authorities claimed to be cutting off the likely outbreak of aggressive leisure activities or violence expected upon the opening of the film *Boulevard Nights*, in which cruising the strip figured prominently (Bright 1995: 99). That weekend saw a 400 percent increase over the usual number of arrests, revealing once again the direct exercise of the repressive law effect on the public leisure spaces of Chicanos. Romero's painting is reproduced on page 64 of the July 11, 1988, *Time* magazine special issue on Hispanic culture.

Popular music has made a recurring theme of Chicano cruising and its more specific manifestation: lowriding. Among the more noteworthy and recognized songs are the early-1960s anthem "Whittier Boulevard" by Thee Midnighters; "Lowrider" by War; "Lowrider (On the Boulevard)," Latin Alliance's rap-sampled homage to War's classic tune; and "On a Sunday Afternoon" and "Bouncin'" by Chicano rappers A Lighter Shade of Brown.

FIVE

1. All translations of the Spanish in Cervantes' poems are taken from the "Glossary of Spanish Words and Phrases" included at the end of *Emplumada* (1981).

2. This tradition of representing the national homeland as woman has been substantially treated in a number of studies. Among those I have consulted are Henry Nash Smith's *The Virgin Land: The American West as Symbol and Myth;* Benedict Anderson's *Imagined Communities: Reflections on the Origin and Spread of Nationalism;* and Marina Warner's *Monuments and Maidens: The Allegory of the Female Form.* For specifically feminist appraisals of this tradition, see Annette Kolodny's *The Lay of the Land: Metaphor as Experience and History in American Life and Letters* and Gillian Rose's *Feminism and Geography: The Limits of Geographical Knowledge.*

3. The masculinist response to colonial violation of women and land may also sublimate a latent male fear of their own potential bodily violation. Such a view is revealed in a foundational nationalist statement issued in 1969 by the Revolutionary Caucus at the Denver Youth Liberation Conference: "Our culture has been castrated through the various institutions of this [racist United States] system" (1969).

4. For a critical account of this school of historicism with particular reference to women, see Antonia Castañeda's "Gender, Race, and Culture: Spanish American Women in the Historiography of Frontier California."

5. There is an important trajectory of writing—critical, theoretical, and literary— by Chicanas that specifically reconsiders the significance of the much-maligned Malinche as an icon of unrecognized female power. In a broad sense, many Chicanas engaged in revising her historico-mythical image stress her ability to deal with the unenviable circumstances of slavery and, later in the conquest, her example of how women of color must and can negotiate multiple oppressions while salvaging some integrity in the process. For a critical account of this trajectory in Chicana writing, see the appropriate chapter in Rita Cano Alcalá's 1997 dissertation. See also Norma Alarcón's 1983 article "Chicana Feminist Literature" for a treatment of Malintzín's revised place in Chicana literary discourse.

EPILOGUE

1. I came across this wonderful imagery from Cather in a 1998 book by Carlo Rotella, *October Cities: The Redevelopment of Urban Literature.* Unfortunately, I discovered this important study too late to be able to engage with it in my own work. I should note, however, that Rotella's work has some uncanny resonances with my own, although with reference to white-ethnic and African-American experience in three cities of fact and feeling far removed from California: Chicago, Philadelphia, and New York.

WORKS CITED

Acuña, Rodolfo F. 1984. *A Community under Siege: A Chronicle of Chicanos East of the Los Angeles River, 1945–1975.* Los Angeles: Chicano Studies Research Center Publications, UCLA, Monograph no. 11.

———. 1988. *Occupied America: A History of Chicanos.* 3d ed. New York: Harper and Row.

———. 1996. *Anything but Mexican: Chicanos in Contemporary Los Angeles.* New York: Verso.

Alarcón, Norma. 1983. "Chicana Feminist Literature: A Re-vision through Malintzín/ or Malintzín: Putting Flesh Back on the Object." In *This Bridge Called My Back: Writings by Radical Women of Color,* ed. Cherríe Moraga and Gloria Anzaldúa, 182–190. New York: Kitchen Table/Women of Color.

———. 1990. "Chicana Feminism: In the Tracks of 'the' Native Woman." *Cultural Studies* 4, no. 1 (October):248–256.

Alcalá, Rita Cano. 1997. "Virgins, Martyrs and Whores: Mexican Cultural Icons of Womanhood in Chicana Literature." Ph.D. diss., University of Texas, Austin.

Alfaro, Luis. 1992a. "Aims and Concerns." Unpublished typescript.

———. 1992b. "Pico-Union." Unpublished typescript.

———. 1994. "Orphan of Aztlán." In *Uncontrollable Bodies: Testimonies of Identity and Culture,* ed. Rodney Sappington and Tyler Stallings, 233–241. Seattle: Bay Press.

Althusser, Louis. 1971. "Ideology and Ideological State Apparatuses: (Notes towards an Investigation)." In *Lenin and Philosophy: And Other Essays.* Trans. Ben Brewster. New York: Monthly Review.

Alvarez, Gloria. 1989. "Contrastes/Contrasts." In *Invocation L.A.: Urban Multicultural Poetry,* ed. Michelle T. Clinton, Sesshu Foster, and Naomi Quiñones. Albuquerque, NM: West End Press.

Anderson, Benedict. 1991. *Imagined Communities: Reflections on the Origin and Spread of Nationalism.* Rev. ed. London: Verso, 1983.

Aptheker, Bettina. 1989. *Tapestries of Life: Women's Work, Women's Consciousness, and the Meaning of Daily Experience.* Amherst: University of Massachusetts Press.

Arias, Ron. 1971. "The Barrio." In *The Chicanos: Mexican American Voices,* ed. Ed Ludwig and James Santibáñez, 123–126. Baltimore, MD: Penguin.

———. 1987. *The Road to Tamazunchale.* 1975. Tempe, AZ: Bilingual Press/Editorial Bilingüe.

Automobile Club of Southern California. 1980. *Guide to Los Angeles Area Freeway System.* Map of Los Angeles.

Bakhtin, Mikhail. 1981. *The Dialogic Imagination: Four Essays.* Ed. Michael Holquist. Trans. Caryl Emerson and Michael Holquist. Austin: University of Texas Press.

———. 1984. *Rabelais and His World.* Trans. Helene Iswolsky. Bloomington: University of Indiana Press.

Banham, Reyner. 1971. *Los Angeles; the Architecture of Four Ecologies.* New York: Penguin Books.

Barnett, Alan W. 1984. *Community Murals.* Cranbury, NJ: Associated University Presses.

Barrera, Mario. 1979. *Race and Class in the Southwest: A Theory of Racial Inequality.* Notre Dame, IN: University of Notre Dame Press.

Barrera, Mario, and Geralda Vialpando, eds. 1974. *Action Research in Defense of the Barrio: Interviews with Ernesto Galarza, Guillermo Flores, and Rosalío Muñoz.* Los Angeles: Aztlán Publications Pamphlet Series.

Baudelaire, Charles. 1970. *Paris Spleen.* Trans. Louise Varese. New York: New Directions.

———. 1993. "Le Cygne." *The Flowers of Evil,* 173–177. Trans. James McGowan. New York: Oxford University Press.

Benjamin, Walter. 1968. *Illuminations.* Ed. Hannah Arendt. Trans. Harry Zohn. New York: Harcourt, Brace & World.

Berman, Marshall. 1982. *All That Is Solid Melts into Air: The Experience of Modernity.* New York: Simon and Schuster.

Binder, Wolfgang. 1985. *Partial Autobiographies: Interviews with Twenty Chicano Poets.* Erlangen, Germany: Verlagg, Palm & Enke.

Boyer, M. Christine. 1983. *Dreaming the Rational City: The Myth of American City Planning.* Cambridge, MA: M.I.T. Press.

Boyer, Paul. 1978. *Urban Masses and Moral Order in America, 1820–1920.* Cambridge, MA: Harvard University Press.

Bright, Brenda Jo. 1995. "Remappings: Los Angeles Low Riders." In *Looking High and Low: Art and Cultural Identity,* ed. Brenda Jo Bright and Liza Bakewell. Tucson: University of Arizona Press.

Brookman, Philip, and Amy Brookman. 1983. Rebel Chicano Art Front (RCAF), audio recording with transcript, rec. October 15, University of California, Santa Cruz, Califas Conference Archives.

Brookman, Philip, and Guillermo Gómez-Peña, eds. 1986. *Made in Aztlán.* San Diego, CA: Centro Cultural de la Raza.

Bruce-Novoa, Juan. 1980. *Chicano Authors: Inquiry by Interview.* Austin: University of Texas Press.

Calderón, Héctor. 1990. "At the Crossroads of History, On the Borders of Change:

Chicano Literary Studies Past, Present, and Future." In *Left Politics and the Literary Profession*, ed. Lennard J. Davis and M. Bella Mirabella, 211–235. New York: Columbia University Press.

Calderón, Héctor, and José David Saldívar, eds. 1991. *Criticism in the Borderlands: Studies in Chicano Literature, Culture, and Ideology*. Durham, NC: Duke University Press.

Camarillo, Albert. 1979. *Chicanos in a Changing Society: From Mexican Pueblos to American Barrios in Santa Barbara and Southern California, 1848–1930*. Cambridge, MA: Harvard University Press.

———. 1984. *Chicanos in California: A History of Mexican Americans in California*. San Francisco: Boyd and Fraser.

Camarillo, Albert, and Pedro Castillo. 1973. *Furia y muerte: Los bandidos Chicanos*. UCLA Chicano Studies Monograph series, no. 4. Los Angeles: Aztlán Publications.

Candelaria, Cordelia. 1986. *Chicano Poetry: A Critical Introduction*. Westport, CT: Greenwood.

Cárdenas de Dwyer, Carlota. 1979. "International Literary Metaphor and Ron Arias: An Analysis of *The Road to Tamazunchale*." In *The Identification and Analysis of Chicano Literature*, ed. Francisco Jiménez, 358–364. New York: Bilingual Review Press.

Castañeda, Antonia. 1990. "Gender, Race, and Culture: Spanish American Women in the Historiography of Frontier California." *Frontiers: A Journal of Women's Studies* 11, no. 1:8–20.

Castañeda-Shular, Antonia, Tomás Ybarra-Frausto, and Joseph Sommers, eds. 1972. *Literatura Chicana: Texto y contexto/Chicano Literature: Text and Context*. Englewood Cliffs, NJ: Prentice-Hall.

Castells, Manuel. 1983. *The City and the Grassroots: A Cross Cultural Theory of Urban Social Movements*. Berkeley and Los Angeles: University of California Press.

Cather, Willa. 1976. *Lucy Gayheart*. New York: Vintage Books. [Originally published by Alfred A. Knopf in 1935.]

Cervantes, Lorna Dee. 1976. "Declaration on a Day of Little Inspiration." *Mango* 1, no. 1:4.

———. 1981. *Emplumada*. Pittsburgh: University of Pittsburgh Press.

———. 1985. Interview. *Partial Autobiographies: Interviews with Twenty Chicano Poets*. By Wolfgang Binder. Erlangen, Germany: Verlagg, Palm & Enke.

Chabram-Dernersesian, Angie. 1992. "I Throw Punches for My Race, but I Don't Want to Be a Man: Writing Us—Chica-nos (Girls, Us)/Chicanas—into the Movement Script." In *Cultural Studies*, ed. Lawrence Grossberg, Cary Nelson, and Paula A. Treichler, 81–95. New York: Routledge.

Champlin, Charles. 1960. "Los Angeles in a New Image: Growing Up as well as Out, the City's Cactus Patch Culture Bursts into Bloom, Civic Pride and Big Business." *Life* 48, no. 24 (June 20):74–90. Photographs by Ralph Crane.

Chávez, John. 1984. *The Lost Land: The Chicano Image of the Southwest*. Albuquerque: University of New Mexico Press.

Chávez Ravine. 1993. Videotape. Dir. Norberto Barba. Los Angeles: Universal Television and National Hispanic Media Coalition.

Chavoya, Ondine. 1989. "Internal Exiles: The Interventionist Public and Performance Art of ASCO." In *Space, Site, and Intervention: Issues in Installation and Site-Specific Art*, ed. Erika Suderberg. Minneapolis: University of Minnesota Press.

———. 1999. "Social Unwest: An Interview with Harry Gamboa, Jr." *Wide Angle* 20, no. 3 (fall).

———. n.d. "Orphan of Modernity: Public Representation and Critical Practice in Contemporary Chicana/o Visual and Media Arts." Ph.D. diss., University of Rochester, Program in Visual and Cultural Studies/Department of Art History.

Chicano Park. 1988. Videotape. Prod. Mario Barrera and Marylin Mulford. Script by Juan Felipe Herrera and Gary Wemberg. Berkeley, CA: Redbird Films.

Cisneros, Sandra. 1984. *The House on Mango Street.* Houston: Arte Público Press.

Citizen's Committee to Save Elysian Park. 1965. "Keep Your Asphalt Out of Beautiful Elysian Park." *Eastside Sun,* March 11, C-2.

Cockcroft, Eva Sperling. 1984. "The Story of Chicano Park." *Aztlán* 15, no. 1: 79–103.

Cockcroft, Eva Sperling, and Holly Barnet-Sánchez, eds. 1990. *Signs from the Heart: California Chicano Murals.* Venice, CA: Social and Public Art Resource Center.

Cockcroft, James. 1986. *Outlaws in the Promised Land: Mexican Immigrant Workers and America's Future.* New York: Grove.

Crawford, Margaret. 1995. "Contesting the Public Realm: Struggles over Public Space in Los Angeles." *Journal of Architectural Education* 49, no. 1 (Sept.): 4–9.

Cuadros, Gil. 1994a. "My Aztlán: White Place." *City of God,* 53–58. San Francisco: City Lights.

———. 1994b. "There Are Places You Don't Walk Alone at Night." *City of God,* 112–114. San Francisco: City Lights.

Cvetkovich, Ann. 1992. *Mixed Feelings: Feminism, Mass Culture, and Victorian Sensationalism.* New Brunswick, NJ: Rutgers University Press.

Davis, Mike. 1987. "Chinatown Two?: The Internationalization of Downtown L.A." *New Left Review* 164:65–86.

———. 1990. *City of Quartz: Excavating the Future in Los Angeles.* New York: Verso.

de Certeau, Michel. 1984. *The Practice of Everyday Life.* Berkeley: University of California Press.

De León, Arnoldo. 1982. *The Tejano Community, 1836–1900.* Albuquerque: University of New Mexico Press.

del Olmo, Frank. 1997. "Is It O'Malley's Last Out or First Down?" Editorial. *Los Angeles Times,* January 12, M-5.

de Roos, Robert, and Thomas Nebbia. 1962. "California's City of the Angels." *National Geographic* (October): 451–502.

Distant Water. 1995. Videotape. Dir. Carlos Avila. Los Angeles, CA: Echo Park Productions.

Downs, Anthony. 1970. "Uncompensated Nonconstitution Costs Which Urban Highways and Urban Renewal Impose upon Residential Households." In *Urban Problems and Prospects,* ed. Julius Margolis and Aaron Wildavsky, 69–106. New York: Columbia University Press.

Durán, Miguel. 1992. *Don't Spit on My Corner.* Houston: Arte Público Press.

Escobar, Edward J. 1983. "Chicano Protest and the Law: Law Enforcement Responses to Chicano Activism, 1850–1936." Ph.D. diss., University of California, Riverside.

Escobedo, Raúl. 1973. "Life Style within the Boyle Heights Community." *Eastside Sun,* April 26.

———. 1974. "Is Boyle Heights Worth Saving?" Interview. *Eastside Sun,* August 8, A-1+.

———. 1998. Interview with author. East Los Angeles, CA, August 28.

Estrada, William. Forthcoming. "The Los Angeles Plaza: Myth, Memory, Symbol, and the Struggle for Place in a Changing Metropolis." Ph.D. diss., University of California Los Angeles.

Fernández, Celestino, and Lawrence R. Pedroza. n.d. "The Border Patrol and News Media Coverage of Undocumented Mexican Immigration During the 1970's: A Quantitative Content Analysis in the Sociology of Knowledge." Working Papers Series. Tucson: University of Arizona Mexican American Studies and Research Center.

Fernández-Kelly, María Patricia. 1995. "Social and Cultural Capital in the Urban Ghetto: Implications for Economic Sociology." In *The Economic Sociology of Immigration: Essays on Networks, Ethnicity, and Entrepreneurship,* ed. Alejandro Portes. New York: Russell Sage Foundation.

Findlay, John M. 1992. *Magic Lands: Western Cityscapes and American Culture after 1940.* Berkeley: University of California Press.

Flores, Juan, and George Yúdice. 1993. "Living Borders/Buscando América: Languages of Latino Self-Formation." In *Divided Borders: Essays on Puerto Rican Identity,* ed. Juan Flores, 199–224. Houston: Arte Público Press.

Fogelson, Robert M. 1993. *The Fragmented Metropolis: Los Angeles, 1850–1930.* Reprint. Berkeley: University of California Press, 1967.

Foster, Nellie. 1939. "The *Corrido*: A Mexican Culture Trait Persisting in Southern California." Master's thesis, University of Southern California.

Fregoso, Rosa Linda. 1993. *The Bronze Screen: Chicana and Chicano Film Culture.* Minneapolis: University of Minnesota Press.

Fried, Marc. 1963. "Grieving for a Lost Home." In *The Urban Condition: People and Policy in the Metropolis,* ed. Leonard J. Duhl, 151–171. New York: Basic Books.

Frieden, Bernard J., and Lynne B. Sagalyn. 1989. *Downtown, Inc.: How America Rebuilds Cities.* Cambridge, MA: M.I.T. Press.

Fuentes, Carlos. 1986. *Aura.* Reprint. Mexico City: Biblioteca Era, 1962.

Galarza, Ernesto. 1971. *Barrio Boy.* Notre Dame, IN: University of Notre Dame Press.

Galarza, Ernesto, Herman Gallegos, and Julian Samora. 1969. *Mexican American in the Southwest.* Photog. George Ballis. Santa Barbara: McNally & Loftin.

Gamboa, Harry. 1991. "In the City of Angels, Chameleons, and Phantoms: Asco, a Case Study of Chicano Art in Urban Tones (or Asco Was a Four-Member Word)." In *Chicano Art: Resistance and Affirmation, 1965–1985,* ed. Richard Griswold del Castillo, Teresa McKenna, and Yvonne Yarbro-Bejarano, 121–130. Los Angeles: Wight Gallery, University of California.

———. 1997. "Phantoms in Urban Exile." *Aztlán: A Journal of Chicano Studies* 22, no. 2 (fall): 197–203.

Gamboa, Manazar. [c. 1996]. *Memories around a Bulldozed Barrio: Book One.* Los Angeles: n.p.

Gans, Herbert J. 1962. *The Urban Villagers: Group and Class in the Life of Italian-Americans.* London/New York: The Free Press; London: Collier-Macmillan Limited.

Gefland, Mark I. 1975. *A Nation of Cities: The Federal Government and Urban America, 1933–1965*. New York: Oxford University Press.

Giedion, Siegfried. 1941. *Space, Time, and Architecture: The Growth of a New Tradition*. Cambridge, MA: Harvard University Press.

Gilroy, Paul. 1987. *There Ain't No Black in the Union Jack*. London: Hutchinson.

Ginsberg, Allen. 1959. *Howl, and Other Poems*. San Francisco: City Lights.

Glendinning, Robert M. 1941. "Zoning: Past, Present, and Future." In *Los Angeles: Preface to a Master Plan*, ed. George W. Robbins and L. Deming Tilton, 173–188. Los Angeles: Pacific Southwest Academy.

Gold, Matea. 1997. "Deep Distrust Stalls Eastside Renewal Plan." *Los Angeles Times*, August 4, B-1, B-3.

Gómez-Quiñones, Juan. 1982. "Canto al trabajador." In *201/Two Hundred and One: Homenaje a la ciudad de Los Angeles/The Latino Experience in Los Angeles*, ed. Los Angeles Latino Writers Association, 25. Los Angeles: Popular Graphics.

Goodman, Robert. 1971. *After the Planners*. New York: Touchstone.

Gordon, Avery F. 1997. *Ghostly Matters: Haunting and the Sociological Imagination*. Minneapolis: University of Minnesota Press.

Gottdeiner, Mark. 1986. "Culture, Ideology, and the Sign of the City." *The City and the Sign: An Introduction to Urban Semiotics*, ed. Mark Gottdeiner and Alexandros Ph. Logopoupos, 202–218. New York: Columbia University Press.

Gottdeiner, Mark, and Alexandros Ph. Logopoupos, eds. 1986. Introduction to *The City and the Sign: An Introduction to Urban Semiotics*. New York: Columbia University Press.

Gramsci, Antonio. 1971. *Selections from the Prison Notebooks*. Ed. and trans. Quintin Hoare and Geoffrey Nowell-Smith. New York: International Publishers.

Griffith, Beatrice. 1948. *American Me*. Boston: Houghton Mifflin.

Griswold del Castillo, Richard. 1979. *The Los Angeles Barrio, 1850–1890: A Social History*. Berkeley: University of California Press.

Griswold del Castillo, Richard, Teresa McKenna, and Yvonne Yarbro-Bejarano, eds. 1991. *Chicano Art: Resistance and Affirmation, 1965–1985*. Los Angeles: Wight Gallery, University of California.

Grossberg, Lawrence, Cary Nelson, and Paula A. Treichler, eds. 1992. *Cultural Studies*. New York: Routledge.

Grossman, Charles P. 1931. *Los Angeles, the Wonder City: A Pictorial Representation of Life in This Great and Growing Metropolis on the West Coast*. Los Angeles: Charles P. Grossman.

Gruen, Victor. 1967. *The Heart of Our Cities, The Urban Crisis: Diagnosis and Cure*. New York: Simon & Schuster.

Guerrero, Lalo. n.d. "Chicas Patas Boogie." *Lalo Guerrero: Early Classic Recordings, 1950–1955*. Compiled by Mark Guerrero.

Guevara, Rubén. 1983. "C/S." With Con Safos. *Los Angelinos: The Eastside Renaissance*. LP. Zyanya/Rhino, RNLP062.

Gutiérrez-Jones, Carl. 1995. *Rethinking the Borderlands: Between Chicano Culture and Legal Discourse*. Berkeley: University of California Press.

Guzmán, Ralph. 1953a. "Let's Get the Story Straight." Editorial. *Eastside Sun*, June 18, 1.

———. 1953b. Editorial. *Eastside Sun*, June 25, 2.

———. 1953c. Editorial. *Eastside Sun*, December 17, 2.

Hansen, Harry, ed. 1967. *California: A Guide to the Golden State*. New York: Hastings House.

Harlow, Barbara. 1991. "Sites of Struggle: Immigration, Deportation, Prison, Exile." In *Criticism in the Borderlands: Studies in Chicano Literature, Culture, and Ideology*, ed. Héctor Calderón and José David Saldívar, 149–163 . Durham, NC: Duke University Press.

Harvey, David. 1993. *The Condition of Postmodernity*. London: Blackwell.

Hartman, Chester. 1974. *Yerba Buena: Land Grab and Community Resistance in San Francisco*. Berkeley, CA: National Housing and Economic Development Law Project, Earl Warren Legal Institute, University of California.

Hayden, Dolores. 1995. *The Power of Place*. Cambridge, MA, and London: M.I.T. Press.

Hebdige, Dick. 1979. *Subculture: The Meaning of Style*. London and New York: Methuen.

Hernández, Guillermo. 1985. "El Trio Casindio and the Royal Chicano Air Force." Booklet accompanying the album, *Chicano Music All Day*. El Trio Casindio and Royal Chicano Air Force. N.p.

Herrera, Juan Felipe. 1987. "Logan Heights and the World." *Facegames*, 58–60. San Francisco: As Is/So & So.

Herrón, Willie. 1972. "Ese Vato Va Marchar." *Regeneración* 2, no. 2.

———. 1983a. "Not Another Homicide." Los Illegals, *Internal Exile*. A&M Records, SP4925.

———. 1983b. "Rampage." Los Illegals, *Internal Exile*. A&M Records, SP4925.

———. 1983c. "Secret Society Man." Los Illegals, *Internal Exile*. A&M Records, SP4925.

Herrón, Willie, and Jesus Velo. 1983. "We Don't Need a Tan." Los Illegals, *Internal Exile*. A&M Records, SP4925.

Higham, John. 1988. *Strangers in the Land: Patterns of American Nativism, 1860–1925*. Reprint. New Brunswick, NJ: Rutgers University Press, 1955.

Hines, Thomas S. 1982. "Housing, Baseball, and Creeping Socialism." *Journal of Urban History* 8, no. 2 : 123–144.

Hirsch, E. D. 1988. *Cultural Literacy: What Every American Needs to Know*. New York: Vintage.

Hobsbawm, Eric. 1965. *Primitive Rebels, Studies in Archaic Forms of Social Movement in the Nineteenth and Twentieth Centuries*. New York: Norton.

Hylen, Arnold. 1981. *Los Angeles Before the Freeways, 1850–1950: Images of an Era*. Los Angeles: Dawson's Book Shop.

Jackson, Helen Hunt. 1884. *Ramona*. Boston, MA: Little, Brown and Company.

Jackson, John Brinckerhoff. 1980. "Nearer Than Eden." *The Necessity for Ruins and Other Topics*, 19–36. Amherst: University of Massachusetts Press.

Jameson, Fredric. 1981. *The Political Unconscious: Narrative as a Socially Symbolic Act*. Ithaca, NY: Cornell University Press.

———. 1988. "Cognitive Mapping." In *Marxism and the Interpretation of Culture*, ed. Cary Nelson and Lawrence Grossberg, 347–357. Urbana: University of Illinois Press.

Judd, Dennis, and Todd Swanstrom. 1994. *City Politics: Private Power and Public Wealth.* New York: Harper Collins.

Kaplan, Caren. 1987. "Deterritorializations: The Rewriting of Home and Exile in Western Feminist Discourse." *Cultural Critique* 6: 187–198.

Klein, Norman M. 1990. "The Sunshine Strategy: Buying and Selling the Fantasy of Los Angeles." In *Twentieth-Century Los Angeles: Power, Promotion, and Social Conflict,* ed. Norman M. Klein and Martin J. Schiesl, 1–38. Claremont, CA: Regina Books.

———. 1997. *The History of Forgetting: Los Angeles and the Erasure of Memory.* New York and London: Verso.

Kolodny, Annette. 1975. *The Lay of the Land: Metaphor as Experience and History in American Life and Letters.* Chapel Hill: University of North Carolina Press.

Kosiba-Vargas, Zaneta. 1988. "Harry Gamboa and the Emergence of a Chicano Art Group, 1971–1987." Ph.D. diss., University of Michigan.

Kovner, Joseph Eli. 1959. "East Welfare Planning Council Is Tool of Mayor's Urban Renewal Committee, as Is West LA Group!" Editorial. *Eastside Sun,* January 8, 1–2.

Latin Alliance. 1991. "Lowrider (on the Boulevard)." Featuring War. *Latin Alliance.* Virgin Records, 2–91625.

Ledut, Raymond. 1986. "Speech and the Silence of the City." In *The City and the Sign: An Introduction to Urban Semiotics,* ed. Mark Gottdeiner and Alexandros Ph. Logopoupos, 114–134. New York: Columbia University Press.

Lefebvre, Henri. 1991. *The Production of Space.* Trans. Donald Nicholson-Smith. Oxford, UK, and Cambridge, MA: Blackwell.

———. 1996. "The Specificity of the City." In *Writings on Cities,* trans. and ed. Eleonore Kofman and Elizabeth Lebas, 100–104. Oxford, UK; Cambridge, MA: Blackwell.

A Lighter Shade of Brown. 1990a. "Bouncin'." *Brown & Proud.* Quality Records, 4XL15154–4.

———. 1990b. "On A Sunday Afternoon." *Brown & Proud.* Quality Records, 4XL15154–4.

Limerick, Patricia Nelson. 1987. *Legacy of Conquest: The Unbroken Past of the American West.* New York: Norton.

Lippard, Lucy R. 1990. *Mixed Blessings: New Art in a Multicultural America.* New York: Pantheon.

Logan, John R., and Harvey Molotch. 1987. *Urban Fortunes: The Political Economy of Place.* Berkeley: University of California Press.

López, Enrique Hank. 1982. "Overkill at the Silver Dollar." In *201/Two Hundred and One: Homenaje a la ciudad de Los Angeles/The Latino Experience in Los Angeles,* ed. Los Angeles Latino Writers Association, 6–8. Los Angeles: Popular Graphics.

Los Angeles County Regional Planning Commission. 1943. "Freeways for the Region." Los Angeles: The Commission.

Los Angeles Department of City Planning. 1941. "A Parkway Plan for the City of Los Angeles and the Metropolitan Area." Los Angeles: The Department, May.

Los Angeles Latino Writers Association, ed. 1982. *201/Two Hundred and One: Homenaje a la Ciudad de Los Angeles/The Latino Experience in Los Angeles.* Los Angeles: Popular Graphics.

Los Illegals. 1983. *Internal Exile.* A&M Records, SP4925.

———. n.d. Manifesto. Photocopy in possession of author.

Loukaitou-Sideris, Anastasia, and Gail Sansbury. 1995–1996. "Lost Streets of Bunker Hill." *California Quarterly* 74, no. 4 (winter): 394–407.

Ludwig, Ed, and James Santibáñez, eds. 1971. *The Chicanos: Mexican American Voices.* Baltimore, MD: Penguin.

Lynch, Kevin. *The Image of the City.* 1960. Cambridge, MA: The Technology Press and Harvard University Press.

Marín, Mariana. 1977. "The Road to Tamazunchale: Fantasy or Reality?" *De Colores* 3, no. 4: 34–38.

Martínez, Eliud. 1986. "Ron Arias' *The Road to Tamazunchale:* A Chicano Novel of the New Reality." In *Contemporary Chicano Fiction: A Critical Survey,* ed. Vernon E. Lattin, 226–238. Binghampton, NY: Bilingual Press.

Mazón, Mauricio. 1984. *The Zoot-Suit Riots.* Austin: University of Texas Press.

McCarthy, Kevin, and R. B. Valdez, 1986. *Current and Future Effects of Mexican Immigration in California.* Santa Monica, CA: Rand Corporation.

McWilliams, Carey. 1949. *North from Mexico: The Spanish-Speaking People of the United States.* New York: J. B. Lippincott.

———. 1976. *Southern California: An Island on the Land.* Reprint. New York: Peregrine Smith, 1946.

Medeiros, Francine. 1975. "*La Opinión,* A Mexican Exile Newspaper: A Content Analysis of Its First Years, 1926–1929." *Aztlán: International Journal of Chicano Studies Research* 6: 43–67.

Medrano, Isabel, and N. Sterlink. 1965. Letter. *Eastside Sun,* May 13.

Mena, Jesús. 1982. "Testimonio de Bert Corona: Struggle Is the Ultimate Teacher." In *201/Two Hundred and One: Homenaje a la ciudad de Los Angeles/The Latino Experience in Los Angeles,* ed. Los Angeles Latino Writers Association, 27–36. Los Angeles: Popular Graphics.

Mesa-Bains, Amalia. 1991. "El Mundo Femenino: Chicana Artists of the Movement— A Commentary on Development and Production." In *Chicano Art: Resistance and Affirmation, 1965–1985,* ed. Richard Griswold del Castillo, Teresa McKenna, and Yvonne Yarbro-Bejarano, 131–140. Los Angeles: Wight Gallery, University of California.

———. 1994. "Land and Spirituality in the Descansos." In *Saber es poder/Interventions,* ed. Richard M. Carp. Los Angeles: ADOBE LA.

Metropolis. 1972. Videocassette. Dir. Fritz Lang. Minneapolis, MN: Festival Films, 1926.

"Mexicans in California." 1930. Report of Governor C. C. Young's Fact-Finding Committee. San Francisco: R and E Research Associates/California Printing Office.

Meyer, Larry L. 1965. "Sinews of a Super City." *Westways* (June): 26–28, 46.

Mies, Maria. 1986. *Patriarchy and Accumulation on a World Scale: Women in the International Division of Labor.* London: Zed.

Mirandé, Alfredo. 1987. *Gringo Justice.* Notre Dame, IN: Notre Dame University Press.

Mohl, Raymond A. 1993. "Race and Space in the Modern City: Interstate-95 and the Black Community in Miami." In *Urban Policy in Twentieth-Century America,* ed. Arnold R. Hirsch and Raymond A. Mohl, 100–158. New Brunswick, NJ: Rutgers University Press.

Mollenkopf, John H. 1978. "The Postwar Politics of Urban Development." In *Marxism and the Metropolis: New Perspectives in Urban Political Economy*, ed. William K. Tabb and Larry Sawyers, 117–152. New York: Oxford University Press.

———. 1983. *The Contested City*. Princeton, NJ: Princeton University Press.

Montoya, José. 1976. "Centro de Artistas, Sacra." *Chismearte* (fall): 6–7.

———. 1980a. "Russian Cowboys, Early Berkeley, and Sunstruck Critics: On Being a Chicano Writer." *Metamorfosis* 3, no. 1: 48–53.

———. 1980b. "Thoughts on La Cultura, the Media, Con Safos, and Survival." *Metamorfosis* 3, no. 1: 28–31.

———. 1985. "Cruzin'." *Chicano Music All Day*. El Trio Casindio and the Royal Chicano Air Force. Instituto de Lengua y Cultura, c/s 284.

———. 1992a. "Cinco de Mayo Poem for '87." In *Information: Twenty Years of Joda*, ed. Antonio Villarreal, 215–216. San Jose, CA: Chusma House.

———. 1992b. "Until They Leave Us a Loan." In *Information: Twenty Years of Joda*, ed. Antonio Villarreal, 117–119. San Jose, CA: Chusma House.

Moore, Joan W. 1978. *Homeboys: Gangs, Drugs, and Prison in the Barrios of Los Angeles*. Philadelphia, PA: Temple University Press.

———. 1991. *Going Down to the Barrio: Homeboys and Homegirls In Change*. Philadelphia, PA: Temple University Press.

Moraga, Cherríe. 1983. Preface to *This Bridge Called My Back: Writings by Radical Women of Color*, ed. Cherríe Moraga and Gloria Anzaldúa, xiii–xix. 2d ed. New York: Kitchen Table: Women of Color Press.

Morales, Armando. 1972. *Ando Sangrando (I am Bleeding): A Study of Mexican American–Police Conflict*. La Puente, CA: Perspectiva.

Moreau, Theresa. 1996. "Offensive Line: Echo Park Residents Mobilize against Possible Football Arena Next to Dodger Stadium." *Los Angeles View*, April 19, 6.

Morín, Raúl. 1963. *Among the Valiant: Mexican-Americans in World War II and Korea*. Los Angeles: Borden Publishing.

Muñoz, Rosalío. 1973. "Our Moving Barrio: Why?" *La Gente* 5 (April): 5, 9.

Negt, Oskar, and Alexander Kluge. 1988. "The Public Sphere and Experience: Selections." Trans. Peter Labanyi. *October* 46 (fall): 60–82.

Neri, Michael. 1973. "A Journalistic Portrait of the Spanish-Speaking People of California, 1868–1925." *Southern California Quarterly* 55, no. 2 (summer): 193–208.

Norte, Marisela. 1983. "Harry Gamboa, Jr., No Movie Maker." Interview. *El Tecolote Literary Magazine* (July): 3, 12.

Omi, Michael, and Harold Winant. 1986. *Racial Formation in the United States*. New York: Routledge and Kegan Paul.

Ovnick, Merry. 1994. *Los Angeles: The End of the Rainbow*. Los Angeles: Balcony Press.

Padilla, Genaro. 1993. *My History Not Yours: The Formation of Mexican American Autobiography*. Madison: University of Wisconsin Press.

Pardo, Mary. 1990a. "Identity and Resistance: Mexican American Women and Grassroots Activism in Two Los Angeles Communities." Ph.D. diss., University of California, Los Angeles.

———. 1990b. "Mexican American Women Grassroots Community Activists: 'Mothers of East Los Angeles.'" *Frontiers: A Journal of Women Studies* 11, no. 1: 1–7.

————. 1991. "Creating Community: Mexican American Women in Eastside Los Angeles." *Aztlán: A Journal of Chicano Studies* 20, nos. 1–2 (spring–fall): 39–72.

Paredes, Américo. 1978. "The Problem of Identity in a Changing Culture: Popular Expressions of Culture Conflict along the Lower Rio Grande Border. In *Views across the Bridge: The U.S. and Mexico*, ed. Stanley Ross, 68–94. Albuquerque: University of New Mexico Press.

————. 1982. *"With His Pistol in His Hand": A Border Ballad and Its Hero.* Reprint. Austin: University of Texas Press, 1958.

Parson, Don. 1982. "The Development of Redevelopment: Public Housing and Urban Renewal in Los Angeles." *International Journal of Urban and Regional Research* 6/7 (September): 393–413.

————. 1993. "'This Modern Marvel': Bunker Hill, Chavez Ravine, and the Politics of Modernism in Los Angeles." *Southern California Quarterly* 75, nos. 3–4 (fall–winter): 333–350.

Pérez, Emma. 1993. "Speaking from the Margin: Uninvited Discourse on Sexuality and Power." *Building with Our Hands: New Directions in Chicana Studies*, ed. Adela de la Torre and Beatriz M. Pesquera, 57–71. Berkeley: University of California Press.

Pérez, Mary Anne. 1994. "Ponen en tela de juicio plan de revitalización." *Nuestro Tiempo*, weekly supplement to the *Los Angeles Times*, July 7: 6, 9.

"El Plan Espiritual de Aztlán." 1972. [Originally published in *El Grito del Norte* 2, no. 9 (1969).] Reprinted in *Aztlán: An Anthology of Mexican American Literature*, ed. Luis Valdez and Stan Steiner, 402–406. New York: Alfred E. Knopf.

Plascencia, Luis F. B. 1983. "Lowriding in the Southwest: Cultural Symbols in the Mexican Community." In *History, Culture, and Society: Chicano Studies in the 1980s*, ed. Mario T. García, Francisco Lomelí, Mario Barrera, Edward Escobar, and John García, 141–175. Ypsilanti, MI: Bilingual Press.

Pool, Bob. 1997. "Respect for Roots." *Los Angeles Times*, January 14, B-2.

"Punishment by Exile." 1972. *La Raza* 1, no. 7 (January): 48–50.

Ramos, George. 1996. "They're No Fans of Chavez Ravine Football Stadium." Editorial. *Los Angeles Times*, January 22, B-3.

Revolutionary Caucus. 1969. Denver Youth Liberation Conference. "Statement." *El Pocho Che* 1, no. 1.

Rich, Adrienne. 1986. "Notes toward a Politics of Location." In *Blood Bread and Poetry: Selected Prose, 1979–1985*. New York: Norton.

Ríos-Bustamante, Antonio, and Pedro Castillo. 1986. *An Illustrated History of Mexican Los Angeles*. Los Angeles: University of California Chicano Studies Research Center.   `

Rodríguez, Luis. 1982. "La veintinueve." In *201/Two Hundred and One: Homenaje a la ciudad de Los Angeles/The Latino Experience in Los Angeles*, ed. Los Angeles Latino Writers Association, 9–10. Los Angeles: Popular Graphics.

————. 1993. *Always Running, La Vida Loca: Gang Days in L.A.* Willimantic, CT: Curbstone.

Romero, Frank. 1988. *The Closing of Whittier Boulevard*. Illustration in *Time*, July 11, 64.

Romo, Ricardo. 1978. "The Urbanization of Southwestern Chicanos in the Early

Twentieth Century." In *New Directions in Chicano Scholarship*, ed. Ricardo Romo and Raymund Paredes, 183–207. La Jolla, CA: UCSD Chicano Studies Program.

———. 1983. *East Los Angeles: History of a Barrio*. Austin: University of Texas Press.

Romotsky, Jerry, and Sally R. Romotsky. 1976. *Los Angeles Barrio Calligraphy*. Los Angeles: Dawson's Book Shop.

Rose, Gillian. 1993. *Feminism and Geography: The Limits of Geographical Knowledge*. Minneapolis: University of Minnesota Press.

Rotella, Carlo. 1998. *October Cities: The Redevelopment of Urban Literature*. Berkeley: University of California Press.

Ruiz, Vicki L. 1990. "A Promise Fulfilled: Mexican Cannery Workers in Southern California." In *Unequal Sisters: A Multicultural Reader in U.S. Women's History*, ed. Ellen Carol DuBois and Vicki L. Ruiz. 264–274. New York: Routledge.

———. 1993. "'Star Struck': Acculturation, Adolescence, and the Mexican American Woman, 1920–1950." In *Building with Our Hands: New Directions in Chicana Studies*, ed. Adela de la Torre and Beatriz M. Pesquera, 109–129. Berkeley: University of California Press.

Sacramento Downtown Association. 1993. Telephone inquiry, July 27.

Said, Edward. 1978. *Orientalism*. New York: Pantheon Books.

Saldívar, José David. 1986. "The Ideological and the Utopian in Tomás Rivera's *Y no se lo tragó la tierra* and Ron Arias' *The Road to Tamazunchale*." In *Missions in Conflict: Essays in U.S.-Mexican Relations and Chicano Culture*, ed. Renate Von Bardeleben, Dietrich Breisemeister, and Juan Bruce-Novoa, 203–214. Tübingen: Gunter Narr Verlag.

Saldívar, Ramón. 1990. *Chicano Narrative: The Dialectics of Difference*. Madison: University of Wisconsin Press.

Salinas, Raúl. 1972. "A Trip through the Mind Jail." 1969. Reprinted in *Literatura Chicana: Texto y contexto/Chicano Literature: Text and Context*, ed. Antonia Castañeda Shular, Tomás Ybarra-Frausto, and Joseph Sommers, 182–186. Englewood Cliffs, NJ: Prentice-Hall.

———. 1995. *East of the Freeway: Reflections de mi pueblo*. Austin, TX: Red Salmon Press.

Sánchez, George J. 1993. *Becoming Mexican American: Ethnicity, Culture, and Identity in Chicano Los Angeles, 1900–1945*. New York: Oxford University Press.

Sánchez, Martha Ester. 1985. *Contemporary Chicana Poetry: A Critical Approach to an Emerging Literature*. Berkeley: University of California Press.

Sánchez, Rosaura. 1995. *Telling Identities: The Californio Testimonios*. Minneapolis: University of Minnesota Press.

Sánchez-Tranquilino, Marcos. 1991. "*Mi Casa No Es Su Casa:* Chicano Murals and Barrio Calligraphy as Systems of Signification at Estrada Courts, 1972–1978." Master's thesis, University of California Los Angeles.

Sandoval, Chela. 1991. "U.S. Third World Feminism: The Theory and Method of Oppositional Consciousness in the Postmodern World." *Genders* 10 (spring): 1–24.

Santillanes, Albert A. 1999. Interview with author. Los Angeles, CA, February 8.

Saxenian, AnnaLee. 1981. "Silicon Chips and Spatial Structure: The Industrial Basis of Urbanization in Santa Clara County, California." Berkeley: Institute of Urban and Regional Development, University of California, Working Paper 345.

————. 1985. "Silicon Valley and Route 128: Regional Prototypes or Historical Exceptions?" *Urban Affairs Annual Review*, vol. 28, ed. Manuel Castells, 81–105. Beverly Hills, CA: Sage Publications.

Schuchardt, William H. 1941. "The Civic Center." In *Los Angeles: Preface to a Master Plan*, ed. George W. Robbins and L. Deming Tilton, 239–252. Los Angeles: Pacific Southwest Academy.

Scott, Mel. 1942. *Cities Are for People: The Los Angeles Region Plans for Living.* Los Angeles: Pacific Southwest Academy.

————. 1949. *Metropolitan Los Angeles: One Community.* Los Angeles: Haynes Foundation.

"The Shaping of Purpose." 1965. *Westways* (June): 29–36.

Shippey, Lee. 1950. Photog. Max Yavno. *The Los Angeles Book.* Boston: Houghton Mifflin.

Silk, J. 1984. "Beyond Geography and Literature." *Environment and Planning D: Society and Space* 2: 151–178.

Smith, Henry Nash. 1950. *The Virgin Land: The American West as Symbol and Myth.* Cambridge, MA: Harvard University Press.

Smith, Richard Austin. 1965. "Los Angeles' Prototype of Supercity." *Fortune* (March): 98–101, 200, 202, 207–208, 210–212.

Soja, Edward W. 1989. *Postmodern Geographies: The Reassertion of Space in Critical Social Theory.* London: Verso.

Soja, Edward W., Rebecca Morales, and Goetz Wolff. 1984. "Urban Restructuring: An Analysis of Social and Spatial Change in Los Angeles." *Economic Geography* 59: 195–230.

Spalding, William Andrew. 1931. *History and Reminiscences: Los Angeles City and County, California.* Los Angeles: J. R. Finell & Sons.

Starr, Kevin. 1997. "The Expression of the City's Transformation." Editorial. *Los Angeles Times*, January 12, M-1, 6.

Stone, William Cutler. 1990. "Bajito y suavecito [Low and Slow]: Low Riding and the 'Class' of Class." *Studies in Latin American Popular Culture* 9: 85–126.

Thee Midnighters. 1983. "Whittier Blvd." *Best of Thee Midnighters.* Zyanya/Rhino, RNLP 063.

Torres, Rudy, and Victor Valle. n.d. *Latino Metropolis.* Minneapolis: University of Minnesota Press. Forthcoming.

Torres, Salvador. 1990. Taped interview. Santa Cruz, CA, June 22.

El Trio Casindio and the Royal Chicano Air Force. 1985. *Chicano Music All Day.* Instituto de Lengua y Cultura, c/s 284.

Trujillo, Larry. 1983. "Police Crimes in the Barrio." *History, Culture, and Society: Chicano Studies in the 1980s*, ed. Mario T. García, Francisco Lomelí, Mario Barrera, Edward Escobar, and John García, 199–242. Ypsilanti, MI: Bilingual Press.

Tuck, Ruth D. 1946. *Not with the Fist: Mexican-Americans in a Southwest City.* New York: Harcourt, Brace.

Urich, Kevin. 1996. "The Houses That O'Malley Demolished." *Los Angeles Reader*, August 9, 11–12, 14, 71.

Valdez, Victoria. 1983. "1949–1959: The Battle of Chávez Ravine." *Caminos* 4, no. 7: 11–14.

Valle, Victor. 1982. "Cuidad de Los Angeles [Parts 1–3]." In *201/Two Hundred and One: Homenaje a la ciudad de Los Angeles/The Latino Experience in Los Angeles*, ed. Los Angeles Latino Writers Association, 24ff. Los Angeles: Popular Graphics.

———. 1991. *Calendar of Souls, Wheel of Fire*. Irvine, CA: Pacific Writers Press.

Vigil, James Diego. 1988. *Barrio Gangs: Street Life and Identity in Southern California*. Austin: University of Texas Press.

Villa, Esteban. 1985. "Southside Park." *Chicano Music All Day*. El Trio Casindio and the Royal Chicano Air Force. Instituto de Lengua y Cultura, c/s 284.

Viramontes, Helena María. 1985. *The Moths and Other Stories*. Houston: Arte Público Press.

———. 1989. "Nopalitos: The Making of Fiction." In *Breaking Boundaries: Latina Writings and Critical Readings*, ed. Asunción Horno-Delgado, Eliana Ortega, Nina M. Scott, Nancy Saporta Sternbach, 33–38. Amherst, MA: University of Amherst Press.

———. 1994. Personal interview with the author. Glendale, CA, June 18.

Wachs, Martin. 1996. "The Evolution of Transportation Policy in Los Angeles: Images of Past Policies and Future Prospects." In *The City: Los Angeles and Urban Theory at the End of the Twentieth Century*, ed. Allen J. Scott and Edward W. Soja, 106–159. Berkeley: University of California Press.

Walker, Alice. 1983. *In Search of Our Mother's Gardens: Womanist Prose*. San Diego, CA: Harcourt Brace Jovanovich.

War. 1975. "Lowrider." *Why Can't We Be Friends?* Avenue Records/Far Out Productions, ECT 71051.

Warner, Marina. 1985. *Monuments and Maidens: The Allegory of the Female Form*. New York: Atheneum.

Weibe, Robert. 1973. *The Search for Order, 1877–1920*. New York: Hill and Wang.

Whyte, William F. 1943. *Street Corner Society: The Social Structure of an Italian Slum*. Chicago, IL: University of Chicago Press.

Williams, Raymond. 1973. *The Country and the City*. New York: Oxford University Press.

———. 1977. *Marxism and Literature*. New York: Oxford University Press.

Wilson, Chris. 1997. *The Myth of Santa Fe: Creating a Modern Regional Tradition*. Albuquerque: University of New Mexico Press.

Workman, Boyle. 1936. *The City That Grew* (as told to Caroline Walker). Los Angeles: Southland Publishing.

Ybarra-Frausto, Tomás. 1978. "The Chicano Movement and the Emergence of Chicano Poetic Consciousness." In *New Directions in Chicano Scholarship*, ed. Ricardo Romo and Raymund Paredes, 81–110. La Jolla, CA: UCSD Chicano Studies Program.

———. 1989. "Rasquachismo: A Chicano Sensibility." *Chicano Aesthetics: Rasquachismo* (exhibition catalog). Phoenix, AZ: Movimiento Artístico del Río Salado.

Zavella, Patricia. 1987. *Women's Work and Chicano Families: Cannery Workers of the Santa Clara Valley*. Ithaca: Cornell University Press.

Zukin, Sharon. 1991. *Landscapes of Power: From Detroit to Disney World*. Berkeley: University of California Press.

———. 1995. *The Culture of Cities*. Cambridge, MA: Blackwell.

PERMISSIONS ACKNOWLEDGMENTS

Grateful acknowledgment is made to the following for permission to use previously published materials:

The excerpt from Luis Alfaro, "Orphan of Aztlán," from *Uncontrollable Bodies: Testimonies of Identity and Culture*, edited by Rodney Sappington and Tyler Stallings, pp. 233–241. Copyright © 1994 by Bay Press, Inc. Reprinted by permission from Bay Press, Inc.

The excerpts from "Aims and Concerns," "Virgin Mary," and "Federal Building," by Luis Alfaro, are used with permission of the author.

The lyrics to "Barrio Viejo," by Lalo Guerrero, are reprinted by permission of the author and Barrio Libre Music. Copyright © 1991.

Portions of Chapter 3 were previously published as "Ghosts in the Growth Machine: Critical Spatial Consciousness in Los Angeles Chicano Writing" and are reprinted with permission of Duke University Press from *Social Text* (spring 1999 issue).

Part of Chapter 4 was previously published as "Marvelous Recreations: Utopian Spatial Critique in *The Road to Tamazunchale*" and is reprinted here, with permission of The Regents of the University of California, from *Aztlán: A Journal of Chicano Studies* 23, no. 1, UCLA Chicano Studies Research Center.

The lines from "Beneath the Shadow of the Freeway" and "Freeway 280," from *Emplumada* by Lorna Dee Cervantes, are used with permission of the author.

The lines from "Poema para los californios muertos" and "Cannery Town

INDEX